CREATING THE UNI

Cities and Society Series

Series Editor:
Chris Pickvance, Professor of Urban Studies, University of Kent, UK

Cities and Society is a series disseminating high quality new research and scholarship which contribute to a sociological understanding of the city. The series promotes scholarly engagement with contemporary issues such as urban access to public and private services; urban governance; urban conflict and protest; residential segregation and its effects; urban infrastructure; privacy, sociability and lifestyles; the city and space; and the sustainable city.

Other titles in the series

Urban Grassroots Movements in Central and Eastern Europe
Edited by Kerstin Jacobsson

Everyday Life in the Gentrifying City
On Displacement, Ethnic Privileging and the Right to Stay Put
Tone Huse

Boosting Competitiveness Through Decentralization
Subnational Comparison of Local Development in Mexico
Aylin Topal

Residential Segregation in Comparative Perspective: Making Sense of Contextual Diversity
Edited by Thomas Maloutas and Kuniko Fujita

Opportunities and Deprivation in the Urban South: Poverty, Segregation and Social Networks in São Paulo
Eduardo Cesar Leão Marques

Beyond the Resources of Poverty: Gecekondu Living in the Turkish Capital
Şebnem Eroğlu

Creating the Unequal City

The Exclusionary Consequences of Everyday Routines in Berlin

Edited by

TALJA BLOKLAND
Humboldt University Berlin, Germany

CARLOTTA GIUSTOZZI
Goethe University Frankfurt, Germany

DANIELA KRÜGER
Free University Berlin, Germany

HANNAH SCHILLING
Humboldt University Berlin, Germany

LONDON AND NEW YORK

First published 2016 by Routledge

2 Park Square, Milton Park, Abingdon, Oxfordshire OX14 4RN
52 Vanderbilt Avenue, New York, NY 10017

Routledge is an imprint of the Taylor & Francis Group, an informa business

First issued in paperback 2020

British Library Cataloguing in Publication Data
A catalogue record for this book is available from the British Library

The Library of Congress has cataloged the printed edition as follows:
Creating the unequal city : the exclusionary consequences of everyday routines in Berlin / [edited] by Talja Blokland, Carlotta Giustozzi, Daniela Krüger and Hannah Schilling.
pages cm
Includes bibliographical references and index.
ISBN 978-1-4724-4542-1 (hardback : alk. paper) – ISBN 978-1-4724-4543-8 (ebook) – ISBN 978-1-4724-4544-5 (epub) 1. Cities and towns—Germany—Berlin. 2. Cities and towns—Growth. 3. Social stratification—Germany—Berlin. I. Blokland-Potters, Talja, editor. II. Giustozzi, Carlotta, editor. III. Krüger, Daniela, editor.
HT169.G32C74 2015
307.760943'155–dc23

2015018234

ISBN: 978-1-4724-4542-1 (hbk)
ISBN: 978-0-367-59725-2 (pbk)

Printed in the United Kingdom
by Henry Ling Limited

Contents

List of Figures

Notes on Contributors

Rebecca Arbter holds a Master's degree in social-cultural studies from the European University Viadrina in Frankfurt (Oder). She worked as a research assistant at the University of Amsterdam and Humboldt University Berlin. Her research interests are in migration studies, social capital theory and gender studies. She is working in the field of political education and anti-discrimination work.

Talja Blokland is an urban sociologist who has worked at Yale University, the University of Manchester and various Dutch universities. Since 2009, she has held the chair of Urban and Regional Sociology at Humboldt University Berlin. Her publications include Urban Bonds (2003), Networked Urbanism (edited with Mike Savage, Ashgate 2008) and various articles on race and ethnicity in the city, poor neighbourhoods, urban violence, gentrification, urban middle classes and neighbourhood relations and everyday interactions.

Imogen Feld is a PhD student and research assistant in the Department of Education at the University Hamburg. Her doctoral thesis is on parental involvement in an international comparison. Imogen Feld majored in sociology at the Philipps-University Marburg and Fatih University Istanbul. She worked as a student assistant at the Philipps-University Marburg and the Berlin Social Research Center. Her research interests are in social inequality, education, citizenship and gender studies.

Nora Freitag is a Master student at Humboldt University Berlin in social sciences. After her first year she went to study at Bogazici University in Istanbul where she is currently writing her Master's thesis on gender in urban transformation processes. Her research interests are in social movements claiming right to the city, gentrification and exclusions from space.

Carlotta Giustozzi is a doctoral researcher in the ERC-funded CORRODE project at the chair for social stratification and social policy at Goethe University Frankfurt. She holds a Master's degree in social sciences from Humboldt University Berlin where she has worked as a research assistant at the chair of urban and regional sociology. She has been a visiting student at the Graduate Center of the City University of New York and co-authored the chapter 'The social dimension of urban transformations' in Mieg and Töpfer's *Institutional and Social Innovation for Sustainable Urban Development*. Her research interests include social stratification, inequality and its manifestation in different national and cultural contexts.

Daniela Krüger is a PhD student and research assistant at the Disaster Research Unit in the Institute of Social and Cultural Anthropology of Free University Berlin and a member of the NYLON network of young scholars in New York, London and Berlin. She studied social sciences at Humboldt University Berlin, the University of Bologna and the City University of New York. Her research interests are in urban sociology, social theory and research on vulnerability and social segregation in the city.

Mirjam Lewek studies social sciences with a focus on migration studies and urban sociology at Humboldt University Berlin and the National Autonomous University in Mexico City. Her main interest lies in the understanding and analysis of migration regimes as processes where manifold legal, economic, social, cultural, and ethnic borders and boundaries are constructed, reified and become manifest in profound inequalities in societies and cities, as much as in the permanent violation of human rights, national and international law. She is committed to political work with and for migrants in Berlin and Mexico City.

Georg Große-Löscher got his MA from the Social Sciences Institute at Humboldt University Berlin. His interests are in social inequality, relational theory, educational inequality in urban settings and the development of educational systems. Following the last one he is currently working for a Berlin based NGO, which is enhancing the culture of learning and teaching in schools and educational institutions.

Hannah Schilling is a doctoral research fellow in the International Graduate Program 'The World in the City' at the Centre for Metropolitan Studies of the Technical University Berlin; fellow of the German Academic National Foundation and member of the NYLON network of young scholars in New York, London and Berlin. In preparation of her dissertation research on precarious youth in Abidjan and Berlin, she worked as a research assistant in the international research program 'Urbanizing Faith' at the chair of urban and regional sociology at Humboldt-University Berlin. Research stays in Madrid and Paris and her studies in social sciences at Humboldt University Berlin have informed her research interest in comparative urbanism, racism and (state) institutions in practice.

Stephan Simon received his MA in social sciences at Humboldt University Berlin and also studied at Sciences Po Toulouse. He currently works as a researcher at the Berlin Social Science Center in a project on the discrimination of migrants in the labour market. His research interests include ethnic discrimination, religious social movements, sociology of religion and social theory.

Preface

AbdouMaliq Simone

When people live in cities, where is it exactly that people live? What is the living that takes place and how is it diffused or enacted spatially across the city, and how are particular instantiations of space made by that living? Neighbourhoods, networks, institutions, circuits and trajectories are various formats for describing, even accounting for, the environments of that living, which in turn are considered to generate particular effects, affordances and constraints. As urban living is something performed by multiple persons, organisms and even things, complex webs of interaction and circumvention continuously unfold, crystallizing into particular collective aggregates, ecologies and conflicts. As a result it is often difficult to know precisely what or who belongs where, about the kinds of effects particular events, actions, implantations and constructions might have and for whom, how far they reach, how particular forces are amplified, cushioned or altered. What are urban analysts supposed to pay attention to in accounting for the differentiations in capacity when it is not clear just how all of the things that take place within city life 'pay attention' to each other? – How they twist and turn, absorb and deflect.

How do lives reach each other, what do they want or need from all the different instantiations of living? How much do particular enactments of living really need to engage all those others taking place in the larger surrounds; how much do they simply need to know that specific ways of doing things are there, somewhere, without necessarily needing to interact with them? When interaction is necessary, how much has to be conceded and recalibrated? In cities where thousands upon thousands of things are going on simultaneously at any given time, how do particular lives know what it is exactly that has meaning to them, that poses serious implications for who they think they are or what they want to be? How far can inhabitants trace the impact of their own actions, and how far and to whom should any moral obligations extend?

What does it mean for lives to have a particular position in relationship to those of others? In cities of varied centrifugal and centripetal forces, then, positions, vantage points, staging areas and exposures are both the by-product of those forces and the very means for attempts to navigate and mediate them. They are the boundaries of what can be conceived and done, but also the tools from which to acquire perspective, enact intentions and consolidate resources. Positions have to take place somewhere; they have to be identifiable, translatable, even as they can be screens behind which many invisible actions occur. Thus position and location always operate in tandem, sometimes reinforcing, sometimes altering the character of the other. All living systems have to manage oscillations between the inclination to both extend themselves outward, maximizing viable staging areas as hedges against contingency and exhaustion, and to consolidate specific boundaries where coherence can be established and entropy minimized. There is no such thing then as either a position or location in and of itself. These are relational matters, and we simply can never know for sure what gives rise to the effective connection among all of the different forms of living that make up the city.

Still, in negotiating always tentative stabilities among these disparate inclinations – movements outwards and inwards, looking at the outside from within and the inside from without – an infrastructure is constituted. The basis of such infrastructure is the interface, or more precisely, a process of inter-facing. Such inter-facing is what Alexander Galloway calls an 'agitation or generative friction among different formats', or different ways of living. Interfaces *compose*, rather than assume, boundaries between inside and outside, figure and ground, here and there, now and then. But as interfaces are sustained because they never fully work – they never fully smooth over, erase, totalize, or subsume the edges that they mark – their particular definitions of the integrity of what they divide are always already on their way somewhere else. As such interfaces, as the basis of social infrastructure, are 'tricksters of orientation' as relations between inside and outside, here and there are always being decomposed and remade. For the capacity to be anything in particular, to have a specific position or location, or a particular set of advantages and statuses, always entails what Celia Lury calls 'what can be as well as what is'.

What this book does then is to examine social infrastructure as the multifarious ways in which connections among residents and ways of living are forged, how they are elaborated and constrained. It explores what residents are able to do with the conditions and resources they have to work with, and how specific practices of connecting with and through the city are both shaped by the differentiating valences of force exerted in the practices of others and also shape specific spaces of operation. The macro-structural scale then is not a pre-existent given. Economic and political conditions do not constitute an overarching environment in which urban practices and livelihoods are explainable. Rather, they are interpretive tools and strategies of assemblage that have to instantiate themselves, reach into the pluralities of lived experiences and actions. They have to find ways of mobilizing and captivating attention and use, to be actively experienced as limitations and potentials. This is not to say that such macro-structural conditions do not constitute a reality. But they do not automatically specify ways in which such a reality is occupied – what urban residents deem possible or not, what they imagine, what they think is transpiring all around them, or how they make decisions.

Urbanization implicitly means that it is possible to manage the oscillations inherent to living systems through continuously reworked engagements with other systems, that it is possible for any particular way of life to continuously sustain, update and increase its efficacy through intersections with ways of living that are different. Coherence, stability and growth need not be exclusively predicated on the institutionalization of particular ways of doing things, of rules, norms, conventions, cultural and social capital. City life, as a particular approximation of urbanizing processes need not adhere to or fulfil such potentialities. The extensiveness and intensity of exclusions, marginalization and disadvantage bear this out time and time again. But where the consolidations of privilege and resourcefulness indeed do produce adverse implications for others this is not so much the failure of urbanization per se but its truncation and partialness. Inhabitants have to have some kind of grip, ensure some kind of on-goingness, and despite their best intentions always 'hold up' the urbanizing process, in both senses of that term.

Behind any skewed city distribution of capacity and resources remain the virtual potentials of the urban. Any encounter, fleeting and durable, can spin off into all kinds of directions and inclinations, as that encounter has enfolded different kinds of desires and perceptions to begin with. The question is where does this spinning off take someone, what will they make it of it, what other encounters will be sought out, avoided or accidentally impelled? This activation of the virtual – all of the encounters a person has inside and outside the house, at work, in the streets, in institutions – informs what they are able to do at any particular time, where they do it, and what it is possible to perceive and pay attention to in a given environment, as each person and way of living acts on and moves through others. For, having something specific – either in terms of location, position, asset, capital, or information – does not guarantee specific trajectories of access or capability; there is always something extra, something supplementary at work, the content of which also changes all of the time.

So cities are replete with differences, some of which are the by-product of what are fundamentally defensive, immunizing manoeuvres against and within the urbanizing processes in which they are situated, and some that are the impulsion of urbanity itself – its capacities to individuate and singularize. How specific residents are situated within the interstices of such distinct difference-making mechanisms is a critical locus of comparison, and is one that this book undertakes in a highly focused way. The book avoids the trappings of conventional categories as well as a reliance on macro-level structures and tactical manoeuvres. Rather, it seeks to understand how any specific city by its very nature precipitates the possibility for productive comparison. This is because each city is replete with both its partiality and a virtual plenitude. The ways in which this double-natured reality is navigated generates a complexion of possibility that the conventional categories of class, capital, opportunity, locational advantage and externality simply can't get at, and thus miss much of what any city actually is.

Acknowledgements

As editors of this volume we would like to send our sincere thanks to the *Lübecker Nachbarschaftspreis*: a prize that we won with the project idea of an edited volume on 'Resourceful Cities' in 2013 and which was generously delivered by the *E-Punkt Lübecker Bürgerkraftwerk* and the City of Lübeck. The application for the prize marked the starting point of this book. Also, we are particularly thankful to the Department of Urban and Regional Studies and the Institute of Social Sciences at Humboldt University Berlin, which offered an inspiring environment for discussions with visiting scholars and colleagues. After all, the actual writing process and submission of this book would not have been possible without the assistance and collaboration of many people.

A special thought here goes to Jenna Büchy who participated in the development and presentation for the *Lübecker Nachbarschaftspreis*. As filmmaker and creative mind, also Tristan Beach helped us prepare the application for the *Lübecker Nachbarschaftspreis* for which we are very thankful.

Concerning the realization of this edited volume, we are very grateful to Claire Jarvis for her patience and guidance through the publishing process with Ashgate. Our gratitude also goes to Ulrike Bialas, Katharina Kruse, Susanna Raab and Robert Vief who helped in preparing the manuscript. Bettine Josties and Emre Karaca shared their illustrative material of Berlin *Kreuzberg* with us, for which we are very thankful. Regarding the creation and preparation of illustrations, special thanks go to Albert Hermann who carefully elaborated the different empirical material. Furthermore, we thank Julia Nast and Christine Barwick for commenting on our draft and the conceptual framework.

The preface by AbdouMaliq Simone is a particular honour to us, as he was a source of inspiration, especially with his work on cityness.

But it is, above all, to our interviewees who constantly are 'in the making' of the city of Berlin, who we would like to express our thanks – as well as to all the authors, who contributed to this project with their thoughts and research ideas. The edited volume entailed a long process of correspondence and meetings. We are thankful to the commitment, patience and interesting debates that made the writing of this book such an inspiring process.

Introduction: Creating the Unequal City

Talja Blokland, Carlotta Giustozzi, Daniela Krüger and Hannah Schilling

Cities are geographical imaginaries: people attribute meanings to spaces or places and perceive, represent and interpret them 'in a particular way, reproducing knowledge and facilitating particular courses of action' (Edensor and Jayne 2011, 24; Said 1994).

Urban practices and interactions increasingly interest urban scholars, especially since more of them find inspiration in 'Global South' cities and scholarship. In 'Global North' cities, austerity, changes in welfare regimes and increased diversity in urban citizenship entitlements due to growing migration require more attention for practices outside the city's formal institutions. With people navigating beyond formal institutions becoming more visible, more and more of us may feel that 'even the semblance of a functional life in cities requires efforts to make them familiar and manageable' (Simone 2010, 1). From this perspective, cities become 'a thing in the making' where '[n]o matter how hard analysts and policymakers might try, practices of inhabiting the city are so diverse and change so quickly that they cannot easily be channeled into clearly defined uses of space and resources or patterns of social interchange' (ibid., 3). This draws attention to the urban social infrastructure – 'a conjunction of heterogeneous activities, modes of production, and institutional forms [that] constitute highly mobile and provisional possibilities for how people live and make things, how they use the urban environment and collaborate with one another' (Simone 2004, 410).

This book is about the relationship between such social infrastructures, inclusion and marginalization. It analyses *how practices, fluid interactions and durable engagements*, concepts we will discuss in more detail below, *include some and marginalize others at the same time*.

That we need to make our cities familiar and manageable, and that this takes effort, is not historically unique. But after other theoretical approaches, from the Chicago School (that saw people merely as adapting to the city and the urban as a given) to more politically oriented perspectives (that saw cities as products of power), and the LA school (where the urban is primarily linked to postmodernism and capitalism) urban studies is in need of more *relaxed* theories which focus more on agents (their practices, their fluid interactions and their durable engagements) without losing sight of big structures and large processes (see Harding and Blokland 2014 for a detailed argument).

Our argument is that understanding three ways of doing the city – practices, fluid interactions and durable engagements – can help avoid a choice for either small-scale individualistic, descriptive approaches or for large scale, governance, political or economics oriented approaches of big processes that nod to agency but eventually explain everything urban by structure, where structure gets various labels (with neoliberalism and revanchism having most contemporary currency). Our book is an attempt to put to test the argument (discussed in more detail in Blokland 2012; Blokland and Savage 2008) that urban studies needs a more relational approach. Marginalization, we claim, is a two-sided process. We discuss various cases of practices that are implicitly connected to practices in other cases: they limit their scope of action, and marginalize, or emerge within boundaries set by marginalization. While these practices are located in different neighbourhoods, we do not compare neighbourhoods, but compare people's ways of securing resources in the city. These ways, as our case studies show, reproduce positions and locations, linking the everyday lives of agents to durable urban inequalities. Before we discuss the main concepts that guide the case studies, we show how this compliments our current knowledge of intra-urban inequalities.

The Usual Lens: Neighbourhoods, Effects and Explanations

Asking how people make the city through practices and how such practices affect the possibilities of others searches for causal mechanisms to understand urban inequality (see Tilly 2001, 365). So far, urban scholars have primarily addressed intra-urban inequalities through the lens of neighbourhood effect studies and studies of residential segregation. Neighbourhood effects literature discusses whether living in specific urban neighbourhoods affects life chances negatively, and has become what Tom Slater (2013) calls a 'cottage industry' of empirical case studies.

Explanations for neighbourhood effects have generally been sought inside the areas where life chances negatively compare to elsewhere, as Small and Newman (2001) show. For instance, the collective socialization model sees lacking 'right' role models as reason why 'deviant' lifestyles develop (cf. Jarrett 1997). The epidemic model, with its assumption that deviant behaviour was contagious, and the oppositional cultural model, saying that segregation creates an anti-mainstream culture, reasons along similar lines (Small and Newman 2001). Such explanations simplify 'mainstream' and 'inner-city' culture as dichotomous and contradictory (ibid., 35–8). A further research strand postulates that poor areas' residents lack social capital, or 'the ability to secure benefits by membership of social networks' (Portes 1998, 6). Their networks may support, but not help to get ahead (Souza Briggs 1997, 1998; Kleit and Carnegie 2011; Farwick 2004).

That neighbourhoods matter for life chances is also discussed as resulting from the spatial stratification of amenities (Helbig 2010; Farwick 2009; Häußermann, Kronauer and Siebel 2004; Häußermann and Kapphan 2004). Here, national and metropolitan welfare regimes mediate neighbourhood effects (see Murie and Musterd 2004, 1458). The location of amenities seems to matter more in less extensive welfare regimes like those in the United States and the United Kingdom, than in regimes based on familial support in combination with the state as in Brazil, or in corporatist or social democratically oriented regimes of Germany or Scandinavia. Scholars have therefore contested that European neighbourhood effects exist (Galster 2012; Musterd 2005; Friedrichs, Galster and Musterd 2003; Kazepov 2004). After all, the welfare state provisions are cut back but still large, even the biggest European cities are limited in size so amenities in other neighbourhoods can be accessed from other areas, and European cities have a relative equal wealth distribution compared to other cities in the world.

However, though European neighbourhoods do not have strong statistical effects as found in the United States (Sampson 2012; Sharkey 2013; Garner and Raudenbush 1991; Leventhal and Brooks-Gunn 2003; Galster 2013) it does not mean that, as geographical imaginations, European cities are not stratified. That neighbourhoods may not (always) produce statistically different outcomes does not mean the affluent of Barcelona's suburbs would change the Good Life for a place in an area imagined as 'bad'. Those who can afford to choose know well that it is not just the leafy trees or hip bars and coffee-shops that make them opt for one place over another. If neighbourhood effects cannot be measured, this is not to say that neighbourhoods do not differ in the qualities of their amenities, the interactions taking place, and the fruitfulness of engagements that people can form there. Statistical effects do not have to occur for neighbourhoods to matter. If a child of parents with little formal education, for example, receives bad teaching at a school in a deprived neighbourhood, their test scores may be low. If this child went to school in an affluent neighbourhood and faced discrimination and exclusion, as teachers treat pupils differently according to what they know about their social class (Rist 1970; Good 1987), then this child may score just as badly in tests. The mechanisms that produce those results, however, are different. In neighbourhood effect studies, first, how locations and the overall city meet people's needs, and second, what barriers to their needs may be linked to whereabouts in the city they live, have not received much attention. Studies on segregation have seen a bit of a wave of studies on middle classes and their social segregation in mixed neighbourhoods or self-segregation in gated communities.

Much of the literature treats residential location from a perspective of individual given preferences, and active choice. Explanations are often limited: the preference to live with people with similar social practices is said to be explained by homophily, but this is tautological. Homophily is not an explanation, but a label that *describes* the preference (Barwick and Blokland 2015).

Atkinson sees 'upper-income colonizing strategies [that] … rang[e] … from the relatively 'open seclusion' of insulation to the incarceration of more extreme fear, wealth and withdrawal' (Atkinson 2006, 822). He describes a tendency among the affluent 'to selectively shield domestic life' (Atkinson 2008, 43). The 'defensive aspect to architectures of home, work and education' allows controlling for risks of exposure to social diversity (Atkinson 2008, 47, 42; cf. Atkinson 2006, 822) and is intensified by links created among the different spheres of daily life through 'capsular modes of transport' (Atkinson 2008, 47). This disaffiliation with other – especially poor – social groups is caused by a 'deeply rooted social fear' reinforced by the avoidance of contact with social danger and spaces of poverty in the city (Atkinson 2008, 47; Atkinson 2006, 819).

Even those who emphasize their preference for diversity in the neighbourhood might not lack fluid encounters, but certainly lack durable engagements with other social groups. As many studies on gentrified neighbourhoods show, gentrifiers express their appreciation of the proximity of other social groups and affirm the importance of social integration, multiculturalism and diversity (Butler 2003; Butler and Robson 2001; and cited in Van Eijk 2010; Ley 1986; May 1996; Zukin 1998). Notwithstanding their cosmopolitanism, they tend not to engage with these others (Blokland and Van Eijk 2010; Van Eijk 2010; Butler and Lees 2006; Smith 1996). Butler argues that these preferences are part of a 'metropolitan habitus in which values such as diversity, social inclusion and social integration form an important element of the narrative of settlement but which, in its practice, is one of social exclusivity' (Butler 2003, 2471). Diversity serves as distinction and the multi-ethnic environment provides a 'social wallpaper' (Butler 2003, 2484).

Most of these arguments assume *intentional* exclusionary practices on the part of the elites or middle classes.[1] Wishes for safety and 'spatial autonomy' are interpreted as an 'expression of a deeper strategy' to exclude others (Atkinson 2006, 819) or the current gentrifiers are assumed to be just 'unwilling to invest social capital' in the neighbourhood they live in (Butler 2003, 2469). Methodologically, the authors infer from their observations to motives, but don't provide the (hard to measure) empirical data that support that this is indeed what the middle classes want, intend or feel.

We think both neighbourhood effects explanations and explanations for the segregating practices of the middle classes need more attention. To explain all differences by composition (social class, as does Slater 2013) rather than context prevents us from seeing that urbanites must realize their capabilities in strongly varying settings. Class does not tell the whole tale of urban inequalities. Surely, the shifting and sorting that bring some to live in leafy affluent areas whereas others cramp in inferior buildings in noisy, dirty, polluted places, results from class structures under market capitalism. The rich segregate from the poor, and when the poor are immigrant or ethnic minority groups, social and ethnic segregation coincide. But as Sharkey (2013) shows for the United States, people live in very poor neighbourhoods over generations, although not in the same neighbourhoods. This challenges Slater's argument that social position comes first, and location after. It points to the necessity to see position and location in tandem and identify

1 With the term middle class we describe the relative positions in social space according to occupation, educational background and/or material wealth (income, savings and property).

the mechanisms behind social (im)mobility and, above all, to treat position and location as relational concepts. In a relational view, Tilly writes (2001, 362) 'inequality emerges from asymmetrical social interactions in which advantages accumulate on one side or the other, fortified by construction of social categories that justify and sustain unequal advantage'.

That position and location have to be seen in tandem becomes visible in the fact, for example, that teachers in Berlin schools are no more often ill in poorer areas than in affluent areas but that when they are sick, the chance that pupils get sent home is higher in the deprived neighbourhoods. Or that the number of remedial and speech therapists in the most affluent Berlin areas per capita children is significantly higher than in deprived neighbourhoods. If we then study outcomes in education or health and do not find neighbourhood effects, it may imply that the poor in deprived areas are doing a whole lot of investment to keep up in outcomes. After all, one would *expect* to find neighbourhood effects where residents face different institutional settings. Intrigued by this patchwork of counterintuitive findings, by sensible and yet unfulfilling arguments of scholars like Slater that position, not location, matters, and inspired by work of scholars who have reported on the often trying circumstances of the lives of the poor as a result of 'marginalization' (Wacquant 1999), we aim to take further this relational understanding of position and location.

In the face of the many criticisms on contemporary debates on neighbourhood effects we have started to think about the city as a whole, rather than neighbourhoods as isolated spatial units, and about the interconnectedness of neighbourhoods and the city as a site of resources, made by people and institutions, accessible to them unequally. We are asking ourselves whether one of the keys to the persistence of urban inequalities (not so much their structural origins) may be spatial. Murie and Musterd (2004, 1457) have pointed out that neighbourhood effects, or the outcomes in life chances for individuals depending on where they live, do not differ simply depending on the statistical features of such areas, but that there is a more complex interaction between a variety of factors that determine the nature of resources brought to bear on life chances. They maintain that neighbourhoods differ in the opportunities they provide people with. Neighbourhoods can be more or less supportive and safe environments and hence affect the quality of life, even when, as is often the case for European cities, statistically strong neighbourhood effects have not been found. With to some extent the exception of Sampson (2012), neighbourhood effect studies have measured differences between neighbourhoods but searched, as we have summarized above, for explanations of these differences within neighbourhoods. So whereas neighbourhood effect studies are always comparative – as various scores for various geographical units called neighbourhoods are being compared – the explanations for these effects rarely are. The explanatory models simply assume that negative neighbourhood effects need to be explained within the areas that 'produce' negative effects.

When we are being very critical for a moment, there is an analogy here with the criticism Jennifer Robinson (2011) has formulated for studies of 'Global South' cities that work with a developmental tradition: the observation of 'otherness' in the 'far-away' place is done through the lens of the 'here', and the explanation is sought in terms of pointing out what the 'far-away' place is not. She advocates a reversed lens and, somewhat similar as those arguing for inner logics of cities (Berking and Löw 2008), to study each place for its own merits and specificity, independently of their geographical classification. In order to 'recalibrate the circuits of knowledge generation and revitalizing the comparative project', she argues 'researchers will need to consider all cities as both resources and sites for theory generation and need to expose theory to interrogation based on this wider world of cities' (Robinson 2011, 17). Similarly, neighbourhood effects have generally been explained by pointing to the deficits of 'disadvantaged' areas.

Robinson's plea for a reversed logic urges us to give up on assuming that what we know as the mainstream is the normal, situationally so and definitively in normative terms (see Misztal 2001 for a further discussion of this difference). In this sense, our book can be read, first, as an exercise in a new form of comparison that hopes to help address some of the problems of explanation in the study of neighbourhoods: we compare the ways in which people use the city to realize their urban lives, or how the city enables and hampers their capabilities, a term we return to below. Whereas we connect our thesis to neighbourhoods as socially and geographically produced spaces, we do not study neighbourhoods as such. We compare practices, fluid encounters and durable engagements of city residents in both deprived and affluent neighbourhoods, but instead of comparing neighbourhoods and treating them as containers within which social life happens, we look at the practices through which people create and secure urban resources, practices that, as our case studies show, reproduce positions and locations, and hence link the everyday lives of human agents to structural, durable inequalities within the city.

Second, we see a need to theorize that even though 'neighbourhood' as such may not produce effects, where we live in and how we live in the city is a spatial expression of a social hierarchy that plays somehow, somewhat, of a role in the social reproduction of urban inequalities. We are saying 'somehow, somewhat' because we do not believe it is possible, eventually, to hammer down exactly in a positivist manner what is the A that causes the B, or isolate the right variables that would explain variance in social reproduction, for example in the mobility, upwards or downwards or not at all, of one generation compared to their parents as if that is what reproduction is all about. Understanding social reproduction or identifying its causes is difficult because of what Bourdieu (1994a) terms the effect of naturalization. By translating social statuses into the physical world social structure appears as a matter of fact and becomes inert. So instead of choosing a macro-scale perspective comparing neighbourhoods, we look at micro-social realities and social relations that may have impact on (and are an expression of) location and position.

Marginalization and Resources versus Disadvantage and Assets

This is not, then, a book on neighbourhoods and neighbourhood effects, or even a book on neighbourhood amenities or institutional differences. We have not studied disadvantage as the accumulation of statistical characteristics of people whose places of residence have concentrated in particular areas of the city over the last decades. We have not moved into poor neighbourhoods to study the lives of poor people. Others have tackled the myth of the behavioural model to explain poverty sufficiently (Perlman 1979; Bourgois 1995; Duneier 1999; Snow and Anderson 1993; Liebow 1967; Newman 1999; Jencks 1991). Disadvantage can be seen as the outcome of processes of marginalization that find spatial expressions in the city elsewhere (in for example middle class areas). An underperforming public sector in a poor neighbourhood may be a disadvantage to the poor who depend on these facilities. Yet, especially in a welfare regime like that of Germany, this in itself may explain different outcomes, but does not explain why such local welfare state institutions are different, as this regime provides them with equal funding. Disadvantage is usually understood as being produced by vectors that determine a structure in which people make their lives, without asking how this structure comes about other than through a macro-sociological lens of labour, migration, or globalization. Urban inequalities are seen more relationally by the authors who contributed to our volume, so that we prefer to speak of marginalization and those subjected to processes of marginalization as marginalized. Disadvantage is too static and suggests too much a developmental path (those advanced are the advantaged, those kept back or staying back the disadvantaged; gentrification then ends the disadvantage of a place, for example). Moreover, disadvantage has in our view theoretical affinity with assets, not resources. As Savage, Warde and Devine (2005) have argued, an analytical distinction has to be made between assets and resources. Whereas the acquisition of assets (i.e. more money) implies the gain of relative advantage over others, the access to resources (i.e. better health status) does not. Resources do not imply gaining power over others but are related to existing structural power differences: everybody can get healthier without deterring the health of 'their neighbours'. To speak of disadvantage implies differences in assets, structurally embedded, whereas marginalization occurs when the access to resources of some is actually impeded by the practices of others. When middle class housing is built by the seaside and the poor are housed near the trash belt, the highway with its noise and pollution or the railroad tracks, the poor are marginalized to the worse places in the city and assets ensure the access to resources (a desirable area to live a healthy life) but the limitation to access of the seaside's fresh air is the consequence of a process of displacement of the poor, or spatial marginalization. When middle class parents use various forms of capital to start their own kindergarten, and set requirements regarding parenting involvement and parenting style for those who want a place for their children, the childcare facility as such is not an asset from which poor children are excluded, but the necessary habitus and the social and cultural capital needed to get a place marginalizes them from the resources that such a kindergarten may entail. Marginalization, then, can be defined as the processes (or frequent combinations and sequences of causal mechanisms, Tilly 2001, 365), explicit as well as subtle, through which specific sections of an urban population are pushed out of resourceful settings, not because of anyone's intentions, but because the mechanisms in place and the capital in various forms that is needed to make them work for oneself are effectively keeping them out and, in some cases, pushing them to the edges: the edges of the city of undesirable high-rises, the edges of urban landscapes where undesirable uses can go unnoticed, the edges of the educational system where there are school places over which no one would even think of competing, and the edges of the medical system where doctors still take patients who are not privately insured.

Conceptual Framework

From our focus on marginalization, all authors in this book start from the thesis that the capabilities, a term we derive from Amartya Sen, to make a life and livelihood in cities depend on the social infrastructure of the city seen as practices, fluid encounters and durable engagements that serve the purpose, whether consciously and rationally strategized as such or not, to create resources (as Sen calls it, embark upon 'valuable combinations of human functionings', (2005, 151)). Some may refer to such practices as 'informal'. We prefer not to speak of a formal-informal divide as it suggests a polarization of two separate segments of urban life which has, as McFarlane and Waibel have put it, an 'implicit idea of formality as the norm and informality as deviation' (2011, 2). Instead, with Altrock (2011) we see informal practices as 'complementary' and 'supplementary': as supporting or standing-in for the work of formal institutions (Altrock 2011, quoted in McFarlane and Waibel 2011, 2). People's spaces to manoeuvre, then, are not the outcomes of a fixed path but eventually result from the effective use of such a pathway and the creation of new paths.

Before we discuss why we think resources and capabilities are useful analytical concepts for our purposes, let us spend a few words on the alternatives, opportunities and capital, as concepts that we do not prefer. Clearly, there is some resemblance of what we call resources with what has been called opportunities, a term used mostly in the context of opportunity structures and originally derived from social movement and contentious political literature from the 1990s (see Tilly and Tarrow 2007; Tarrow 1998; McAdam, Tarrow and Tilly 1996; McCarthy and Zald 1977; Benford and Snow 2000). We prefer resources over opportunities because the latter concept suggests that there is an existing structure with a fixed set of opportunities that people may or may not access in behaviour along lines of exit, voice and loyalty (Hirschman 1970). This way of thinking is rational choice influenced. While this in itself is not a problem, it clashes with the idea of a social infrastructure and the weaving and knitting of the urban fabric: a fabric, understood in the tradition of Simmel's web of group affiliations (1955), produced by social life not as a fixed, clearly demarcated space but rather as a plurality of interacting agents in encounters and engagements, where the weaving stands metaphorically for the brief encounters and the knitting symbolizes the networks of durable engagements (cf. Blokland 2000). Our assumption is, as stated above, that cities are dynamic and are ever in the making. In addition to the economics, the labour market opportunities, the housing market, the geographical or ecological setting, the built environment and political position of the city in the country and the region, there is a *social* infrastructure not immediately visible and measurable in the way that urban statistics usually do. We maintain that, whereas it is not the only nor an isolated issue, this social infrastructure impacts marginalization through the ways in which it affects people's resources to realize their capabilities, for example to position themselves in the city.

This understanding of the social fabric as a social infrastructure diverts somewhat from the literature that works with social and other forms of capital. A long-recognized and extensively discussed aim of the literature on economic, social and cultural capital is to go beyond simply having a characteristic, a skill, a tie or a bag with money and achieve some goal with it through exchange. It aims to theorize how such assets are turned into capital by making them profitable to achieve something *else* and how *accumulation* occurs. How this happens, and how some assets can be made profitable in certain fields whereas others are not, however, is less clear.

This is particularly true for the concept of social capital. If the use of the concept of social capital has to follow the economic logics of investment and profit (and some have criticized this, see Fine 2001) then many exchanges may support but are not social capital. From relatively specialized and not widely used, the concept has been popularized especially by Robert Putnam (1995), who defined it as 'features of social organization such as networks, norms and social trust that facilitate coordination and cooperation for mutual benefit' (ibid., 67). Social capital has also been defined in more instrumental terms, referring to people's possibilities to get by or get ahead through mobilizing resources by virtue of their memberships of groups and networks (Portes 1998; Souza Briggs 2005; Lin, Cook and Burt 2001). In the literature, social capital to get by is the support that helps individuals to meet their daily needs, often associated with strong ties with kin, close neighbours and intimate friends (Dominguez and Watkins 2003, 112–13). Social capital to get ahead as social leverage through ties that help people's upward social mobility by providing access to information, for example about employment, is typically expected to be provided by weak ties (Boissevain 1974; Campbell, Marsden and Hurlbert 1986; Granovetter 1973). Weak ties are hence expected to function as bridges, but what features determine whether there is bridging remains vague, so that we do not know how exactly bridging works (cf. Leonard and Onyx 2003, 191; Blokland and Noordhoff 2008, 109).

After all, just the presence of a tie does not mean that this bridge sees any traffic. Blokland and Van Eijk (2010) have shown that the bridging ties of residents with a migration background in a mixed neighbourhood in Rotterdam tended to be ties with native Dutch residents with a lower social status than the immigrants themselves. Superficially, such ties seem to fit within the idea that mixed ties are bridges, but it is not necessarily the case that such bridges provide means to do things people value. Similarly, Blokland and Noordhoff (2008) have shown that people living in poverty in the Netherlands may have ties that measured superficially could be seen as social capital because they are ties with people differing from themselves, whereas in fact these ties cannot, for other reasons of avoiding dependency, shame, lack of reciprocity, be activated. The means are there, but provide a different set of substantive possibilities. More concretely, a Black single mother may not call on the White lawyer whom she knows from a community activist group when her son gets into trouble, whereas a White professor who gets accused of a criminal activity when her ex-husband reports her for 'theft' has no problem asking a parent in school who is also a lawyer for help. Measured as potential social capital, both have the means, but only one has the access.

In fact, the same tie may be capital to some and not to others. Blokland and Nast (2014) show in their recent article how in a mixed school where parents of pupils differing in social status and ethnicity develop child-oriented social capital then when they share the same educational and child raising values, and only then boundaries of class and ethnicity can be overcome. Implicitly then, they also show that educational values are not either 'middle class' or working or lower class. Even the concept of economic capital, suggesting it is not just money for exchange but a return on investment that can be transferred into other forms of capital, may be empirically complicated to measure, and money may not turn out to be transferrable capital in this sense in all cases. Note that in the literature on capital and fields, the question whether any economic capital can be turned into any other form of capital has not been extensively researched (see Khan 2011 for an exception). Particularly in the German context, the convertibility of economic resources into cultural capital is limited by a strong public education system. Hence, money does not get people in the 'right' elementary schools in the public school system of Berlin, for example, which is dominated by the middle class. In terms of the choice of school there is a tendency of middle class parents in Berlin to circumvent formal regulations of registering their child in the public elementary school nearby. Money, as such, does not get people into the 'right' elementary school within the public school system of Berlin. Even if they buy out of the system by going to private schools, those schools are not a guarantee to a better education than the good public schools in the city at all. This indicates that social skills, connections, and being able to attune to the type of expectations the school has of parents seem to help people get places, although there is no systematic empirical evidence to support this.

Here again it becomes clear that weak ties that provide information, for example, do not automatically mean capital that can be made profitable: a rich person interested in a private school in an upper class neighbourhood of Berlin may learn from other parents in the elementary school that 'connections' are needed to get a place for the preferred school, as one mother tells another. She attended the school herself as a child and knows many people there. She knows who to talk to and they know her, and that is how she got a place. This information, however, does not provide the new, in-coming parent without a local biography with this type of access. In an elementary school in the same area, there is one classroom with a very good teacher team. The children landing with these teachers in the first grade come more often from the kindergarten next to the school than first graders who went to other kindergartens, and often tend to know each better from the kindergarten than the other new children in the school. Newcomers may have the same information ('these are the best teachers in the school') and even hear this from the same parents, but the mere piece of information does not necessarily include them in the clique of parents who are 'in the know': knowledge is shared, but knowledge of an informal way to get something done does not open up that way in itself. This becomes possibly even more visible in situations where bribing is expected, as was long the case in former eastern European countries: to get a permit to build in Czech towns, for example, was known to depend on paying off some officials. As this is publically known but officially non-existent, people are secretive about first, having bribed, and second, sharing the ways of how to do such bribing with outsiders. Whereas one may have enough economic capital to build a castle, they may still be unable to build as much as a chicken pen, because unfamiliarity of outsiders with local bribing practices makes it impossible to bribe in the right way.

All these examples show that there is a difference between having something and being able to put it to use, and scholars who have worked with social and other forms of capital have overlooked such subtleties too much. Of course there have been many other grounds to be critical of the concept of social capital that seems to have had its high days by now (although a substantial amount of quantitative studies are still produced (Aldrich 2012; Li and Choi 2014; Fasang, Mangino and Brückner 2014; Lewandowski and Streich 2012; Franzen and Freitag 2008; Field 2003), some of which we share and some of which we do not. We do not suggest that conceptual frameworks that build on forms of capital cannot be useful, but consider a capability approach with a focus on resources more fruitful for the purposes of our book. Bourdieu's perspective can be said to be more relational than the perspectives discussed so far. However, his analysis is primarily an analysis of social class, and for contemporary urban inequalities, we need a broader scope. Moreover, Bourdieu discusses forms of capital primarily for its exclusionary practices, and was less interested in how forms of capital also work in inclusive ways. With resources and capabilities we are thus inspired by Amartya Sen, not a usual choice for urban scholars (see Drilling 2004 for an exception). Sen's capability approach sees opportunity in terms of capabilities: 'the opportunity to achieve valuable combinations of human functionings' (Sen 2005, 151) – or what a person is able to do or be. This view differentiates between first, whether a person is able to do things she values doing and second, whether 'she possesses the means, instruments and permissions to do so' (ibid.). This perspective, Sen argues, resists an overconcentration on simply means: the same set of means may, after all, provide a different set of substantive possibilities to different people.

There is variability in how means and actual opportunities are related: means, instruments and permissions, then, in our framework, are resources in so far as they can be actualized to become capabilities, depending on physical and mental conditions, variations in non-personal resources, environmental diversities and the relative position of an agent vis-à-vis others (ibid., 153). In the example of the private school or the first graders' classroom, while one may share the information that certain connections may give access, the limited places available make the ability to have the absolute advantage of getting a place in this school or this classroom depend on a relative position. Being able to broker access through ties for one's own child depends on others not being able to do so. This is not because other parents may particularly want to keep this access to themselves, but because they want to do well for their own children, which means here that they must keep some 'differential advantage' (Sen 1983, 156): therefore, Sen concludes with a similar example of enjoying a quiet beach that only you know about, 'your absolute achievement – not merely your relative success – may depend on your position in some other field' (ibid.). This, then, is the connection between 'absolute deprivation in terms of a person's capabilities' and 'relative deprivation in terms of commodities, incomes and resources'. Agents, in other words, are in our view not, as Bourdieu maintains (1994a, 111), just defined by their relative position in social space, but also by their capabilities, and these go further than mere dispositions and habitus. Following this line, our book will show how not just having the means, instruments and permissions of people to achieve in their eyes valuable combinations of human functionings matter, but also whether a person is able to do the things she values doing, which depends on more than just having the assets. This also shows that where mechanisms of exclusion work to the disadvantage of some, a perspective that simply claims that the middle classes out of revanchist sentiments (Smith 1996) do not *want* others to realize their capabilities is too easy and too narrow. It puts the empirical unverifiable 'motives' of middle classes at central stage. Finding that many middle class interview partners in empirical projects talk politically progressively about the world they would wish for, but in their own actions realize capabilities through hoarding opportunities so that these become only their resources, can be dismissed as saying that interview partners simply answer the researcher what is socially desirable. Apart from the question whether in today's 'Global North' cities left-wing orientations are socially desirable, this argument is problematic because it first assumes that the researcher knows what the middle class interview partners 'really' think without having any evidence. Second, it starts from the idea that middle class interview partners are more likely to adhere to socially desirable imaginations and therefore that their answers are less reliable than the answers of other interview partners. This is methodologically problematic. And it is theoretically unnecessary: all we need, as our book shows, is a more careful conceptual framework to analyse the practices, fluid encounters and durable engagements of urbanites and a more careful language that refrains from bashing either the poor or the middle classes for having the 'wrong' motives (see in more detail Blokland 2012).

We have defined social infrastructure above as composed of practices, fluid encounters and durable engagements. Practice follows the Bourdieusian perspective on the sociology of practice. For Bourdieu, structured and structuring dispositions and habitus are constructed through practices and directed at practical functions (and here we see an analogy with Sen) (Bourdieu 1994b, 95). Habitus thus connects capabilities to inequality in substantive possibilities as Sen described them: a person matches his subjective aspirations with objective probabilities, as Bourdieu says:

> not because agents consciously adjust their aspirations to an exact evaluation of their chances of success, like a gambler organizing his stakes on the basis of perfect information about his chances of winning. In reality, the dispositions durably inculcated by the possibilities and impossibilities, freedoms and necessities, opportunities and prohibitions inscribed in the objective conditions … generate dispositions objectively compatible with these conditions and in a sense pre-adapted to their demands. (ibid., 97)

Habitus governs practice, not as a determining set, but 'within the constraints and limits initially set on its interventions' (ibid., 98). We focus on practices because we agree with Bourdieu that social scientists should avoid the suggestion that 'all traces of life … appear as the realization of an essence that seems to pre-exist them' (ibid., 99; see also Tilly's criticism (1984) on essentializing individuals or Gouldner (1970) on the under-socialized and over-socialized person; also Wrong (1999)). Practices, in short, rather than intentions, create resourceful sites for some, while marginalizing others and limiting the scope for their practices to live and make a livelihood. We separate fluid encounters and durable engagements from other practices as the forms of sociability itself through which urbanites create resources. These two terms identify not what people do, but name the actual relation created, maintained or altered while doing something.

So far, the relational perspective has heavily leaned on network understandings of personal ties. We stretch the concept of ties in two ways. First, in addition and complementary to personal networks, we see the urban texture as woven rather than knitted, flowing and flexible as a web of affiliations (Simmel 1955) by brief encounters (Blokland and Nast 2014). The fluidity of encounters, more than that they are brief, is most important. The accidental, unplanned interactions we will talk about when Sub-Saharan immigrants learn about opportunities through talking to other 'Africans' on the subway, in shops or in the church without a proper 'tie' emerging, or when middle class residents learn about chances for their children whilst chatting at the playground with people whom they do not identify as 'network' can broker situations in which resources emerge – this, also, is one of the forms of interactions that the social capital approach has difficulties grasping. Second, we prefer durable engagements over ties to name associations between people that last longer than a moment. The social ties that network research usually measures belong to these, but also the attachments between people who we will meet in this book: members of the same church or the same leisure club, as in the case of a group of girls, or people meeting frequently at a square. Such engagements do not constitute a network in the sense that network generators would bring people to talk about these others. Yet they are, as the empirical chapters will show, important for living and making a living in the city. The conceptual difference with fluid encounters is that they come with a different set of expectations of social behaviour – the expectation to greet in an African church is different than the expectation to greet someone on the subway because he is 'African' too – and that they are likely to repeat as people engage in an institutional setting that provides them with a regular focus for contact. Such engagements may change into personal ties, like friendships, over time. Fluid encounters will rarely do so. Together with our common understanding of people's networks, these durable engagements constitute the knitted fabric of the social infrastructure. The fluid encounters contribute to the fabric too, but more like the threads of a woven cloth: they touch in passing but do not bind.

Durable engagements, fluid encounters and practices are not taking place in a vacuum but are spatially, socially and historically grounded. Being situated in a specific context shapes the ways in which people see the right to the city as a right to protect or enhance their or other people's positions, for example how they are situated in terms of access to resources. Eventually, one may say that they are just pursuing self-interests. The choice, however, to let self-interest prevail over other possible, also substantial, rationalities or emotions, is informed by moral orientations about deservingness, rights and belonging. The assumption that people ever have a purely instrumental-rational orientation decontextualizes and individualizes human agents and does not contribute to precise understandings of their practices. Hence, understanding moral orientation as a practice, not an individualistic and abstract notion (see the critique of Lamont and Aksartova 2002 on Ignatieff 1999 and Beck 1998), helps see it as a device to draw boundaries between the 'good' and the 'bad' (see Lamont and Molnár 2002). This categorization, part of the individual's cultural repertoire for encounters and engagements, legitimizes in/exclusions (see ibid.; Small, Harding and Lamont 2010; Silverstein 2001).

Taking moral orientations as a special feature of practices also enables us to see ambivalences between moral orientations and consequences of practices, as highlighted in our example above of accessing the right schoolteachers. But we will also see moral orientations, especially in the chapters on the church and the mobilization of ethnicity where Sub-Saharan immigrants try to find work, that result in inclusion rather than marginalization. Their combination of positions and locations, for example the particular places in the city where they live, may provide what Bourdieu has called 'spatial profit' (Bourdieu 1999, 123–30). Moral orientations include how people define obligations to share or to give, and hence the rights to exclude or draw boundaries, turning them from symbolic into social (Lamont and Molnár 2002). Daily activities of connecting, sharing and opportunity hoarding (Tilly 2001) organize interactions in encounters and engagements. The recognition of moral orientations, legally and socially, and their guidance to further practices has to be contextualized. For instance, the German welfare regime with its encompassing notion of welfare and equality has generated an urban landscape of public institutions that are, notwithstanding the influence of neoliberalism, largely intact. Welfare regimes do not simply transfer social benefits (where neoliberal politics have certainly been enforced). Welfare regimes are also about how institutions, whether state-run or state-funded, transfer services to urbanites. Such transfers do not simply happen as the movement of something from one place, person, or thing to another. The ultimate outcomes of a transfer of anything from a medicine prescribed by a doctor, a reading skill to a student in first grade, or a German language skill to an immigrant in a language course is less interesting than the process of transfers. The skills, expectations, chances and possibilities on both the side of the agent in the public institution actually doing this and on the side of the agent who is 'receiving' impact such processes just as much as a formal set of regulations of entitlements and rights may do. Our focus therefore lies on moral orientations and recognition as a dimension of practices through which people live and make a living in the city (cf. also Maynard-Moody and Musheno 2003).

The continuous reshaping of the city resulting from such practices tends to strengthen the urban imaginaries of some urban places and institutions over others. Such imaginaries reinforce spatial divisions in the city and limit the right to all places for all. To use some of the examples in this book, the *drinkers* on a Berlin square in a deprived neighbourhood face the double stigma of the imagery of the neighbourhood and of their social status; the Sub-Saharan immigrants face the marginalization of being Black and the practices of 'racist neighbourhoods' that constitute no-go areas for them, and some of the Arabic- and Turkish-German girls withdraw in their neighbourhood's youth club, not having the 'urban literacy' (Simone 2010) to traverse the neighbourhood borders.

In short, then, each of our chapters works with the following concepts. **Capabilities** is used for having something and put it in use (a valuable combination of human functionings), being able to do something (physical, mental condition, environmental diversities, non-personal resources, relative position) and, in addition to either one of these, and indispensable, having the means, instruments, or permissions to do so. **Resources** are these means, instruments and permissions, structured by habitus and dispositions. Resources can become capabilities when they can be used to achieve a human functioning that the person involved holds for valuable. They are created through the social infrastructure of practices, fluid encounters and durable engagements. This **social infrastructure** of practices, weaving **fluid encounters**, and knitting **durable engagements** are intertwined with **moral orientations**. Urbanites create resources through both fluid encounters and durable engagements. Whereas the first are accidental and unplanned, durable engagements are more long-lasting, although not necessarily personal, and come with a different, often more tight set of expectations regarding social behaviour, especially in institutional contexts.

On Comparison

This book takes the thought of the city as a thing in the making away from where this argument was developed, in the 'Global South' cities from Jakarta to Dakar. We take the idea to Berlin, where the city's 'capacity to provoke relations of all kinds' (Simone 2010, 3) may be less obvious. This capacity to provoke all kinds of relations, after all, is a feature of a city that is relatively planned and institutionally structured.

We hence follow urban scholars who are currently pleading for new forms of comparisons and methods under the flag of 'comparative urbanism'.

Comparative urbanism brings a challenging set of criticisms to mainstream urban studies. Scholars like Jennifer Robinson, Colin McFarlane, Ananya Roy and Aihwa Ong plead for the 'comparative gesture' (Robinson 2006), which takes comparisons not only as a method 'but as a mode of thought that informs how urban theory is constituted' (McFarlane 2010, 725). These scholars enthusiastically propose a research agenda that differs from classic approaches as it uses comparisons as analytical lenses to reveal circuits of knowledge. Moreover, it challenges the traditional units of comparison (i.e. entire cities) and the unidirectional connections between them (i.e. cities from the 'Global South' are compared to the standards of the 'Global North'), as they are seeing all cities as both resources and sites for theory generation. They aim to expose theory to interrogation based on this 'wider world of cities' (Robinson 2006, 17). However, this scholarship of comparative urbanism has until now achieved less in showing how, precisely, their aim can be put to practice.

Few uncommon comparisons have so far been made in substantive empirical projects. We suspect that one of the reasons for this may be that the debate has been instigated by geographers who do not come from social science methods backgrounds. Moreover, we think that the comparative urbanism discussion may not have resulted in clarity as to what exactly needs to be compared: if we do unlikely comparisons and see cities as each unique, then *what* do we compare? Policies, forms of governance, poverty, or inequality, to name a few, all seem unsuitable for such an approach if comparison is to generate theory. If we were to compare such themes between cities, we can find that they are the same or they are different, and may be tempted to explain variation by the particularities of one place or another. This would, in the end, invite an endless cottage industry of case studies, and some of that has been happening so far: many housing studies scholars have found that 'yes, people in our poorest neighbourhood are stigmatized too' or 'well, gentrification works a little different in my case than in yours'. The dominance of descriptive case studies and theorizing by geographers in urban studies, and the remarkable silence of sociologists who theorize in the field, may explain this. Maybe comparison is becoming the new mantra of our social science era, and is too easily understood as comparing two places. Can comparison not be thought of differently and made truly unusual? Sociology may hold a surprisingly easy answer to this. If we accept that social life is patterned – and we would have to give up the discipline if we did not want to start with that – and start our investigations by searching for, as Charles Tilly has long advocated, the processes and mechanisms that help explain the occurrence of social phenomena (Tilly 1984 and 2004), then our task is to find the phenomena that we consider interesting or important, define them as sociologically the same even though they may seem empirically very different, and work out what the mechanisms and contexts are that bring these phenomena to be two variations of the same social fact, experience or event. In other words, precisely because they seem very different when looked at only through a positivist empirical, descriptive lens, they do, when theorized, present two variations of social life produced by the same mechanism or process.

Comparative urbanism, then, becomes an exercise in explaining social phenomena in and of the city through comparison whilst attempting to figure out the relationship between agent, structure and context in the process, rather than just the more traditional agency and structure (see for a study that implicitly makes this argument Sharkey 2013).

With Berlin as one place where we find various cases, we take on the invitation for a new comparative urbanism: we look at the city's social infrastructure – and contrast unusual groups within the city. We think that in doing so, we can learn something about the processes and mechanisms of inclusion versus marginalization, rather than pointing to the outcomes of such processes (for example inequalities in positions, assets and locations) as evidence that they have taken place.

Berlin[2] is composed of twelve districts with their own constituencies and political governance structures. About 3.3 million inhabitants live in Berlin. Almost 11 per cent are non-German citizens from 185 countries. The largest group with about 102,000 people has a Turkish nationality and the second largest with about 45,000 people is Polish. Including the second generation, about 25 per cent of the population has a so called 'migration background'. Berlin's rate of unemployment is about 11 per cent and its rate of underemployment was about 15 per cent. Berlin has 39 Universities or Colleges, 670 public and 140 private schools (2013), almost 8,000 physicians, 80 hospitals and 4,000 dentists. The national and local state provides access to services and amenities on a broad scale, and relatively speaking what is usually called the 'informal sector' is limited. But Berlin is also a city of, for example, squatters, homeless people including Roma families from Romania and Bulgaria now seeking shelter in parks in *Kreuzberg*, a 'Thai Park' where Thai immigrants sell food informally to tourists and visitors and bottle collectors trying to earn a living by collecting empty bottles in parks where others relax (cf. Haid 2013) and an underground economy of drugs. Nonetheless, both national welfare provisions in terms of unemployment benefits, welfare checks and health insurances and local welfare state arrangements like public schools and social work institutions provide a broad range of services for

2 The statistics in this section are derived from the Statistical Office for Berlin-Brandenburg (2014), the Press and Information Office of the Federal Government (2013) of Berlin and the Senate Administration for Education, Science and Research (2013).

citizens *and* create limitations on the capacity to provoke relations of all kinds. One may, with Foucault (1982), argue that this is the control of the state, or with Wacquant (2010) that this is 'managing the poor', or, instead, with Marshall and Bottomore (1992), that the German national and local state defines itself, with democratic legitimization, as a nation state with a broad conception of citizenship, including a right to participation. For our aim, it does not matter much how one prefers to see this. The point is that the state provides social services, and still does so extensively notwithstanding the worries about neoliberalization, and that such provisions may do people good, but analytically do mean that the space of manoeuvre in the city is different than it is in the *favelas* of São Paulo or the slums of Hyderabad. Whether as a caring and emancipating state or a civilizing force (see De Swaan 1988; Elias 1982), the role of the state, locally and nationally, is a different one. Without judging this in moral terms, seeing like a state (Scott 1990) may not rule everyone's life, but the institutional and built infrastructure of the city of Berlin shows a continuous presence of the state.

The development of industrial welfare states historically showed a formalization of labour, but informal forms of work have survived and sometimes grew (Pfau-Effinger and Sakač Magdalenić 2010). Such informal activity and provoking of relations outside the official welfare state regime suggests that the citizenship conception on which the welfare regime is built is far from inclusive. As Lebuhn (2013) has argued, with the decreasing border control at territorial national borders, citizenship has become urban and state control and state provision have become less a territorial matter and more a matter of entitlement and rights to access in the city. This book starts from the point of view that comparatively speaking a city like Berlin may appear 'in line' with the regulations of its welfare regime, but that within the framework defined by the obvious, visible city, there is another social infrastructure where people create practices, interactions and engagements within. The ways in which they mobilize their capacities to generate material or immaterial benefits from a variety of sources depend not just on state and market, but also on people as infrastructure.

The Structure of this Book

Each of our chapters, then, discusses practices of urban life of a non-representative set of agents in various networks and sociality: we return time and again to the triad of practices, fluid encounters and more durable engagements. The agents are non-representative for a reason: we aim to show that the mechanisms and processes that underlie the unequal access to resources, linked to their spatiality, are at work across the urban context, not defined by the categorical characteristics of the groups of residents. Different from what is often believed in mainstream public discourse, exclusion and inclusion do not depend on the characteristics of the groups, but are about the production of group boundaries as such. Hence this is not a book about a specific ethnic group, and not about a specific social class.

This is a book about how residents of an ordinary city, Berlin, go about creating a resourceful city – and how their practices have marginalizing consequences.

Empirically, the odd comparisons that we make have required an odd combination of methods. Each of the authors of the chapters has conducted face-to-face interviews and/or observations. We rely on 89 interviews and observation accounts of various places and groups of people, scattered over the city of Berlin[3] from the middle class home-owning groups in *Lichterfelde*, located in the district *Steglitz-Zehlendorf*, to the socially and ethnically mixed districts of *Kreuzberg*, *Wedding* and *Neukölln*. *Kreuzberg* and *Neukölln* are undergoing stark processes of gentrification, but all three districts are also publically labelled as 'problematic'. In *Kreuzberg*, we primarily interviewed middle class residents as this area is quickly moving away from being 'problematic' in the public imagery.

We organize our book in two parts. We start with an emphasis on marginalized neighbourhoods as not resulting exclusively from internal logics but from citywide processes, such as the urban elite's creation of spatial imaginaries and their hoarding of opportunities. The creation of 'spaces of fear' for Sub-Saharan immigrants and the consequences for this group's everyday practice is the topic of the chapter by Mirjam Lewek. The city, she argues, is often celebrated as the 'natural home' of cosmopolitanism, expressed as open-minded encounters with others. Lewek critically engages with the imaginary of the open-minded city, by looking at a market-oriented cosmopolitanism's function for sustaining spatial profit for some and excluding others from places and resources in the city. Through the everyday life stories of Sub-Saharan immigrants, she points to the consequences for their creation of capabilities, putting emphasis on the city's accessibility for them.

The accessibility of resources in the city might also be hampered implicitly by those residents who do have the right resources allowing them to move freely within the city. Carlotta Giustozzi, Talja Blokland and Nora Freitag focus on this group of residents and look at residential choices of middle class families with small children in Berlin and the school choices for their children. Here, they demonstrate that the awareness of middle class parents about the importance of transmitting cultural capital to their children in a globalizing labour market creates anxieties over schools, anxieties that bring them to practices that enhance the already existing segregation in schools and neighbourhoods.

In the next chapter Talja Blokland and Georg Große-Löscher further trace the practices of middle class families reproducing their cultural capital through schooling thereby showing how these practices (re)produce a segregated school landscape. As they conclude, the interviewed parents secure educational resources through fluid encounters and durable engagements to circumvent catchment area regulations and thus get their offspring into what they perceive as the 'right' school. While they prefer to live in socially mixed neighbourhoods, they do not

3 See the map in the appendix for a detailed overview of our research areas and sites in Berlin.

necessarily practice diversity – instead, some of these parents express anxieties and racist assumptions about the immigrant 'other'.

Giustozzi then zooms into the practices of middle class women of German ethnicity. As we have argued, to understand mechanisms and processes that produce unequal outcomes, only saying that 'class has done it' no longer suffices, and a broader scope, intersecting class and, as in this chapter, gender, is necessary. Giustozzi shows how mothers create resources in the city to secure the positions of their children, using the advantages of their neighbourhoods to do so, here a middle class enclave in mixed *Kreuzberg* and the predominantly single-family homes quarter in *Lichterfelde*. As mothers, they go through a stressful life stage, as they have to establish careers while raising small children. This chapter discusses in particular how the gender roles of women as mothers come into existence by making use of neighbourhood-based resources, and reflects on marginalization as an unintended consequence of intended behaviour along the lines sketched above of absolute advantage through relative positions.

In the second part of the book, we focus on those urbanites living at the margins of the city and their practices of realizing their capabilities. Here, we discuss both the role and effectiveness of institutions in providing access to resources. We show that fluid encounters and durable engagements emerge within institutional settings and beyond – for example in the public realm and how they are used to deal with marginalization in urban contexts.

Imogen Feld brings together marginalization with practices of durable engagements in her discussion of young women's orientations towards the future as they are about to enter vocational training or higher education. Their capabilities to create lives and livelihood differ depending on the resources they can create: most clearly they depend not just on means and instruments, but very much on being able to do the things they value doing (permissions in the broad sense and recognition on a meta-level). The girls' club where Feld interviewed the young women is an institution where interactions are organized and moral orientations are created that strongly influence the young women's potentials vis-à-vis a school system that marginalizes them and a family context in which they endure economic and racial marginalization.

Stephan Simon takes us back to Sub-Saharan immigrants in Berlin, and presents their routes and structures (Simone 2010, 1) of engaging in durable relationships within such an institutional context, an African Pentecostal church. His chapter shows that sites, or what in social capital literature are often called 'foci', that are relevant to people's lives may not be linked to the place where their bed stands, for example their residential neighbourhood. He also shows that capabilities here depend on people's capacity to take part in the 'doing of community': means, instruments and permissions making durable engagements possible and moral orientations profitable.

Like Simon, Rebecca Arbter discusses the creation of resources in and of the city by Sub-Saharan immigrants. But she does so through asking whether social networks as they are usually defined in the analyses of economic opportunities (finding and keeping a job) do or do not provide ties that Sub-Saharan immigrants use. What kind of fluid encounters or durable engagements do they use, what moral orientations guide to what extent information of job chances is shared, and why do such practices produce only limited social mobility for the people involved? Arbter argues that the standard Anglo-Saxon understanding of networks may not be accurate for understanding how Sub-Saharan immigrants make a livelihood in the city, and that the relevance of such social networks must be reconsidered. Instead, the concept of fluid encounters helps us understand how capabilities can be realized in contemporary cities like Berlin.

Daniela Krüger focuses on people's ways of gaining social recognition within a neoliberal regime of poverty. This regime reflects on everyday experiences of alcohol- and drug-using, predominantly German low-income Berliners. Krüger shows how they use a public square and its design to organize interactions and define moral orientations, distancing themselves from public images of the square and the associated substance abuse. While the square provides them a sanctuary from everyday exclusions, it also requires them to position and locate themselves actively. Programmes of urban redevelopment and police operations challenge the boundary drawing of the studied groups and exemplify the impact of policy strategies on such a setting. Still, through their durable engagements within their groups and their fluid encounters with others, their practices create a location of visibility and social recognition, albeit an unstable one.

Hannah Schilling again takes the capabilities of Sub-Saharan immigrants who visit a Pentecostal church in Berlin as a starting point, but elaborates on the informal social infrastructure that develops here beyond the institutionally fostered community building discussed by Simon. She shows how the participation in a Pentecostal church can become a resource for Sub-Saharan immigrants who face specific processes of marginalization in the city. Religiosity then becomes a source for moral orientations, cultural capital and provides access to people that serve them as infrastructure (Simone 2004). It enables marginalized citizens to overcome spatial and institutional barriers to gain recognition, and opens access to alternative sites for the creation of resources.

In the conclusion, then, we summarize the perspective put forward in this book. We argue that to understand the city as in the making, it makes sense to think of urban inequalities through the lens of a resource perspective. Such a perspective can take into account that agents in the city can make their lives and livelihoods, and how such practices may include and marginalize, but can meanwhile acknowledge structural barriers. The consequence of such a perspective, here empirically grounded in the practices of as diverse groups as middle class German parents, Arabic- and Turkish-German girls, and Sub-Saharan immigrants and alcohol- and drug-using disadvantaged Berliners, is a plea for the relational study of urban resources. It asks for attention for the ways in which moral orientations and organizations of interactions impact capabilities, not just because people are heterogeneous and vary in their assets, but also because the urban social infrastructure creates spatial differences (or, in Sen's term, variations in non-personal resources and environmental diversities) and different relative positions of urban residents vis-à-vis others. The book hence takes issue with the way the 'urban' is currently often understood in neighbourhood effect studies, the subfield that currently dominates the field of the study of intra-urban inequalities. We propose to take seriously 'spatial profit' not simply as a label that links location to position, but as a relational (unintended) result of inward orientations and practices expressed spatially by some groups at the expense of others.

References

Aldrich, Daniel P. 2012. *Building Resilience: Social Capital in Post-Disaster Recovery*. Chicago: University of Chicago Press.

Altrock, Uwe. 2011. 'Conceptualising Informality: Some Thought on the Way Towards Generalisation'. In *Urban informalities. Reflections on the formal and informal*, edited by Colin McFarlane and Michael Waibel, 171–93. Farnham: Ashgate.

Atkinson, Rowland. 2006. 'Padding the Bunker: Strategies of Middle-Class Disaffiliation and Colonisation in the City'. *Urban Studies* 43 (4): 819–32.

———. 2008. 'The Flowing Enclave and the Misanthropy of Networked Affluence'. In *Networked Urbanism: Social Capital in the City*, edited by Talja V. Blokland and Michael Savage, 41–58. Aldershot, England; Burlington, VT: Ashgate.

Barwick, Christine and Talja V. Blokland. 2015. 'Segregation durch Diskriminierung auf dem Wohnungsmarkt'. In: *'Ich habe nichts gegen Ausländer, aber ...' – Alltagsrassismus in Deutschland*, edited by Britta Marschke and Heinz Ulrich Brinkmann, 229–43. Berlin-Münster-Wien-Zürich-London: Lit Verlag.

Beck, Ulrich. 1998. 'The Cosmopolitan Manifesto'. *New Statesman* 20: 28–30.

Benford, Robert D. and David A. Snow. 2000. 'Framing Processes and Social Movements: An Overview and Assessment'. *Annual Review of Sociology* 26: 611–39.

Berking, Helmuth and Martina Löw. 2008. *Die Eigenlogik der Städte: Neue Wege für die Stadtforschung*. Frankfurt/Main: Campus-Verlag.

Blokland, Talja V. 2000. 'Unravelling Three of a Kind: Cohesion, Community and Solidarity'. *Netherlands Journal of Social Sciences* 36 (1): 56–70.

———. 2012. 'Blaming Neither the Undeserving Poor nor the Revanchist Middle Classes: A Relational Approach to Marginalization'. *Urban Geography* 33 (4): 488–507.

Blokland, Talja V. and Floris Noordhoff. 2008. 'The Weakness of Weak Ties: Social Capital to Get Ahead Among the Urban Poor in Rotterdam and Amsterdam'. In *Networked Urbanism: Social Capital in the City*, edited by Talja V. Blokland and Michael Savage, 105–25. Aldershot, England; Burlington, VT: Ashgate.

Blokland, Talja V. and Gwen van Eijk. 2010. 'Do People Who Like Diversity Practice Diversity in Neighbourhood Life? Neighbourhood Use and the

Social Networks of 'Diversity-Seekers' in a Mixed Neighbourhood in the Netherlands'. *Journal of Ethnic and Migration Studies* 36 (2): 313–32.

Blokland, Talja V. and Julia Nast. 2014. 'From Public Familiarity to Comfort Zone: The Relevance of Absent Ties for Belonging in Berlin's Mixed Neighbourhoods'. *International Journal of Urban and Regional Research* 38 (4): 1142–59.

Blokland, Talja V. and Michael Savage. 2008. *Networked urbanism social capital in the city.* Aldershot, England; Burlington, VT: Ashgate.

Boissevain, Jeremy. 1974. *Friends of friends: Networks, manipulators and coalitions*. Oxford: Blackwell.

Bourdieu, Pierre. 1994a. 'Social space and symbolic power'. In *The Polity reader in social theory*, edited by Wolfgang J. Mommsen, 111–20. Cambridge: Polity Press.

———. 1994b. 'Structure, habitus and practices'. In: *The Polity reader in social theory*, edited by Wolfgang J. Mommsen, 95–110. Cambridge: Polity Press.

———. 1999. *The Weight of the World. Social Suffering in Contemporary Society*. Cambridge: Polity Press.

Bourgois, Philippe I. 1995. *In Search of Respect. Selling Crack in El Barrio.* New York: Cambridge University Press.

Butler, Tim. 2003. 'Living in the Bubble: Gentrification and Its 'Others' in North London'. *Urban Studies* 40 (12): 2469–86.

Butler, Tim and Garry Robson. 2001. 'Social capital, gentrification and neighbourhood change in London: a comparison of three South London neighbourhoods'. *Urban Studies* 38: 2145–62.

Butler, Tim and Loretta Lees. 2006. 'Super-Gentrification in Barnsbury, London: Globalization and Gentrifying Global Elites at the Neighbourhood Level'. *Transactions of the Institute of British Geographers* 31 (4): 467–87.

Campbell, Karen E., Peter V. Marsden and Jeanne S. Hurlbert. 1986. 'Social resources and socioeconomic status'. *Social Networks* 8 (1): 97–117.

De Swaan, Abram. 1988. *In care of the state: Health care, education, and welfare in Europe and the USA in the modern era*. Oxford: Polity Press.

Dominguez, Silva and C. Watkins. 2003. 'Creating networks for survival and mobility: Social capital among African-American and Latin-American low-income mothers'. *Social Problems* 50 (1): 111–35.

Drilling, Matthias. 2004. *Young urban poor: Abstiegsprozesse in den Zentren der Sozialstaaten.* Wiesbaden: VS Verlag für Sozialwissenschaften.

Duneier, Mitchell. 1999. *Sidewalk.* New York: Straus and Giroux; Farrar.

Edensor, Tim and Mark Jayne (eds). 2011. *Urban Theory Beyond the West.* Abingdon, Oxon; Burlington, VT: Routledge.

Elias, Norbert. 1982. *The Civilizing Process. Sociogenetic and Psychogenetic Investigations*. Oxford: Blackwell.

Farwick, Andreas. 2004. 'Segregierte Armut. Zum Einfluss städtischer Wohnquartiere auf die Dauer von Armutslagen'. In *An den Rändern der Städte:*

Armut und Ausgrenzung, edited by Hartmut Häußermann, 286–314. Frankfurt am Main: Suhrkamp.

———. 2009. *Segregation und Eingliederung: Zum Einfluss der räumlichen Konzentration von Zuwanderern auf den Eingliederungsprozess*. Wiesbaden: VS Verlag für Sozialwissenschaften / GWV Fachverlage.

Fasang, Anette E., William Mangino and Hannah Brückner. 2014. 'Social Closure and Educational Attainment'. *Sociological Forum* 29: 137–64.

Field, John. 2003. *Social Capital*. London; New York: Routledge.

Fine, Ben. 2001. *Social Capital versus Social Theory: Political Economy and Social Science at the Turn of the Millennium*. New York: Routledge.

Foucault, Michel. 1982. 'The subject and power'. *Critical inquiry* 8 (4): 777–95.

Franzen, Axel and Markus Freitag. 2008. *Sozialkapital: Grundlagen und Anwendungen*. Wiesbaden: VS Verlag für Sozialwissenschaften.

Friedrichs, Jürgen, George Galster and Sako Musterd. 2003. 'Neighbourhood Effects on Social Opportunities: The European and American Research and Policy Context'. *Housing Studies* 18 (6): 797–806.

Galster, George C. 2012. 'The Mechanism(s) of Neighbourhood Effects. Theory, Evidence, and Policy Implications'. In *Neighbourhood Research. New Perspectives*, edited by Maarten van Ham, David Manley, Nick Bailey, Ludi Simpson and Duncan Maclennan, 23–56. Dordrecht, Heidelberg, London, New York: Springer Verlag.

———. 2013. 'Neighborhood Social Mix: Theory, Evidence, and Implications for Policy and Planning'. In *Policy, Planning, and People: Promoting Justice in Urban Development*, edited by Naomi Carmon and Susan S. Fainstain, 307–36. Philadelphia: University of Pennsylvania Press.

Garner, Catherine L. and Stephen W. Raudenbush. 1991. 'Neighborhood Effects on Educational Attainment: A Multilevel Analysis'. *Sociology of Education* 64 (4): 251–62.

Good, Thomas L. 1987. 'Two Decades of Research on Teacher Expectations: Findings and Future Directions'. *Journal of Teacher Education* 38 (4): 32–47.

Gouldner, Alvin W. 1970. *The Coming Crisis of Western Sociology*. New York: Basic Books.

Granovetter, Mark S. 1973. 'The Strength of Weak Ties'. *American Journal of Sociology* 78 (6): 1360–80.

Haid, Christian. 2013. 'Contentious Informalities – The Narratives of Picnicking at Berlin's Thai Park'. *dérive – Zeitschrift für Stadtforschung*: 43–8.

Harding, Alan and Talja V. Blokland. 2014. *Urban Theory: A Critical Introduction to Power, Cities and Urbanism in the 21st Century*. Los Angeles: SAGE.

Häußermann, Hartmut and Andreas Kapphan. 2004. 'Berlin: Ausgrenzungsprozesse in einer europäischen Stadt'. In *An den Rändern der Städte: Armut und Ausgrenzung*, edited by Hartmut Häußermann, Martin Kronauer and Walter Siebel, 203–34. Frankfurt am Main: Suhrkamp.

Häußermann, Hartmut, Martin Kronauer and Walter Siebel. 2004. 'Stadt am Rand: Armut und Ausgrenzung'. In *An den Rändern der Städte: Armut und*

Ausgrenzung, edited by Hartmut Häußermann, Martin Kronauer and Walter Siebel, 7–42. Frankfurt am Main: Suhrkamp.

Helbig, Marcel. 2010. 'Neighborhood does matter! Soziostrukturelle Nachbarschaftscharakteristika und Bildungserfolg'. *Kölner Zeitschrift für Soziologie und Sozialpsychologie – Sonderheft* 62 (4): 655–79.

Hirschman, Albert O. 1970. *Exit, Voice, and Loyalty: Responses to Decline in Firms, Organizations, and States*. Cambridge, MA. Harvard University Press.

Ignatieff, Michael. 1999. 'The Grandeur and Misery of Cosmopolitanism'. Paper presented at the conference 'Re-imagining Belonging: Self and Community in an Era of Nationalism and Post-Nationality', Center for International Studies, Aalborg University, Denmark, May 1999.

Jarrett, Robin L. 1997. 'Resilience among Low-Income African American Youth: An Ethnographic Perspective'. *Ethos* 25 (2): 218–29.

Jencks, Christopher. 1991. *The Urban Underclass*, Washington, DC: Brookings Institution.

Kazepov, Yuri (ed.). 2005. *Cities of Europe: Changing Contexts, Local Arrangement and the Challenge to Urban Cohesion*. Malden, MA: Wiley-Blackwell.

Khan, Shamus R. 2011. *Privilege: The Making of an Adolescent Elite at St. Paul's School*. Princeton, NJ: Princeton University Press.

Kleit, Rachel G. and Nicole B. Carnegie. 2011. 'Integrated or Isolated? The Impact of Public Housing Redevelopment on Social Network Homophily'. *Social Networks* 33 (2): 152–65.

Lamont, Michele and Sada Aksartova. 2002. 'Ordinary Cosmopolitanisms: Strategies for Bridging Racial Boundaries among Working-class Men'. *Theory, Culture & Society* 19 (4): 1–25.

Lamont, Michele and Virág Molnár. 2002. 'The Study of Boundaries in the Social Sciences'. *Annual Review of Sociology* 28: 167–95.

Lebuhn, Henrik. 2013. 'Local Border Practices and Urban Citizenship in Europe: Exploring Urban Borderlands'. *CITY. Analysis of Urban Trends, Culture, Theory, Policy, Action*. 17 (1): 37–51.

Leonard, Rosemary and Jenny Onyx. 2003. 'Networking Through Loose and Strong Ties: An Australian Qualitative Study'. *Voluntas: International Journal of Voluntary and Nonprofit Organizations* 14 (2): 189–203.

Leventhal, Tama and Jeanne Brooks-Gunn. 2003. 'Moving to Opportunity: An Experimental Study of Neighborhood Effects on Mental Health'. *American Journal of Public Health* 93 (9): 1576–82.

Lewandowski, Joseph D. and Gregory W. Streich. 2012. *Urban Social Capital: Civil Society and City Life*. Burlington, VT: Ashgate.

Ley, David. 1986. 'Alternative Explanations for Inner-City Gentrification: A Canadian Assessment'. *Annals of the Association of American Geographers* 76 (4): 521–35.

Li, S.C. and T.H. Choi. 2014. 'Does Social Capital Matter? A Quantitative Approach to Examining Technology Infusion in Schools: Does Social Capital Matter?' *Journal of Computer Assisted Learning* 30 (1): 1–16.

Liebow, Elliot. 1967. *Tally's Corner. A Study of Negro Streetcorner Men.* Boston: Little, Brown and Company.

Lin, Nan, Karen S. Cook and Ronald S. Burt. 2001. *Social Capital: Theory and Research.* New Brunswick, NJ: Transaction Publishers.

McAdam, Doug, Sidney G. Tarrow and Charles Tilly. 1996. 'To Map Contentious Politics'. *Mobilization* 1 (1): 17–34.

McCarthy, John D. and N. Mayer Zald. 1977. 'Resource Mobilization and Social Movements: A Partial Theory'. *American Journal of Sociology* 82 (6): 1212–41.

McFarlane, Colin. 2010. 'The Comparative City: Knowledge, Learning, Urbanism'. *International Journal of Urban and Regional Research* 34 (4): 725–42.

McFarlane, Colin and Michael Waibel. 2011. 'Introduction: The Informal-formal Divide in Context'. In *Urban informalities. Reflections on the formal and informal*, edited by Colin McFarlane and Michael Waibel, 1–12. Farnham: Ashgate.

Marshall, Thomas H. and Thomas B. Bottomore. 1992. *Citizenship and Social Class*. London: Pluto Press.

May, Jon. 1996. 'Globalization and the Politics of Place: Place and Identity in an Inner London Neighbourhood'. *Transactions of the Institute of British Geographers, New Series* 21 (1): 194–215.

Maynard-Moody, Steven and Michael C. Musheno. 2003. *Cops, Teachers, Counselors.* Ann Arbor: University of Michigan Press.

Misztal, Barbara A. 2001. 'Normality and Trust in Goffman's Theory of Interaction Order'. *Sociological Theory* 19 (3): 312–24.

Murie, Alan and Sako Musterd. 2004. 'Social Exclusion and Opportunity Structures in European Cities and Neighbourhoods'. *Urban Studies* 41 (8): 1441–59.

Musterd, Sako. 2005. 'Social and Ethnic Segregation in Europe: Levels, Causes, and Effects'. *Journal of Urban Affairs* 27 (3): 331–48.

Newman, Katherine S. 1999. *No Shame in my Game. The Working Poor in the Inner City.* New York: Knopf and the Russell Sage Foundation.

Perlman, Janice E. 1979. *The Myth of Marginality: Urban Poverty and Politics in Rio de Janeiro.* Berkeley, Los Angeles: University of California Press.

Pfau-Effinger, Birgit and Slađana Sakač Magdalenić. 2010. 'Informal Employment in the Work-Welfare Arrangement of Germany'. In *Informal Work in Developed Nations*, edited by Enrico Marcelli, Colin C. Williams and Pascale Joassart, 66–83. London, New York: Routledge.

Portes, Alejandro. 1998. 'Social Capital: Its Origins and Applications in Modern Sociology'. *Annual Review of Sociology* 24 (1): 1–24.

Press and Information Office of the Federal Government. 2013. *Berlin heute. Berlin. Faszinierende Metropole, mitten in Europa.* Accessed 26 September 2013: www.berlin.de/rbmskzl/_assets/publikationen/berlin_heute_2013_.pdf.

Putnam, Robert D. 1995. 'Bowling Alone: America's Declining Social Capital'. *Journal of Democracy* 6 (1): 65–78.

Rist, Ray C. 1970. 'Student Social Class and Teacher Expectations: The Self-Fulfilling Prophecy in Ghetto Education'. *Harvard Educational Review* 40 (3): 411–51.

Robinson, Jennifer. 2006. *Ordinary Cities: Between Modernity and Development*. London: Routledge.

———. 2011. 'Cities in a World of Cities: The Comparative Gesture'. *International Journal of Urban and Regional Research* 35 (1): 1–23.

Said, Edward W. 1994. *Culture and imperialism*. London: Vintage.

Sampson, Robert J. 2012. *Great American City: Chicago and the Enduring Neighborhood Effect*. Chicago, London: University of Chicago Press.

Savage, Michael, Alan Warde and Fiona Devine. 2005. 'Capitals, Assets, and Resources: some Critical Issues'. *The British Journal of Sociology* 56 (1): 31–47.

Scott, James C. 1990. *Domination and the Arts of Resistance: Hidden Transcripts*. New Haven: Yale University Press.

Sen, Amartya. 1983. 'Poor, Relatively Speaking'. *Oxford economic papers* 35 (2): 153–69.

———. 2005. 'Human Rights and Capabilities'. *Journal of Human Development* 6 (2): 151–66.

Senate Administration for Education, Science and Research. 2013. 'Ausgewählte Eckdaten aus der IST-Statistik der allgemein bildenden Schulen Schuljahr 2013/14' Accessed 7 February 2015. http://www.berlin.de/imperia/md/content/sen-bildung/bildungsstatistik/eckdaten_allgemeinb_schulen_2013_14.pdf?start&ts=1418717067&file=eckdaten_allgemeinb_schulen_2013_14.pdf.

Sharkey, Patrick T. 2013. *Stuck in Place: Urban Neighborhoods and the End of progress toward racial equality*. Chicago: The University of Chicago Press.

Silverstein, Paul A. 2001. 'Rethinking Comparative Cultural Sociology: Repertoires of Evaluation in France and the United States'. In: *Rethinking Comparative Cultural Sociology: Repertoires of Evaluation in France and the United States*, edited by Michele Lamont and Laurent Thevenot, 529–31. Cambridge: Cambridge University Press.

Simmel, Georg. 1955. *Conflict and the Web of Group-affiliations*, New York: The Free Press.

Simone, AbdouMaliq. 2004. 'People as Infrastructure: Intersecting Fragments in Johannesburg'. *Public Culture* 16 (3): 407–29.

———. 2010. *City Life from Jakarta to Dakar: Movements at the Crossroads*. Abingdon: Routledge.

Slater, Tom. 2013. 'Your Life Chances Affect Where you Live: A Critique of the 'Cottage Industry' of Neighbourhood Effects Research'. *International Journal of Urban and Regional Research* 37 (2): 367–87.

Small, Mario L. David J. Harding and Michèle Lamont. 2010. 'Reconsidering Culture and Poverty'. *The ANNALS of the American Academy of Political and Social Science* 629 (1): 6–27.

Small, Mario L. and Katherine S. Newman. 2001. 'Urban Poverty after the Truly Disadvantaged: The Rediscovery of the Family, the Neighborhood, and Culture'. *Annual Review of Sociology* 27 (1): 23–45.

Smith, Neil. 1996. *The New Urban Frontier: Gentrification and the Revanchist City*. London, New York: Routledge.

Snow, David A. and Leon Anderson. 1993. *Down on their Luck. A Study of Homeless Street People*, Berkeley: University of California Press.

Souza Briggs, Xavier de. 1997. 'Moving up versus Moving Out: Neighbourhood Effects in Housing Mobility Programs'. *Housing Policy Debate* 8 (1): 195–234.

———. 1998. 'Brown Kids in White Suburbs: Housing Mobility and the Many Faces of Social Capital'. *Housing Policy Debate* 9 (1): 177–221.

———. 2005. 'The geography of opportunity: Race and Housing Choice in Metropolitan America'. Accessed 17 September 2014. http://site.ebrary.com/lib/academic completetitles/home.action.

Statistical Office for Berlin-Brandenburg. 2014. *Zenus 2011. Land Berlin am 9. Mai 2011.* Accessed 12 September 2014. https://www.statistik-berlin-brandenburg.de/zensus/gdb/ bev/ be/11_Berlin_bev.pdf.

Tarrow, Sidney G. 1998. *Power in Movement: Social Movements and Contentious Politics*. New York: Cambridge University Press.

Tilly, Charles. 1984. *Big Structures, Large Processes, Huge Comparisons*, New York: Russell Sage Foundation.

———. 2001. 'Relational Origins of Inequality'. *Anthropological Theory* 1 (3): 355–72.

———. 2004. 'Observations of Social Processes and Their Formal Representations'. *Sociological Theory* 22 (4): 595–602.

Tilly, Charles and Sidney G. Tarrow. 2007. *Contentious Politics.* Boulder, Colorado: Paradigm Publishers.

Van Eijk, Gwen. 2010. *Unequal Networks: Spatial Segregation, Relationships and Inequality in the City*. Delft, Netherlands: Ios Press.

Wacquant, Loïc D. 2010. 'Crafting the Neoliberal State: Workfare, Prisonfare, and Social Insecurity'. *Sociological Forum* 25 (2): 197–220.

Wacquant, Loïc J.D. 1999. 'Urban Marginality in the Coming Millennium'. *Urban Studies* 36 (10): 1639–47.

Wrong, Dennis H. 1999. *The Oversocialized Conception of Man.* New Brunswick, NJ: Transaction Publishers.

Zukin, Sharon. 1998. 'Urban lifestyles: diversity and standardisation in spaces of consumption'. *Urban Studies* 35: 825–39.

PART I
Making the City Work: Practices of Segregation

Chapter 1

Spaces of Fear and their Exclusionary Consequences: Narratives and Everyday Routines of Sub-Saharan Immigrants in Berlin

Mirjam Lewek

Introduction

> The Negro who ventures away from the mass of his people and their organized life finds himself alone, shunned and taunted, stared at and made uncomfortable ... he remains far from friends and the concentrated social life of the church and feels in all its bitterness what it means to be a social outcast (Du Bois 1967 [1899], quoted in Sibley 1995, 146).

Racial segregation in cities has been an urban reality for centuries (Sibley 1995), and even today, Du Bois's quote resembles the situation of Berlin. This chapter discusses racial segregation in Berlin today. It sketches the effects on segregation of those perceived as – and labelled by the middle class cosmopolites as – deviant, working class and Eastern German right-wing radicals for the capabilities of Sub-Saharan immigrants in creating a resourceful setting, while coping with a situation of marginalization. In short, subtle practices of the middle classes, as some of the upcoming chapters will show, marginalize immigrants. In their creation of durable engagements, middle class residents seclude themselves from others and produce spatial fringes in which urban cosmopolitanism is literally absent. While not demonstrably motivated by explicit racism, such practices are racist in their consequences. They sharply contrast with the picture commonly painted of cities like Berlin as cosmopolitan, a stage for open encounters between people of diverse backgrounds, especially in race and ethnicity. Marketing campaigns and tourist guides celebrate the city as the natural home of cosmopolitanism, although such campaigns champions only parts of the city. Other parts of the city, in contrast, show another social reality of right-wing violence that adds to the marginalization of non-White Germans and immigrants. As we will argue, an instrumental usage of the concept of cosmopolitanism serves expansionist economic politics of the neoliberal city (market cosmopolitanism) and deviates from actual practices of immigrant populations moving in European cities, like the creation of capabilities through moral orientations, durable engagements and fluid encounters (immigrant cosmopolitanism). Berlin reflects both these understandings of cosmopolitanism. This chapter discusses the role of market-oriented cosmopolitanism in creating spatial voids that marginalize people from places and resources in the city. How does it shape the creation of capabilities in the everyday life of Sub-Saharan immigrants? How is market-cosmopolitanism linked to the accessibility of the city for them?

In semi-structured, in-depth interviews, we asked 40 Sub-Saharan immigrants, with at least five years of residence in Berlin, about their perception of the city and specifically of their neighbourhood, their access to the housing and job markets, their leisure time activities and personal ties. In this chapter, we focus primarily on questions about moving through the city, feeling safe or comfortable in certain areas. With a map of Berlin, the interview partners were asked to mark areas, which they 'didn't know', 'knew and liked' and 'knew and did not like' (see Figure 1.1 and Figure 1.2). Interview partners revealed a clear spatial pattern of city perception and city use: the avoidance of East Berlin.

First, we dismantle the discursive construction of Berlin as a cosmopolitan city. Second, we point to the voids and absent spaces in that image, namely the East Berlin region (see Figure 1.3). East Berlin became a commonplace for 'spaces of fear', which affected in particular the free movement of non-White Germans and immigrants. Third, the marginalized consequences of such places for this group of Berliners are then analysed through the lens of narratives and everyday routines of Sub-Saharan immigrants in Berlin.

As we have seen in the introduction, the capabilities of residents are framed by their structural positions and their spatial locations, and the ways in which their locations are produced by marginalization from other sites in the city. The unequal access of different social groups to the job and housing markets and other types of urban resources impacts people's capabilities. We will see here how they are spatial. Next, we will see what alternative roads to resources those marginalized develop.

Cosmopolitanism and Geographical Imaginaries

Race and Space as Intertwined Constructs in the Cosmopolitan City

The increasingly popular term 'cosmopolitanism' wavers between political-philosophical ideas of world-citizenship, descriptive-analytical approaches to think beyond narrow national categories and empirical findings of 'really existing cosmopolitanism' as an unintended side effect of everyday life in a globally intertwined world (see Beck 2006, 17), turning it into the 'cultural habitus of globalization' (Ang 2001, quoted in Ley 2004, 159). City marketing campaigns in various cities promote cosmopolitanism to attract business, investors, international tourists, consumers and prosperous residents. As Young et al. (2006,

1688) argue, these campaigns create a 'geography of difference' through defining acceptable and unacceptable forms of difference in a hegemonic discourse about the 'cosmopolitan city'. Marketing campaigns concentrate on certain areas, formulating their particular cosmopolitanism and the cosmopolitan lifestyle they offer and require. Following this, campaigns encode a specific vision of the cosmopolite who belongs in this cosmopolitan place (see Young et al. 2006, 1697).

Cities are presented to be the natural home of cosmopolitanism – and Berlin seems to be one of them. The official Berlin web page reveals its ambitions to become a leading international business site, drawing on its cosmopolitan character. The senate and business marketing departments sketch Berlin as an extraordinary business location, well situated in Germany and the European Union and therefore close to its important markets, offering a terrific inner city infrastructure, internationally connected, equipped with a highly qualified but reasonable work force, an international culture and a specific dynamism of innovation.[1]

In creating and promoting cosmopolitan identities for places and people who are meant to inhabit them, it becomes clear who and where these specific characteristics are missing. Non-cosmopolitan places and people are first of all defined by their absence (see ibid, 1702–3). The promoted market cosmopolitanism is expressed in a marketed lifestyle and in consumption practices requiring certain cultural and economic capital, which clearly excludes non-consumers and people missing valid cultural capital and/or economic means (see Kothari 2008, 500–501). This hierarchical and elitist understanding of cosmopolitanism simultaneously produces the non-cosmopolitan, for example the person lacking the correct type of difference: non-western immigrants and ethnic groups marked by skin colour and the respective prejudices, members of subcultures and the less wealthy (see Young et al. 2006, 1705–6; Ley 2004, 160).

Thus in the construction, perception and expression of a cosmopolitan identity (of the individual and the city) lies the imagination of the other, based on race, class and ethnicity (see Kothari 2008, 501). As David Harvey discusses in his essay on 'Cosmopolitanism and the banality of geographical evils' (2000), this applies to social groups and to place and space: '... the evil (if such it is) arises out of the dreadful cosmopolitan habit of demonizing spaces, places and whole populations as somehow "outside the project" (of market freedoms, the rule of law, of modernity, of a certain vision of democracy, of civilized values, of international socialism, or whatever)' (ibid.,15). Especially the working class appears as the opposite to a cosmopolitan middle class (see Young et al. 2006, 1706). Working class neighbourhoods are therefore hardly considered as potential cosmopolitan places and usually are left out of respective image campaigns and urban politics. This is true for Berlin too, as Lanz (2007) shows in his analysis of the discursive construction of Berlin as an 'occidental, multicultural and cosmopolitan immigrant

1 See a self-description by Business Location Center (2014) at http://www.businesslocationcenter.de (Accessed 2 August 2014) and a marketing video by Business Location Center (2010) 'Berlin – the place to be'.

city'. Political attempts to label Berlin as a multicultural and cosmopolitan world city were intertwined with discriminatory and racist discourses throughout the long immigration history of the city.

The traditional working class districts contribute to the 'spatial construction of the other' in the unified city (Lanz 2007, 146 ff.). Within this urban landscape of exclusion, boundaries between places and people labelled as cosmopolitan and non-cosmopolitan appear. Social categories of race and ethnicity are constructed to form visible subjects in specific space and time contexts (Keith 2005, 6–7 and 18–19). Hence forms and processes of racial discrimination, as exclusionary practices, become evident in a certain place at a specific time, using both geography and history as narrative structures to naturalize the reproduction of social inequalities (see Keith 2005, 18).

This was the case for so called 'guest' and 'contract' workers in Berlin. Here, the declining western districts *Neukölln*, *Kreuzberg* and *Wedding* had become immigrant quarters, populated by 'guest workers' families and following generations, which were never given a chance to escape their 'migratory background'. Besides becoming the cities' multicultural sites, as their culture was literally multi, they were stigmatized as 'ghettos' and even 'parallel societies', where ethnicity and cultural dispositions could be blamed for causing pressing social problems, decay, criminality etc., while deeper structures of inequality and racism were obscured (see Lanz 2007, 69 ff., 151–2, 157–8). In socialist East Berlin the relatively small numbers of foreign 'contract workers' were actively and officially segregated from locals and isolated in hostels in *Marzahn*, *Hohenschönhausen* and *Lichtenberg*, where then especially immigrants from the former Soviet Union settled after the fall of the Iron Curtain (ibid., 111 ff., 149). Together with *Friedrichshain* and *Prenzlauer Berg* (both branded as 'bourgeois' in built structures and therefore left to decay under communism), these neighbourhoods were mapped and labelled as places of social decline with high numbers of unemployment and welfare recipients (ibid., 149; cf. Holm 2006 on the development of the social composition in *Prenzlauer Berg*). Different to the western districts where immigrants had been present in larger numbers for some time already, another logic of externalization helped to exclude Eastern areas in public as the 'racist other'.

Lanz presumed (2007, 132) that an increase in violence against foreigners and non-White Germans in East Berlin in the early 1990s could be influenced by a discriminatory discourse about asylum misuse and overwhelming foreign presence in the city and Germany as a whole. But rising numbers of racist attacks were explained by external conditions (crucial social changes in East Berlin) and the deviant behaviour of individuals. Instead of recognizing structural and institutional origins of racism in mainstream society, residents of East Berlin were discursively marginalized as 'the other' narrow-minded people with racist moral orientations, juxtaposed against the otherwise cosmopolitan population (ibid., 132 ff.).

In sum, two mechanisms of exclusion in the promotion of cosmopolitanism externalized certain areas and their inhabitants in a mutual way. First, in the discourse of the cosmopolitan, attractive city, non-cosmopolitan places and people were constructed and then excluded from image campaigns. But there is no empty space. So, second, precisely the excluded places were left to convert into 'spaces of fear', as we will see later, with the marginalized residents becoming potential suspects (neo-Nazis) or victims (non-White Germans and the visible immigrant population).

Besides image campaigns promoting Berlin's cosmopolitanism, the existence of non-cosmopolitan places and people are not a secret to city officials. The report of the 'Office for the Protection of the Constitution' on political right-wing violence in Berlin identified 'places of intensified right-wing violence' in the Eastern districts *Lichtenberg*, *Niederschöneweide*, *Prenzlauer Berg* and *Rudow* in the west (see Verfassungsschutz Berlin 2007). These places of intensified right-wing violence are above-average scenes of crime and places of residence of the suspects. The report further reveals that the named districts are also places marked by right-wing extremism in a broader sense (measuring above-average votes for the right-wing extremist party *NPD* and density of places of residence, meeting points and activism of right-wing extremists). The time and sites of right-wing extremist violence reported by the *Verfassungsschutz* in 2007 coincide with the 'spaces of fear' later described by our interviewees and the points in time our interviewees see these spaces as being the most dangerous: during evening hours, at night and especially on weekends.

Although institutional and structural racism, the prevalence of right-wing extremist and racist opinions in mainstream German society, and related realities of everyday racism have been investigated and discussed in recent years (see Decker et al. 2012 and 2010; Stöss 2007; Terkessidis 2004), neo-Nazis are still regarded as a marginal problem located in the East of Germany and Berlin (see Stöss 2007, 49 ff.; Buchstein and Heinrich 2010, 34 ff.; Heinemann and Schubarth 1992) and externalized to certain social groups and areas (for a discussion see Bürk 2012, 27 ff. and 228 ff.; Döring 2008, 22–3; Terkessidis 2004, esp. 67 ff.). Market cosmopolitanism and its promotion support this process of spatial and social externalization of right-wing extremism and racism in the city of Berlin: marginalized as a deviance that is not its 'true' character. This not only allows for their violent manifestation in marginalized spaces (although not only there), the constructed non-cosmopolitan places and people also serve as a scapegoat and excuse not to face right-wing extremism and racism as a pressing problem in German society. Since Berlin is presented and perceived as open-minded, multicultural and cosmopolitan, racism must be denied as part of its city-culture. As Young at al. (2006, 1706) state, marketing campaigns only create the image of cosmopolitanism including certain places and urban dwellers and excluding others. Meanwhile the very residents of the cosmopolitan city articulate, live and fix the geography of difference in space. So the prevalence of right-wing extremism and racism performed by neo-Nazis in East Berlin, causes the avoidance of this part by their potential victims, as we will see below.

The Divided City

'Spaces of Fear': Narratives and Everyday Routines of Sub-Saharan Immigrants

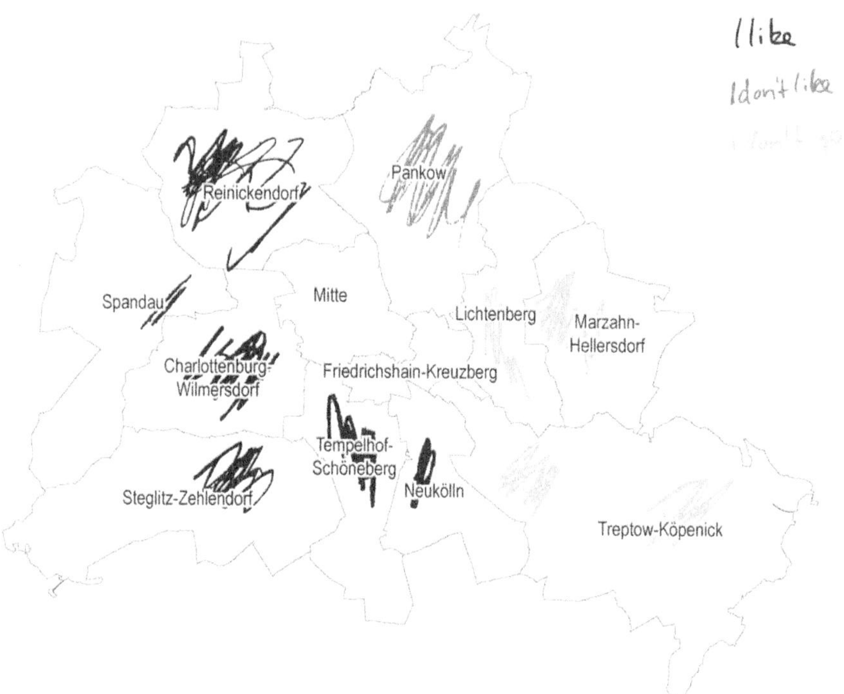

Figure 1.1 Mental map by Sub-Saharan immigrants I
Source: © albertherrmann.de on the basis of the author's fieldwork material

The common imaginaries for East Berlin expressed by Sub-Saharan immigrants whom we interviewed originally can best be described as 'spaces of fear'. As Thomas Bürk writes, in the last decade the public, political and academic discourse on 'spaces of fear', 'no-go areas' and 'national liberated zones'[2] spatialized right-

2 The term 'national liberated zones' refers to a strategic concept promoted by the extreme right-wing party NPD (*Nationaldemokratische Partei Deutschlands*) in the early 1990s. It aimed at a spatial hegemony through the occupation/appropriation of mainly geographical, but also political, virtual and temporal spaces and places and the construction of an infrastructure for right-wing extremism (see Bürk 2011, 29; Schulze 2011, 16; Bundschuh 2004, 10 ff.). Although describing first of all a strategic aim of Germanys extreme right-wing scene, which luckily was never achieved in all its dimensions, 'national liberated zones' were broadly discussed in the media and geographically attached to areas

Figure 1.2 Mental map by Sub-Saharan immigrants II
Source: © albertherrmann.de on the basis of the author's fieldwork material

wing extremism in Germany and located it in the area of its former socialist territory (see Bürk 2011, 25). The terms 'zones' or 'spaces of fear' emerged in the 1980s feminist debates about urban planning according to female needs and aimed at locating and avoiding potential or real places of violence against women (see Bürk 2011, 21 and 26 ff.; Schulze 2011, 19–20). By the turn of the millennium, the term was more frequently used to geographically address the presence of right-wing extremists and the related fears of their potential victims, non-White Germans and immigrants, especially in Germany's Eastern states and cities (see Schulze 2011, 19–20). As a more individual categorization of space based on the rather 'irrational' feeling of fear, 'spaces of fear' are constructed from the perspective of potential victims in scenes of (extreme right-wing) crime and places of neo-Nazi presence (see Bürk 2011, 26–7). As danger is geographically localized and communicated between individuals as well as in the media, real and potential

and cities in Eastern Germany (see Bundschuh 2004, 15; Bürk 2011, 30; Döring 2008, 93–4; Schulze 2011, 16).

victims develop a mental map of 'spaces of fear', which may then affect their daily life (see Döring 2011, 60–61). The extensive and undifferentiated use of such terms and concrete mapping of respective areas in the media are discussed critically (see Döring 2011, 61–2; Bürk 2012, 269): the geographically located danger does not only imply a deceptive security everywhere else and induces potential victims to retreat or stay away. It also cements a powerful image that is hard to deconstruct and can strengthen the position of neo-Nazis while simultaneously hindering the mobilization of counterforces. It suffices for our purpose to note that the pattern of avoiding East Berlin by Sub-Saharan immigrants shows a spatial reality of the city that affects their capabilities. The following sections show how the interview partners have found ways to make their city in the context of this reality.

Figure 1.3 Map of Berlin with former course of the Berlin Wall
Source: © albertherrmann.de

Avoiding East Berlin

The 'spaces of fear' which the interviewees described were not the mere imaginations, but were mapped on areas in Berlin of right-wing extremists' presence and violence, as we described in the section before. Differences in the districts named by the interviewees as 'spaces of fear' and 'real' places of intensified right-wing violence identified by the governmental report can be explained by the collective construction of such 'spaces of fear'. Once labelled as such by concrete events, the 'collective memory' of such violence in the group of potential victims produces a durable image of danger, which makes the re-appropriation of those places difficult, or even impossible (Döring 2011, 58). This seemed to be the case for *Marzahn*, a district that Sub-Saharan immigrants frequently mentioned. Charly, who was born in Ghana in 1966, came to Germany in 1990 and located 'no-go areas' in our interview:

> Interviewer: Are there certain places in Berlin where you go?
> Charly: Yeah I go everywhere, apart from *Marzahn*. That is a no-go area, as a foreigner.
> Interviewer: What is that?
> Charly: No-go means where it is risky.
> Interviewer: Which areas are those for you, for example?
> Charly: *Marzahn* area. You don't go there, it's not safe. As far as I know.

Even though Charly was naturalized in Berlin in 2006, he stills stated that *Marzahn* was not safe 'as a foreigner'. He may have had a German passport, but he was acutely aware of the ascription of a status as a foreigner that had not changed with acquiring German nationality. The discussion of the Berlin map at the end of the interview revealed that there were more districts in former East Berlin where he did not go because he did not feel safe:

> Interviewer: So you don't like *Lichtenberg, Marzahn, Hellersdorf, Treptow, Köpenick*?
> Charly: This is not safe, for me it is not safe. You must know where it is safe and where it is not.
> Interviewer: What makes the place unsafe?
> Charly: Because they attack foreigners. ... I don't know the name of the German federation [refers to GDR], this is not good. ... if you go there it is your own risk, because it is not safe for foreigners. I was in Adlon [Hotel in Berlin], because President Kufuor from Ghana came .... At that time in Germany, Ghana was playing the world cup ... and the police and other people were talking, there were Americans also and the police was telling them: no-go area. So this is how I came to know, that in certain places 'we are not encouraging you to go there'. Because some of the people are awful. ... Every society's country has bad people.

As Charly explains, he had been informed about no-go areas in Berlin during a public event of the World Cup in Germany 2006, where, according to him, the police officially advised non-White people to avoid the Eastern districts. Indeed, in a radio interview at the time, a former public official warned Black visitors about areas in the East, where, if a Black person would go there: 'It is possible he wouldn't get out alive' (Spiegel-Online 2006). Berlin's African council and other initiatives of people of colour issued travel warnings for cities and areas in Eastern Germany for 'dark skinned' guests (Schulze 2011, 17; Bürk 2011, 29–30). Charly's statement and the cited media articles show that in contrast to the Anglo-Saxon perception of 'no-go areas' as places that hint at unsafety, for example because they are supposed to be dominated by street-crime and gang violence of racialized minorities, in Germany the term is closely connected to neo-Nazi presence and extreme right-wing violence against the non-White Germans and immigrants (see Schulze 2011, 17).

Others had friends who lived or had lived in East Berlin, warning them like Justice. He was born in Ghana in 1972 and came to Berlin in the late 1990s. He worked in *Prenzlauer Berg*, an Eastern district right next to the centre that by then had fully been gentrified. He lived in *Reinickendorf*, located in the North of former West Berlin:

> Interviewer: Are there areas in Berlin which you don't feel safe or secure?
> Justice: I have other friends who used to tell, some of them are staying in the East, some part of the East, *Friedrichshain*. And they tell me the story about the places and some are in the East somewhere, somewhere not far, *Pankow*. I have colleagues too, who are staying in *Pankow* and at times they have difficulty when they [are] coming home, with these Nazis.
> Interviewer: So, could you name the areas where you wouldn't go for example, or that you don't think are secure?
> Justice: Yeah, for instance, deep in the East, somewhere in *Pankow*. I know maybe by this time it has changed, but there are certain places I will not live.

Apart from brief encounters and friendships in which people personally learnt about these places, there also seemed to be a general knowledge or common sense about the East as being dangerous for 'people from Africa' without links to such encounters or ties. Rachel, who was born in Zambia in 1973 and came to Berlin in 2008, worked in the central district Berlin-*Mitte* and also lived in the western district *Reinickendorf*:

> Interviewer: But do you know places in Berlin where you don't feel safe?
> Rachel: Yes. *Marzahn*. Yes. I have never been there (*laughs*) but I've just been told, so to say. It's a place where there are very particular … living around there. I know there are people from Africa living there but it's not very safe.

The common perception of East Berlin districts as dangerous places can be traced in social media as well. On the website *Atlantablackstar.com*, people of colour are warned by Moore (2014) not to venture into East Berlin:

> Africans and other dark-skinned people in Berlin, … and other cities know [that] certain areas in the Eastern part of Berlin, such as *Marzahn* and *Hellersdorf*, are 'no-go' areas where they are certain to be attacked or killed. It is also reported that German police routinely ignore these racist attacks and Germans, in general, are in denial about the depth of racism in their society.

On various blogs people post questions whether Berlin is 'safe' to visit for Black tourists and whether the rumour is true that areas should be avoided. People sharing their experiences referred to the wonderful multicultural character and openness of the Germans, but also noted that whether or not the outskirt areas are racist 'spaces of fear' or not is irrelevant because there is 'absolutely nothing' to see there for visitors anyway. A question posted on the webpage *Toytown Germany* (2009) by a Black woman planning to move to Berlin about where to live and which areas to avoid received many replies, calling Berlin 'nice and international' and telling the immigrant all would be 'cool' if she avoided *Marzahn* and *Lichtenberg*. But the housing prices there are low, the amenities and public transport good, and the public spaces green (see Senate Department for Urban Development and the Environment 2013). Defining these discursively and through collective memory as no-go areas directly affects the resources of dark-skinned residents of the city.

Unfortunately, the imagination is not just a construct whereas tourists may follow the marketed image of cosmopolitan Berlin and never venture out East, the everyday experiences of the Africans living there shed a different light on the matter. Some of the interviewees had personal experiences that forced them to leave and avoid the area. Tom was born in 1970 in Benin and came to Berlin in 2000. He lived in *Wartenberg*, a neighbourhood in *Lichtenberg* with his wife for several years until he was attacked by a group of neo-Nazis on the way from the train station to his house:

> Tom: … It happened in *Wartenberg*. Back then, I worked in the late shift and then Nazis attacked me … I worked during the night and then … during the nights I was always by myself [on the way home] and once I met these Nazis and they attacked me ….
> Interviewer: And you went home from your work in *Spandau*?
> Tom: Yes, *Spandau*, yes and then … the police officer said alright, there are such cases [of right-wing violence] in *Wartenberg*, when you work the night shifts … [and then take] the subway or walk home alone, it's dangerous.
> Interviewer: The police told you that?
> Tom: Yes, yes, it's really dangerous … they have many such cases there [and] then we said, somewhere they have nicer city, districts, well yes that's better. … yes, they [the police] told me, where *Mitte* [central district of Berlin] is, it is better. … It is better to live in *Mitte* also then for after the work …. Here, in this district [*Neukölln*] it is okay, until now I have my peace (*laughing*), I had no problems.

Alarming in his story is not just the attack, or that Tom reported there were many people at the train station who saw the group of neo-Nazis following him but did not interfere. There was even a man who passed him when he was being beaten up and did not interfere, call the police or support him later as a witness. Alarming is also the poor performance of Germany's juridical system where the court case did not lead to any criminal conviction, although Tom recognized two of the neo-Nazis who attacked him in the data-base of Berlin's police department for 'politically motivated crime – right'. Alarming, however, is above all that the police told Tom to leave East Berlin as quickly as possible and move into the central circle line area because as a Black he would not be safe in *Wartenberg*, especially not during the night hours coming back from work.

The police declaring an area unsafe to a Black resident of Berlin might be the well-meant and wise but unofficial advice of one police officer. But it reveals that government institutions recognize certain areas of open and violent racism in Berlin and do not even pretend to provide substantial protection for non-White citizens there. In this case, they 'solved' the problem by encouraging potential victims to leave the district because of the intolerance, discrimination and crime caused by the presence of neo-Nazis. From our perspective of resources and capabilities, it is clear that this limits the Sub-Saharan immigrants in their movement within the city, excluding them from an area where, for example, housing is cheap and spacious, the schools are not overfull, public transport is efficient and green space is abundant. All that East Berlin's districts have to speak against them is their reputation, and possibly their rather suburban, quiet environment. They are not dilapidated, low quality and badly maintained outskirt areas. They are not hip, maybe dull, but certainly liveable except for migrants and people of colour.

As shown above, the interview partners did not regard just any Eastern district as a zone of potential danger for people of colour, but differentiated between areas and temporalities. Ilya, who was born in 1955 in Ghana and lived in *Rudow* since 2000, mentioned, again, *Marzahn* as an area that he avoided: '*Marzahn* is a place for neo-Nazis. And [I] would not like to go there in the night, during the day it's all right, but in the night. After 8 p.m'.

Maison, who was born in Ghana in 1976 and came to Berlin in 2003 where he worked and lived in *Marienfelde*, replied similarly:

> Maison: … There are several no-go areas for me. *Marzahn, Lichtenberg*. I wouldn't just go there at night. …
> Interviewer: What is a no-go area for you?
> Maison: No-go, because I'm afraid. I don't want to be assaulted or abused, just because of racism. It didn't happen to me, but I heard of, people are, for example, assaulted or … I heard of such things.

Like Ilya, he referred to certain districts as no-go areas in a specific time of the day, saying he wouldn't go to *Marzahn* or *Lichtenberg* at night. For Maison, no-go areas were marked by his own fear. He was afraid of becoming a victim of racist attacks in these areas, because he had heard about 'such things'. So certain districts were perceived as dangerous at specific times for people of colour. Not going there protected him against becoming a victim of racist attacks. This did not only create a deceptive security from racist attacks and discrimination everywhere else in the city and helped Berlin to maintain its cosmopolitan image *despite* racist attacks. Moreover it limited Sub-Saharan immigrants' free movement through the city, and their access to resources of housing and employment.

In contrast, *Rudow* in West Berlin's *Neukölln* surfaced as a place of intensified right-wing violence in statistics whereas at the same time it happened to be one of the districts with the highest Sub-Saharan immigrant population and presence (see Taube and Borja 2011, 214). Even if identified as a place of neo-Nazi presence and activities, there was no sign of an existing or emerging 'space of fear' for non-White Berliners as it was the case for Berlin's Eastern districts. Still, *Neukölln* was far from only causing positive associations. Interview partners described it as noisy, dirty and full of dog shit, frequented by street boys, drinkers, homeless and generally less affluent, rather suspect residents. Especially, interview partners who did not live in *Neukölln* evaluated this area negatively – it did not have a problematic reputation among Sub-Saharan immigrants living there. Ilya was not afraid of the neo-Nazis living in *Rudow*:

> Interviewer: Is there something you would like to change in *Rudow*?
> Interviewee: ... Yes. The neo-Nazis have a spot here. But until now, we haven't had any confrontations.
> Interviewer: What do you mean, they have a spot?
> Ilya: There is a particular place that is known for the presence of neo-Nazis. They live nearby and have a kiosk there, where they gather almost daily, at the train station in *Rudow*. But until now, nothing bad happened. And I think, a prayer can change things there. You know that neo-Nazis are hostile to foreigners, but God is protecting us and until know, nothing bad happened. And we pray for these people, too. That they see the truth in life, so that foreigners are human, too ....
> Interviewer: Well, you would not feel safe then, at the kiosk?
> Ilya: For me, this is not an issue. I don't buy there. After I noticed that this is a kiosk for neo-Nazis I don't buy there. But I'm not afraid of these people.

Through everyday fluid encounters, Ilya identified a shop close to the train station as a 'neo-Nazi spot' where 'they met almost every day'. Fluid encounters can hence establish a familiarity – knowing about certain potential dangers rather than not being prepared for them – that Ilya did not have with *Marzahn*. We will now move to those interview partners who did continue to live in these areas.

'Resisting Fear' and Residing in Berlin's East

Armand, who was born in 1983 in Cameroon, came to Berlin in 2005 to study at the Technical University in *Charlottenburg* and lived in Berlin's Eastern district

Lichtenberg. While others denounced this area as a no-go area, he stated the place was 'quite cool'. He has not had any bad experiences, although initially he did not want to live there because of 'many Nazis'. Many friends had told him they were 'verbally provoked' there. Although he did not have such experiences himself, he expressed that he would still prefer to live in another district. John expressed even more confidence about living in *Lichtenberg* as a Sub-Saharan immigrant. He was in his late thirties, born in Ghana and came to Germany in 2002 and to Berlin in 2006 for his PhD. When asked whether he has heard of attacks by neo-Nazis in the area, he denied it. He liked the place because of its quietness, he felt safe there and was moving freely. However he did know that 'the people' had reservations about *Lichtenberg* as a place of Nazis and often wondered how he came to live there:

> John: Yeah, people would say that when you are about to tell someone that you are living here: how come?'
> Interviewer: What do you mean by that?
> John: They have the impression that there are Nazis here and you can easily be attacked. And so the people have reservations when you tell them that you are living here. ... Yeah, I feel comfortable. And I feel safe. Having in mind that I have not experienced any bad things. You only feel unsafe when you experience something, or you hear something strange or something ... I don't know what to say but I have not experienced anything, so I walk open-minded, freely, and you know, it also sometimes depends on the individual.

Later, when discussing the map of the city, he added that he nevertheless was 'a bit careful' because he was told about Nazis in *Lichtenberg*: 'This place is quiet [*Lichtenberg*]. I like this place because of its quietness. But I'm also a bit careful because people have told me there are Nazis there, and you have to be careful'.

Demba, who was born in the late 1960s in Nigeria, came to Berlin more than 20 years ago. He lived in the western part of the city, in *Tempelhof* and worked in *Mitte* and *Kreuzberg*. He thought that times had changed in Berlin's Eastern districts, and that they no longer were dangerous places for Black people. He believed that the number of attacks had decreased and that such attacks, moreover, could happen anywhere in the city, so he did not attach feelings of safety to certain places. He stressed his view of an increasing diversity or growth of the 'foreign population' in the previously notorious areas as the driving force of change:

> Interviewer: And are [there] places in Berlin that you don't feel safe, or you don't like or you ...?
> Demba: Feeling safe is a feeling. You can be anywhere and then you don't feel safe. It's just a feeling. But before, a long time ago, it used to be a dangerous place for Black people like me, dangerous place. But now not any more. But I still think once in a while, once in a while, here, here [points on the map] they attack Black people.
> Interviewer: In *Marzahn*, in *Pankow*, in *Köpenick* and *Lichtenberg*?

Demba: Yeah yeah yeah ..., but not any more like before. Maybe once in the year, maybe [every] two years. I call it sporadic, just as it can happen here in *Kreuzberg*. So, but before, it used to be very very scary.
Interviewer: Ok, so you are optimistic.
Demba: The things are getting better. ... Because a lot of foreigners are going there, they are living there, so, the people are moving, spreading everywhere so it is getting better.

While John and Demba took a particular personal stand towards the alleged danger of Berlin's Eastern districts for people of colour, some simply rejected to give up their personal freedom of movement in the city. This attitude is explicitly expressed by Arthur, who was born 'around' 1969 in Uganda. He came to Berlin in 1997 where he lived in *Alt-Mariendorf* and worked in *Kreuzberg*. Initially, he had lived in a small town in Brandenburg, *Königs-Wusterhausen*, at the Eastern outskirts of Berlin. He described the town as a 'small centre of neo-Nazis'. But living there made him able to live anywhere else, in his view:

Interviewer: Are there places in *Alt-Mariendorf* where you don't feel safe?
Arthur: Nope! No, like I said before, first of all I lived here and then in *Königs-Wusterhausen*, you know exactly what is there.
Interviewer: (*laughing*) No, I don't know what is there.
Arthur: Well, yes, it is like a small centre of neo-Nazis, yes.
Interviewer: Really? What was it like living there?
Arthur: I was at the train station in *Königs-Wusterhausen*. I met these Nazis several times. Thank god ... I haven't been harmed or so. When you can make it here, you can live everywhere else [in the city].

Discussing the map of the city later, Arthur stated that he did not fear people because Jesus accompanied him. Still, he rather avoided dirty and noisy places. He suggested that actually the neo-Nazis were the ones who were afraid. He had decided to become 'brave' and ignore people who offended him:

Arthur: Nope, I can, now, live everywhere else. Because now I know, I don't know I have no problems anymore. Although there are [some] people that say 'I don't walk late at night' and things like that. But I have my Jesus, Jesus accompanies me, and he protects me, and fear, no, I don't have that. Why should I? Afraid of a human being?
Interviewer: I mean some people are afraid in certain districts ....
Arthur: I'm not afraid of a Nazi or that neo-Nazis come to me or so, but I'm afraid of places that are noisy, or where it is dirty, filthy or things like that, but I'm not afraid of getting attacked, no I don't have that.

There has been a time Arthur felt more afraid, but then he decided that fear was the 'wrong' feeling:

> Therefore I decided to, how to say … yes, being brave. Actually, normally, you are afraid, but actually these people are also afraid of us! You know?! … That's why I'm actually brave … Even if someone says something [racist], I cope with it … and keep going.

Arthur's practice of resisting fear in Berlin's East is morally orientated at his religious belief. His moral orientation helped him to confront racism in his fluid encounters in his everyday experience and enabled him to use resources in parts of the city that other interviewees did not access.

In contrast to those interview partners who mapped no-go areas in Berlin's East and to others that expressed practices of resistance while moving through the city and finding a place to live, some interview partners were indifferent towards the East of Berlin. They simply did not know the Eastern districts, had nothing to do there and hence did not go there. Much more striking were the accounts of those who did have such mental maps.

In sum, we found clear spatial patterns of the perception and use of the city by Sub-Saharan immigrants as a response to racist practices of exclusion. Meanwhile, Sub-Saharan immigrants created spaces that enabled the hoarding and distribution of resources, as we will see in the chapters of Simon, Schilling and Arbter. This practice helped people to find ways of making a living in the city, which in turn caused the formation of collective identities as 'Africans' or 'Blacks', as expressed in our interviews.

Creating Alternative Spaces of Immigrant Cosmopolitanism

Besides the exclusionary effects of market cosmopolitanism, urban studies have discussed non-elitist forms of 'real cosmopolitanism', based on the unspectacular everyday encounters of people of various origins in the city: 'actual existing cosmopolitanism … produced "from below"' (Kothari 2008, 501). It includes a set of moral orientations and/or practices towards 'the other', which stretch social, economic, cultural and political networks in Western contemporary cities far beyond the limits of nationality and ethnicity. This 'immigrant cosmopolitanism' can be seen as a resourceful strategy[3] to make a living in an urban environment characterized by discrimination and social and economic marginalization (ibid., 501 and 509).

Taube and Borja find Afro-shops to be self-created safe public spaces for people of African origin in Berlin (see 2011, 219 ff.). They argue that the shared experience of being of colour and the related issues of racism, exclusion and

3 We say resourceful strategy and not practice because the 'immigrant cosmopolitanism' refers to a set of practices and moral orientations that helps to play creatively with the rules of the game that structure the making of an urban livelihood in Berlin, and this despite and within the limited means one gets as an immigrant in this city. We understand strategy here in the sense of Bourdieu's theory of practice (see 1994, 151–61).

discrimination lead to the construction, self-perception and -representation of a We-group identity, of an African consciousness that transcends ethnic and national boundaries and frontiers. Afro-shops are found to be open places and spaces of multi-culture, where ethnic boundaries are questioned and crossed rather than enforced (ibid., 222). Far beyond being mere places of consumption, Afro-shops are hubs, Taube and Borja maintain, of information, communication and mutual support, build (personal) bridges to 'home' and provide at least an economical link to the receiving society (ibid., 219). Apart from crossing ethnic and national boundaries of the vast African continent, clients, owners, products and local networks cannot be reduced only to Africa. In a shop in *Wedding* an Indian owner sold African, Asian and Arabic products to its diverse customers, as one of them told us:

> Personally, I like to go to [... this shop] for my needs. Because this is a very interesting shop, which is from a Indian owner, who is selling African and Arab products and Chinese products, ... so actually international, but you don't find European products there (*smiling*) and this is the great thing about it, no matter what you're looking for, if it is not European you will find it there. That's where I get my smoothing cream for my hair, artificial hair for braiding. Plantains and so on, exotic fruits.

In another Afro-shop in *Neukölln*, Russian immigrants found a 'private social worker', Michael from Togo, who studied in 'Leningrad' and helped immigrants in Berlin to handle German bureaucracy. As an act of 'African solidarity' he helped out with legal issues and translated the legal jargon to Russian, English and French, to only name the European languages:

> Interviewer: And what kind of people are they? Last time you mentioned that they aren't only from Ghana and Togo and so on but also Europeans ...?
> Michael: Well, I speak Russian, I speak French and I speak [English]. There are Russians in Berlin whom I know, who don't speak German very well. .
> Interviewer: So, not only people who know of the Afro-shop know you, but also others? Where are they from?
> Michael: ... The church and the club of course, they come from Nigeria, Kenia, Tanzania, Ghana, Senegal.

Afro-shops can be seen as vital places of a migrant cosmopolitanism in Berlin. Being more than just a shop, they provide a public space for interaction, business, information, beauty, exchange and mutual support. This comes quite close to Du Bois's impression and vision of Berlin in the 1920s and to Gilroy's idea of an 'evasive, multicultural future', which is '... prefigured everywhere in the ordinary experiences of contact, cooperation, and conflict across the supposedly impermeable boundaries of race, culture, identity, and ethnicity' (Gilroy 2004, viii).

Following Gilroy and other important contemporary thinkers on cosmopolitanism, the fluid encounters in the diverse reality of contemporary cities already express a real and powerful cosmopolitanism that is able to transcend the manifold constructed differences in Western societies. In other words: immigrant cosmopolitanism anticipates a different society. At sites of 'immigrant cosmopolitanism' like the Afro-shops, social space is produced within the context of mainstream racism in the city. Here, interchange and solidarity seam to clear the ground for ways of hoarding and distributing resources. That said, generally absent from these sites for fluid encounters and the development of public familiarity seem to be the German residents themselves: as the next two chapters address, even when living in highly diverse areas, the families we interviewed live rather secluded lives.

Conclusion

Du Bois found Berlin of the 1920s to be a wide-open, cosmopolitan city (Lenz 2012, 77). As Lenz points out, in his novel *Dark Princess* Du Bois chose it to be the scene for 'the meeting of representatives of all the "darker people of the world"' (ibid.). Discussing the ambiguous relation of Du Bois and Berlin, Lenz (ibid., 80) sees the city in the novel presented as 'a public space of a global non-Western/ non-White alliance … [which] projects Du Bois's vision of a transnational, global dialogue between Western and non-Western, African as well as Asian cultures'.

The idea of Berlin as cosmopolitan is still vivid and popular (see Lanz 2007). As we have seen, a limited idea of cosmopolitanism used by the entrepreneurial city as a marketing campaign referred only to certain social groups and places and hence excludes others. Since the imagination (or more precisely the discursive construction) of Berlin as a cosmopolitan and open-minded city always had to go along with contradictory racist and narrow-minded realities, this 'outside' of cosmopolitan Berlin needed to be constructed as a part of the cosmopolitan self-perception. Non-cosmopolitans were found in East Berlin, where the deep-rooted racism and right-wing extremism of the whole society surfaced in violent attacks. While intolerance could be externalized to being a sign of abnormal individual failure in socially declining areas, the immigrant population of Berlin was equally excluded. Culture and ethnicity were found to explain urban social problems in Berlin, instead of social inequality and discrimination, which becomes particularly visible in our discussion of school segregation later on. With the externalization of racism and right-wing extremism to East Berlin, the problem was literally placed outside of the city-culture and the society as a whole.

This allowed Berlin to continue promoting its open-mindedness and cosmopolitanism alongside the news of racist attacks, which in turn severely affected the capabilities of Sub-Saharan immigrants for moving through the city. The Eastern districts were relatively speaking left to neo-Nazis with their spatial ambitions of 'national liberated zones' or foreigner-free areas, which they of course never fully achieved. What they did achieve was the construction of 'spaces of fear', which are expressed by the Sub-Saharan immigrants in the interviews and substantiated and confirmed by government reports and police announcements.

Immigrants have always been a constitutive and transformative force in the city. But the brighter realities of immigrant cosmopolitanism are also bound to place. It blossoms only where racism is not already inscribed in space. Since East Berlin is marked and avoided as a 'space of fear' for some, immigrant cosmopolitanism is less likely to develop. It might be the case that the Afro-shops our interviewees spoke of, functioning as public spaces of immigrant cosmopolitanism and mostly located in Berlin's Western districts, do not say much. Historical explanations can be given why less immigrants of African origin live in East Berlin and the Eastern districts are far from being homogenous places only inhabited by narrow-minded right-wing extremists.

Still, the mere fact that 'spaces of fear' exist and persist is alarming, even if they only exist for some. In the understanding of Berlin as an open-minded city (independent of image campaigns) its residents cannot wait until either more places are being occupied by neo-Nazis (south of *Neukölln*), or enough 'cosmopolitan warriors' enter and inhabit the Eastern districts to show how 'spaces of fear' are really deconstructed (*Lichtenberg*). It is rather time to take a close look to see what spatial realities hide behind the comfortable image of cosmopolitanism. Such realities severely hamper the freedom of movement of Sub-Saharan immigrants in Berlin. As the next two chapters will discuss, their access to resources is already limited, as is the case for other migrant groups, by the spatial profits that the middle classes organize through their patterns of segregation. For Sub-Saharan immigrants this marginalization is severed by the districts where racist practices can be openly expressed and, relatively unchallenged, keep them out.

References

Ang, Ien. 2001. *On not speaking Chinese: living between Asia and the West*, quoted in David Ley. 2004. 'Transnational Spaces and Everyday Lives'. *Transaction of the Institute of British Geographers, New Series* 29: 151–64.

Beck, Ulrich. 2006. *The Cosmopolitan Vision.* Cambridge: Polity Press.

Bourdieu, Pierre. 1994. *Raisons pratiques. Sur la théorie de l'action.* Paris: Seuil.

Buchstein, Hubertus and Gudrun Heinrich. 2010. 'Einleitung'. In *Rechtsextremismus in Ostdeutschland. Demokratie und Rechtsextremismus im ländlichen Raum*, edited by Hubertus Buchstein and Gudrun Heinrich, 13–55. Schwalbach: Wochenschauverlag.

Bundschuh, Stephan. 2004. 'Rechtsextremismus und Sozialraum'. In *Sozialraumorientierung und Auseinandersetzung mit Rechtsextremismus in der Jugendarbeit*, edited by Deutsches Jugendinstitut Arbeitsstelle Rechtsextremismus und Fremdenfeindlichkeit, 10–21. Halle: Deutsches Jugendinstitut Arbeitsstelle Rechtsextremismus und Fremdenfeindlichkeit.

Bürk, Thomas. 2011. 'Geographie der Angst'. In *Kämpfe um Raumhoheit. Rechte Gewalt, 'No Go Areas' und 'National befreite Zonen'*, edited by Christoph Schulze and Ella Weber, 21–36. Münster: unrast transparent.

———. 2012. *Gefahrenzone, Angstraum, Feindesland?* Münster: Westfälisches Dampfboot.

Business Location Center (BLC). 2010. 'Berlin – the Place to Be'. Accessed 2 August 2014. http://www.youtube.com/watch?v=ZTYoX_EwOq8&list=PLDB80CED18527D04A.

Decker, Oliver, Johannes Kiess and Elmar Brähler. 2012. *Die Mitte im Umbruch. Rechtsextreme Einstellungen in Deutschland 2012.* Bonn: Dietz.

Decker, Oliver, Marliese Weissmann, Johannes Kiess and Elmar Brähler. 2010. *Die Mitte in der Krise. Rechtsextreme Einstellungen in Deutschland 2010.* Berlin: Friedrich Ebert Stiftung.

Döring, Uta. 2008. *Angstzonen. Rechtsdominierte Orte aus medialer und lokaler Perspektive.* Wiesbaden: VS Verlag für Sozialwissenschaften.

———. 2011. 'Alltag und Angst in der Zone'. In *Kämpfe um Raumhoheit. Rechte Gewalt, 'No Go Areas' und 'National befreite Zonen'*, edited by Christoph Schulze and Ella Weber, 53–63. Münster: unrast transparent.

Du Bois, William E.B. 1967 [1899]. *The Philadelphia Negro. A Social Study.* New York: Schocken Books. 296–7, quoted in David Sibley, *Geographies of Exclusion. Society and difference in the West*, 137–56. New York: Routledge.

Gilroy, Paul. 2004. *After Empire. Melancholia or Convivial Culture?* Oxfordshire: Routledge.

Harvey, David. 2000. 'Cosmopolitanism and the Banality of Geographical Evils'. *Public Culture* 12: 529–64.

Heinemann, Karl-Heinz and Wilfried Schubarth. 1992. *Der antifaschistische Staat entlässt seine Kinder. Jugend und Rechtsextremismus in Ostdeutschland.* Köln: PapyRossa.

Holm, Andrej. 2006. 'Urban Renewal and the End of Social Housing: The Roll Out of Neoliberalism in East Berlin's Prenzlauer Berg'. *Social Justice* 33 (3 (105)): 114–28.

Keith, Michael. 2005. *After the Cosmopolitan? Multicultural Cities and the Future of Racism.* Oxon and New York: Routledge.

Kothari, Uma. 2008. 'Global Peddlers and Local Networks: Migrant Cosmopolitanisms'. *Environment and Planning* 26: 500–516.

Lanz, Stephan. 2007. *Berlin aufgemischt: abendländisch, multikulturell, kosmopolitisch? Die politische Konstruktion einer Einwanderungsstadt.* Bielefeld: Transcript.

Lenz, Günter H. 2012. 'Radical Cosmopolitanism: W. E. B. Du Bois, Germany and African American Pragmatist Visions for Twenty-First Century Europe'. *Journal of Transnational American Studies* 4 (2): 65–96.

Ley, David. 2004. 'Transnational Spaces and Everyday Lives'. *Transaction of the Institute of British Geographers, New Series* 29 (2): 151–64.

Moore, A. 2014. 'Eight of the Worst Countries For Black People to Travel'. Accessed 18 July 2014. http://atlantablackstar.com/2014/01/08/8-worst-countries-black-people-travel/.

Schulze, Christoph. 2011. 'Einleitung'. In *Kämpfe um Raumhoheit. Rechte Gewalt, 'No Go Areas' und 'National befreite Zonen'*, edited by Christoph Schulze and Ella Weber, 13–20. Münster: unrast transparent.

Senate Department for Urban Development and the Environment. 2013. 'Berliner Mietspiegel 2013'. Accessed 31 July 2014. http://www.stadtentwicklung.berlin.de/wohnen/mietspiegel/de/download/Mietspiegel2013.pdf.

Sibley, David. 1995. *Geographies of Exclusion. Society and difference in the West.* New York: Routledge.

Spiegel-Online. 2006. 'Is Eastern Germany Safe for Foreigners? Racism Warning Has German Hackles Raised'. Accessed 18 July 2014. http://www.spiegel.de/international/is-eastern-germany-safe-for-foreigners-racism-warning-has-german-hackles-raised-a-416904.html.

Stöss, Richard. 2007. *Rechtsextremismus im Wandel.* Berlin: Friedrich Ebert Stiftung.

Taube, Jana and Alejandra Borja. 2011. 'Afro-Shops. Eine Brücke zwischen verschiedene Welten?' In *Marginale Urbanität: migrantisches Unternehmertum und Stadtentwicklung*, edited by Felicitas Hillmann, 209–28. Bielefeld: Transcript.

Terkessidis, Mark. 2004. *Die Banalität des Rassismus. Migranten zweiter Generation entwickeln eine neue Perspektive.* Bielefeld: Transcript.

Toytown Germany. 2009. 'Moving to Berlin as an African-American Woman'. Accessed 18 July 2014. http://www.toytowngermany.com/lofi/index.php/t132062.html.

Verfassungsschutz Berlin. 2007. 'Rechte Gewalt in Berlin 2003–2006'. Studienreihe Im Fokus. Berlin: Senatsverwaltung für Inneres und Sport, Abteilung Verfassungsschutz.

Young, Craig, Martina Diep and Stephanie Drabble. 2006. 'Living with Difference? The "Cosmopolitan City" and Urban Reimaging in Manchester, UK'. *Urban Studies* 43 (10): 1687–1714.

Chapter 2

Secluding: Middle Class Segregation in Schools and Neighbourhoods

Carlotta Giustozzi, Talja Blokland and Nora Freitag

Introduction

'So it's mum, dad, two children and a small front yard'. Suzi, mother of two children with a university degree, with a tone of irony in her voice described her neighbourhood, *Kreuzberg* in Berlin's inner city, in our interview. She had found a place, a 'village in the city', that she felt was appropriate for her family. In cities, many middle class families with young children cluster together in homogenous, privileged residential areas. Among social scientists, social segregation is often seen as problematic, as it reinforces social inequality (Small and Newman 2001). Most of the literature on segregation looks at disadvantaged neighbourhoods and seeks explanations within these areas (see Small and Newman 2001 for an overview). Some describe middle class urbanites as revanchist purposively trying to exclude the poor (Atkinson 2006; 2008; Butler 2003). How these residential practices of middle class families come about is not often asked. Here, we focus on the residential choices of these middle classes and show how they are linked directly to an important aspect of social reproduction: ensuring cultural capital for the offspring through getting what middle class parents believe to be the right schools. In other words, neighbourhoods, schools and kindergartens form resourceful settings for which the access is structured by matching habitus and forms of capital. Those who enter the 'right' neighbourhood and educational infrastructure for their offspring are capable of secluding themselves from the rest of the city. Supporters of cosmopolitanism and tolerance and diversity, the choices they make for their children don't, as we will see, always match such moral orientations. This allows us to further explore the ambivalence of moral orientations in practices that we have mentioned in our introduction. Whereas middle class secluding practices have been noted by others (Butler 2003; Atkinson 2006; 2008), such studies have primarily looked at gentrifiers. In contrast, we compare gentrifiers with urban middle classes in an area not undergoing upgrading. Moreover, while they have registered social contamination, we think there still is some work to do to understand these practices if we are not willing to assume that it is just what they want. As we will see, they seclude themselves from urban infrastructures that they find less ideal – not from others in the first place. Chapter 3 then asks what strategies middle class parents use to achieve places in preferred institutions, and reflects on the exclusionary consequences and the role of racism. Here, we first show how unreflexively marginalization emerged.

As urban resources are limited, residents struggle for access to housing, work and schools, even when they may not always experience this as such or reflect on it. This struggle is both individual, as when individuals try hard to organize resources for their kids, and structural, as boundary work of inclusion and exclusion makes it a struggle between social groups. Following Bourdieu (1992), we argue that different social classes create lifestyles that enable them to exchange resources and get them to function in a valuable way. They meanwhile segregate from other social classes in the city, to ensure the reproduction of their social positions. Here, we look in particular at how and why parents decide to settle in certain places, a practice that, although not intentionally so, creates an inward orientation of inclusion of people with similar positions at the expense of marginalizing others. Scholars who studied middle class urban or metropolitan habitus concluded that the middle classes intentionally segregated from lower situated 'useless' others in the city (Butler 2003) or were so inwardly orientated that there was little room for reflection (Watt 2009).

This chapter then traces the gaps between actual practices and moral orientations: whereas many of our middle class interview partners supported the idea of a multi-cultural, cosmopolitan, inclusive city, they saw their decisions as 'natural' or 'logical' as they were able to realize what they saw best for their children (Bourdieu 2002, 125).

In our study, the parents' choice for 'good' over 'bad' areas conflicted with their moral orientations towards segregation, but effectively segregated them from less well-off citizens in Berlin. As individuals are the producers and the products of class habitus, they may remain blind to how their practices – and the logics of their own reproduction of positions – harmonize social groups (Bourdieu 1992, 59). Parents, with their need to care for their children, are particularly likely to do so:

> Reproduction strategies, the set of outwardly very different practices whereby individuals or families tend, unconsciously, to maintain or increase their assets and consequently to maintain or improve their position in the class structure, constitute a system which, being the product of a single, unifying generative principle, tends to function and change in a systematic way. (Bourdieu 2002, 125)

The interviews on which we draw in this chapter and in Chapter 4 were conducted with parents in *Kreuzberg* and *Lichterfelde*, both urban areas that differ in terms of the housing stock and social structure. *Kreuzberg* has a long history of immigration and squatting but has increasingly gentrified, so that now quite a few sub-districts are inhabited by White middle class families, especially in areas like the one around *Viktoriapark*. The streets are accessible but privately owned, the architecture sets the development off from the rest of the area clearly.

Figure 2.1 Area around *Viktoriapark* in *Kreuzberg*
Source: © Bettine Josties and Emre Karaca

Figure 2.2 The *Swiss Quarter* in *Lichterfelde*
Source: © Daniela Krüger

The second neighbourhood is the *Swiss Quarter* in *Lichterfelde*, an area located outside the inner ring of apartments and mainly single family houses that are owner-occupied, built in the last decade. Whereas the streets are not gated, the streets, green spaces and children's playgrounds are privately owned.

Both areas have square metre prices above Berlin's average. Twenty interviews were conducted in each of the neighbourhoods, using an open interview topic list as well as some questions with fixed answers.

In another study typifying Berlin's districts, *Kreuzberg* was classified as 'creative' and *Lichterfelde*, where the *Swiss Quarter* is located, as 'bourgeois' (Gemeinnützige Hertie-Stiftung 2009). As we will see, their reproduction strategies create – despite these differences – similar forms of marginalization.

Residential Choices: 'Nice' Neighbourhoods

Kreuzberg*: Practices of Creating Islands in the City*

Many interview partners had quite fixed ideas about the type of neighbourhood they wished for. It had to be safe for the children, either urban or in contrast rather quiet, and with good kindergartens and schools. Michael and Sophia, in their thirties, had lived in *Steglitz*, an urban middle class district outside the ring, in the past, but that was 'too quiet' to their taste: they liked to be able to get out of the door for a breakfast or a coffee, and *Steglitz* had not offered them much. They had always liked to come out to the *Bergmannstraße*, a highly gentrified street in *Kreuzberg*. Here the classical Berlin curry sausage can be eaten in a vegetarian version. Cola of an organic variety is served in some of the establishments, and a Turkish-German owner of a kebab house had turned his place into a coffee bar with hard wooden panels where drinking coffee is advertised as an 'experience' as he sailed on the waves of the commercial gentrification. Realizing that their *Steglitz* apartment was becoming too small with a baby on the way, they reacted quickly when they saw a 'to let' sign on an apartment during one of their visits to the street. They went for breakfast there regularly, so why then not just move there? The apartment was privately owned, and the owner had insisted on a personal meeting to see what they were like, but they had not had any problem getting the apartment. They liked the area, and thought it was better than where some of their friends 'deep into *Kreuzberg*' lived. Sophia did not specify what she meant by 'deep', but it carries the notion of something more intense, more severe, as going deep into the woods or the jungle rather than staying on the more manageable edges of the wilderness, in other words a frontier (Smith 1996). Sophia did not think they would stay at *Bergmannstraße* forever, as the area was too loud at night with all the bedrooms except for one facing the street. Many of their friends had moved to the greener middle class suburban neighbourhoods in the South once their children were older. The presence of like-minded people in the area meant a lot to them now. Sophia had recently started to take her three months old baby to baby-massage, where she met 'like-minded people'. A colleague with a one year old had recommended the place to her. She also attended a class to 'build back' (sic) after pregnancy with a friend who delivered her baby two weeks after her. Michael and Sophia had created an island of durable engagements with friends and acquaintances in *Kreuzberg* that supported the lifestyle they found important for themselves. They reflected little on the presence of people not 'like-minded', or those assumed not to be. Connections with their neighbours were just casual fluid encounters of 'hello', there were 'mostly elderly' or people with older children in their building and they had their friends elsewhere. They had an island, oriented around practices with the baby and their consumption behaviour in a variety of bars, cafés and restaurants, and enjoyed living where they did.

Christine was 44, a medical doctor, living with her husband and three children, the youngest two and the oldest 10 years old, near *Viktoriapark* in 'what is called a townhouse', she said laughingly. They were well off, with a monthly income of over €4,000 after tax, and had lived in their house with five rooms for five years. The connections to the other families in their development were open, children played with each other, adults knew each other and each other's children. They had shared an apartment with friends whom they knew from their studies before. The apartment became too small when both couples had children, and they initially had looked for a bigger place together, somewhere in the inner city, not necessarily *Kreuzberg*, but had not found a suitable place. They had looked at the *Viktoriapark* development too but it had been too expensive for their budget at that time. But then they happened to receive an inheritance, so they could go for it. They had researched the area, where they did not know anyone else, especially for the quality of the Kindergartens. Christina had invested a lot so far in providing her children with the cultural capital she thought was important for them. She was very active in introducing her children to theatre and music when they were even younger, but she did not 'drag her children to cultural events so much anymore' as they preferred 'to hang around the house'. Her own life had become very strongly focused on work and family. She did not like to leave her children with a babysitter to go out with Frank because they 'are not really nice to strangers':

> They don't jump to strangers, they will say hello, not that they are rude, but they won't start … one really has to stretch oneself, to get into a good contact with them. Because they are saturated, I mean, I don't think that is weird, that just is that they are saturated, they don't need the attention of others. I mean, I know this different too, often you have children that really try, they really enjoy it when someone plays with them a little or reads to them, but that is not the case with our children.

While Christine did not explicitly say so, one could read in her comments that the privileges she sought for her children were less of an economic kind – which she could take for granted given their economic capital – but of a social and cultural kind: her children received so much, with being read to by their own parents, that they did not need further resources – again, Christine and Frank too had created a safe island for their family.

Ada, a freelance actress, lived with her partner and two very small children in a *Kreuzberg* apartment for three and a half years. They liked *Neukölln*, the inner city neighbourhood where her boyfriend had lived (she came from *Schöneberg*, a less inner-city area to the south), but when they were moving in together, they did not want to move there: with a baby on the way, they thought it was hip, but 'not necessarily' where one would live with children. She thought this part of *Kreuzberg* was a little more 'decent': leaving the underground, you did not 'walk right into the arms of a drug dealer' as was the case in another part, in her experience, which she did not think was right when her children were a little older and would be going around the neighbourhood by themselves. She liked the parks in her area, and the very multicultural character that was nevertheless not aggressive. 'It somehow simply does not have an aggressive, fighting to survive kind of atmosphere here'. At the end of the interview, she referred back to her own statement, and showed exactly the ambivalence between moral orientations and practices: she pointed out that she liked going out in the areas in *Kreuzberg* and *Neukölln* about which she had made her comment on 'aggressive' – she elaborated a little on the behaviour of young men and street codes there and found these areas 'also exciting'. Happy to consume the exciting diversity and slight rough edges of these areas nearby in fluid encounters, Ada, then, too, had started to build an island for her family. Such findings match with the quantitative analysis by Van Eijk and Blokland, that people who had moved to a mixed neighbourhood because they liked its diversity may have done so from a moral orientation, but also as part of consumption related to a specific urban middle class lifestyle. They did not necessarily have diversity in their social networks (Van Eijk and Blokland 2010).

More than in the *Swiss Quarter*, where cultural diversity was not omnipresent in the streets so being positive about diversity could be done from a safe distance, the *Kreuzberg* interview partners had to come to terms with their own moral orientations of supporting diversity on the one hand and their daily experiences. Ada stated she actually liked the atmosphere of *Kreuzberg* with its diversity, 'probably because I grew up with foreigners'. Having newly arrived in the area, her classifying of the immigrants who had often lived there for years as *foreign* is remarkable. She had an incident at a bus stop once when someone threw a bottle on the ground – someone she labelled as 'a Turkish young man'. She used that incident, however, to reveal how ambivalent she was about the question of diversity, when she commented that such an incident could also have happened in *Steglitz*, *not* saying it had to be an incident with a *foreigner*, but rather suggesting that 'bad behaviour' could occur anywhere. During the interviews, all interview partners were asked to mark areas where they did not feel comfortable on a map. They all tended to mark the same districts as 'problematic', but those living in the inner-city mixed area *Kreuzberg* were more precise in their description. Sophia, a mother living in *Kreuzberg* compared *Steglitz* as a more 'solid', less 'stressful' area with 'less foreigners' but was not worried too much about it, as after all she lived in *Kreuzberg*'s 'gentrification zone'. When people did comment on the presence of immigrants, stating sometimes that one hardly 'noticed' the migration background because it was 'integrated migration' and sometimes labelling other areas as 'extreme' because of the immigrants, they seemed more concerned about appropriate behaviour in public spaces as civil, respectful and crime-free spaces and *sometimes* suggested that immigrants, especially young males, behaved inappropriately. Some indeed did imply that immigrants cared less about their environment and were more tolerant towards loud or even criminal behaviour. Though the families cited here lived in an ethnically diverse neighbourhood in *Kreuzberg* they did not practice diversity. For them embracing the image of a cosmopolitan, creative and authentic environment went along well with distancing themselves from their neighbours. Informed by fluid encounters with residents of the neighbourhoods, interviewees expressed their discomfort with residents who, as they thought, did not share their moral orientation. There is a similarity here with residents in our second research area, the *Swiss Quarter* – still, the actual choice for residence in the latter area was particularly different, showing an overall tendency for self-segregation that harmonized this middle class neighbourhood and provided its residents with spatial profit.

Swiss Quarter*: Practices of Residential Segregation*

The families in the *Swiss Quarter* and in *Kreuzberg* shared a desire for a safe environment in which the children could play outside, and valued having neighbours with whom they could get on well. Quite a few indicated that their moral orientation of a not segregated, inclusive city as ideal conflicted directly with their own residential practices. This ambivalence, often absent in many of the studies on the urban middle classes, challenges the idea of a deliberate, intended *choice* to exclude the poor and immigrants from their environments. John and Silvia had an ideal mixture of cultural diversity, but would not want to live in areas with 'too high' concentrations of immigrants with their children. They saw, however, how their own practice contributed to the very process they rejected. They had moved to the *Swiss Quarter* in 2008, and preferred the area over *Wedding* or *Neukölln*, inner-city neighbourhoods with fewer places for children to play and a high population density. They had moved from *Wedding* where it had become 'decayed' and would not want to live in *Neukölln*, because the social composition there was 'unpleasant':

> That should be distributed better, so I find that here with us also, here it is really so, it is, well, one-sided, see? A certain mixture is also absent here, I don't think that is so good either. But … then I prefer it here over there, see. This one-sidedness all the time … yeah … that results then also all the time again in this … let me call it ghettoization, yes? Includes us also into that.

Tim and Matilda, a graphic designer and a certified nurse in their late forties, interviewed together, lived in *Wedding* before they moved to *Lichterfelde*, first into an apartment and then into a house in the *Swiss Quarter* two years ago with their teenage children. They used irony to critically reflect on their own practices, that contrasted with what they thought was good for the city. After the birth of their second child, when they had to 'deal with Kindergarten, schools and so on' and it became 'very clear' to them that *Wedding* did not offer the environment in which they wanted their children to grow up. *Lichterfelde* was not the only possibility, but at least it was 'more quiet and eh … more posh' and (ironically in tone) 'pretending to be socially better'. Their ambivalence became clear too, when they commented that they enjoyed living with people who had 'similar ideas' as they did. Speaking in their terms, one feels oneself 'a little well situated' here 'with our Prussian understandings of a good life'. The next step from the rental apartment to the homeownership of a house in the *Swiss Quarter* was a logical step, as the children could stay in their schools and their many sports clubs and music classes. Moving elsewhere in the city had not been a discussion anymore.

While in *Kreuzberg* many couples had studied in Berlin, were born in the city or had come to Berlin at a younger age, the interview partners in the *Swiss Quarter* had often moved to Berlin with their families for professional reasons. The choice of the residential location was a choice for spatial profit: the place they had moved to offered the right combination of housing quality, neighbourliness, amenities and, above all, good quality schools. Daniela, a musician in her late thirties, whose partner worked in the pharmaceutical industry, grew up in a village herself. The *Swiss Quarter* was an 'acceptable alternative' to the big city. She was pleased with the outside space for the children and talked about their friends and how boys and girls played football together outside on a green between the houses. Her youngest daughter went to the catchment area school, where Daniela was active in the PTA. She had studied the available data and Internet site of the school carefully before they decided on the house when they moved from Frankfurt to Berlin for her husband's job. The older daughter attended a nearby *Gymnasium*. In Daniela's case, then, the residential choice was heavily influenced by the school choice: they actually bought a house in the catchment area of a school she liked. Katharina, who worked in a pharmacy and was married to a banker, was not too positive about the *Swiss Quarter* when she first saw it on a house hunt when her husband moved jobs, as all the houses appeared the same. But when they had moved to Berlin with two small children seven years ago, she did not see many alternatives: coming from a 'proper middle class area' in München, she did not even look anywhere else, but now she knew she would not have wanted to move to 'something like *Kreuzberg*'.

Now that we have seen how residential choices included the ambivalence of a moral orientation in favour of a cosmopolitan, diverse city with segregating practices to safeguard what parents saw as the best interests of their children, let us move on to what concerned all of them most: the battle over good kindergarten and school places. We will not discuss in detail through what processes parents managed to get different schools than the ones to which they were allocated. This is the subject of Chapter 3 later on. Neither will we discuss extensively the importance of ethnicity and race, as we will return to this too in Chapter 3, but will meet some arguments that will later also be found by the parents interviewed there.

Educational Choices: 'Nice' Schools and Kindergarten

Segregation at the Age of Two: Kindergarten Places

Compared to schools and housing, having access to social ties within a network of friends and neighbours, for example durable engagements of people one personally knew rather than superficial fluid encounters, was more important for the choice and access to kindergarten places. Compared to the allocation of school places the access to kindergarten places is remarkably non-transparent, opaque and unregulated. The fierce attempts of the local state to regulate access to schools by catchment areas and strict procedures (although they can be circumscribed) contrast with the enormous freedom of parents in kindergarten choice and agency to start their own alternative forms of day care. As parents often get school places allocated on the basis of the argument that children from a kindergarten should be able to stay with their friends – friends of course who have been carefully selected for them by their parents when they were toddlers – part of the school segregation and the marginalization of children who do not attend kindergartens or attend the large state institutions starts not when children reach the school age, but long before at the doorsteps of the kindergartens.

The issue of finding the right kindergarten and schools for children was more complicated and ambivalent for the families in *Kreuzberg* than it was for those in the *Swiss Quarter*: as we have seen, some had moved there for the purpose of accessing the as 'good' or 'nice' defined schools. Kindergarten places were hard to come by, as elsewhere in the city. Edith, a jewellery artist working from home, married to a lawyer and mother of four children, had her youngest children initially in a church-based Kindergarten, but she did not like the staff. She hence moved the youngest three children to a kindergarten based on anthroposophist principles, which implied a few adjustments: the children were, for example, not supposed to watch television, which she thought was a good thing but got her into some difficulties with her oldest son, already in the catchment area school, whose peers did watch. She liked the principles as long as one did not overdo them. When her daughter had to enter elementary school, her experiences with the catchment area school had not been great. She never had a feeling that the teachers really cared much and thought that they made their jobs easy by not paying the weaker students or the ones that had social adjustment issues much attention. She therefore submitted an application for her daughter to the *Waldorf* elementary school. As she came from the kindergarten with the same principles, she had a good chance to get in – as she did – but Edith had worried quite a bit about it. With her son in a normal school, she was not sure how convinced the director was that she really supported the school's principles.

John and Silvia had had some problems finding a proper kindergarten, but found one through friends they knew from the neighbourhood. The topic had simply come up when they had had breakfast together, and they went to visit the kindergarten that their friends had recommended right away. The centre was small, it had many staff members per child, and the toddlers were immersed in English with one of the staff members being a native speaker who only communicated in English with the children. In the stories of acquiring kindergarten places, the relevance of the residential area became clear: with many kindergartens nearby, but few available places, word of mouth and getting introduced and be spoken for was necessary to find out what the good institutions were and how to get a place there. Most of these kindergartens were so-called 'parent-initiative' kindergartens, a popular alternative in Berlin to the state-led, often large institutions. These kindergartens were organized as associations with a board of directors elected by parents and hired professional staff. The freedom to design the profile, to define what was expected in 'participation' from parents, to set the fee – usually higher than the subsidy parents received from the state – and to select the children they admitted was great. While many officially said to have waiting lists, the procedures of moving up such lists were not transparent. In *Lichterfelde*, selection may have been primarily a matter of being connected to parents who already had a place. Sonya, who had moved from abroad back to Germany when her husband, working for a pharmaceutical company, had been relocated and had never lived in Berlin and had no local network, found a *Gymnasium* for her teenage daughters easily, but struggled more to find a kindergarten for her son. Not being connected to other parents, it took her six months to find a place; her son got into a bilingual kindergarten eventually because he had learnt to speak English abroad already.

In *Kreuzberg*, it is likely that support for the specific profiles of the kindergartens, about which parents were interviewed, may have worked as a selection mechanism beyond personal networks, and, as such ideas about special programmes were so closely related to cultural capital, may have reproduced boundaries between various groups. This is not to say that no immigrant children attended such kindergartens. In fact, there were many bilingual and 'multicultural' kindergartens in *Kreuzberg*. But a specific, culturally defined habitus was needed to acquire a place there.

Christine's youngest daughter went to a private carer (*Tagesmutter*), where various children in the neighbourhood had gone to, whom she found through word of mouth. Her sons had both attended a musical kindergarten, found, too, through word of mouth.

Jason, an architect, and his wife, a bookseller, and two daughters had lived in a smaller apartment in the same building where they lived now. They liked *Kreuzberg* and happened to learn – not specifying how – about the free apartment. Whereas they had not thought about children when they moved to *Kreuzberg*, it had 'a useful kindergarten and two schools for the children' nearby. With a net income of reported €2,000 a month, they are not as affluent as some other families in the area, and lived in a smaller apartment than most interview partners. They were thinking about moving, as the new owner of their apartment had increased the rents, but did not want to leave the area because of the kindergarten and the school. Their daughter did go to a school nearby, but not the catchment area school. That many children in the area went to their school was a selection of all those living there, namely children of parents with whom they had shared the same small kindergarten, and others that managed to get their school preferences acknowledged rather than get the local school allocated:

> Because our children go to school directly in the neighbourhood, and they went to kindergarten there too, and eh, most of the children there come from the immediate neighbourhood of course, so that is why we have many contacts … of whom the children then go in the same class as our daughter, eh … then one knows them of course.

As a matter of fact, few *Kreuzberg* interviewees sent their children to the allocated school. It became clear from the interviews that they, living in a 'diverse' area, had more worries about the schools than did people in similar class positions in the *Swiss Quarter*.

Schools: Alternatives to the Catchment Area School

School quality is a difficult theme, and there is not much reason to assume *a priori* that schools in the *Swiss Quarter* and its environment were any 'better' than schools in *Kreuzberg*. For example, an analysis of the equipment of schools in the material sense, like the number of computers per child in the school, reveals that schools in deprived areas were better equipped, not worse. Rates of illness among teachers did not differ statistically between neighbourhoods, although the number of hours that students were not receiving any teaching due to illness of the teachers was higher in deprived areas than in rich neighbourhoods. The problem with schools is, of course, that these statistics do not mean much to parents who, concerned to reproduce their social position, seriously look at schools and ask whether *their* particular child would flourish there. The uniqueness of the little individual that is their child becomes the focus of their choice, at least in their experience and understanding. So a neighbourhood school in the catchment area may be fine, it just may not work for their child: this seems to be the line of argumentation in these interviews (which, of course, did not focus solely and exclusionary on school choice, but see Chapter 3 for a more detailed analysis of middle class parents' choices).

In both the *Swiss Quarter* and *Kreuzberg*, middle class residents struggled with catchment area schools. The catchment area school of the *Swiss Quarter* was said to be too full, as the relatively new housing development had brought so many new children to the area, but the prospect of a new additional building was comforting, so people believed this would get better soon. The school had a good reputation; it was sometimes said to not deal too well with children with learning difficulties, but the parents we talked to did not have such children. Only Daniela had taken her son out of the school a few years ago. Daniela's daughter, now 15, changed to a fast-track on a *Gymnasium* after fourth grade, and only attended the elementary school for two years. Her son went to a private school after fourth grade, where he changed to when Daniela and her husband were dissatisfied with the catchment area elementary school but did not think the step to the *Gymnasium* was right for him. There was an intake interview with the school director:

> Let us say, it simply has to be a fit. He needs to be convinced that it is the right school for the child. They only have 40 places, twenty of which are filled up with kids coming from their own elementary school, and then 20 places are open. Then you got 120 children applying and then they have to see, well, you can't influence it, you go to the interview and either it fits or it does not ... No idea how they do that, who fits and who does not. We never learnt what criteria they use.

She was happy that she did not have to go through the normal process of getting a place at a *Gymnasium*, as she heard many 'terrible' stories of other parents, who, when they did not get a place in one of the most popular schools, ended up having their children in *Gymnasiums* that they did not wish them to go to. By switching after the fourth grade and moving their son into a private school, this family managed to maximize their own agency in the school choice.

So did Jason, the *Kreuzberg* architect, and his wife. As we see in this example, as well as in the next one, the choice for a different school than the catchment area school was motivated by beliefs about some qualitative aspects about the school of their preference, not simply by a negative opinion about the specific catchment area school as such. Jason's children did not go to the catchment area school, but to a school with an 'integration concept' where children with handicaps and without handicaps learnt together. Their children had no handicaps, but Jason and his wife thought that the principle on which this school was based was important to the socialization of their children, who would learn in a context of diversity – diversity as able and disabled, not thought of primarily in ethnic, racial or class terms. To get a place, they registered at a fake address in the catchment area. That did 'not work' in the case of their second daughter, who was given a place at the catchment area where they actually lived. Her parents gave it a try 'but we had to conclude that it really did not work out'. When they realized that the school had 'not delivered what their child needed' (not further specified in the interview) they managed to change schools through the 'way of the small favours' about which Jason did not tell more. It was 'luckily' easy to get the school change through, because 'those in charge' (the school director and the teachers) had known Jason and his wife already, so the move was 'quick and uncomplicated'.

Christine, the doctor from *Kreuzberg*, avoided the catchment area school, too. Although she and her husband wished for their children to go to a state school, they were concerned about the rather mass-oriented after-school programmes of many of the state schools, where staff had too little time for the individual needs of children. The state of Berlin has reorganized some of its schools into all-day schools from the early morning until 4 pm, with various organized activities for children in music, arts and sports after classes. Christine was in principle supportive of this policy, but was critical about its implementation, as Berlin schools remained under-resourced to provide high quality after-school activities. The alternative school that Christine and her husband had found had a *Schülerladen*, a small after-school programme initiated by parents and run by a private foundation:

> Christine: Well, ehh ... Max and Stephan go to [a different school than the catchment area school], but it is a perfectly normal state school. We have applied for that school, because at least we thought it would be really good, because of the after school program, and we find that good ... because it is not a normal after-school program, it is much smaller, and at the time they had an intern that had cooked and played football with them. That is a smaller group, with two youth workers and an intern, three people for twenty, not always changing youth workers [as] in one of those big institutions ... maybe it was the wrong decision because we have to transport them there ... But we ended in the Montessori class, by accident, and that is good of course, and then the after school program.
> Interviewer: Was that accidental then, the Montessori class?
> Christine: No, we have applied, it could have been different, we did not know that they ... we had said if there is a Montessori class - because it is not an entire Montessori school, it also had a normal after school, and then this department with the *Schülerladen* and then [classes] with or without Montessori. ...
>
> [W]e just applied for the school and then we have said, if there is a place in the Montessori [class], then we like to have it. *Ganztagsschule* is coming up in the elementary schools, that is clear, and that is politically also right, but those people have to think that the quality has to change, because the way it is at the moment, in those after school programs, they merely keep them there.

Aware of the resulting segregation of such choices, Christine still presented her choice as the natural thing to do for one's children, assuming anyone who had the cultural capital to understand the ins and outs of the after school system would do the same, even though that may not be politically correct (PC):

> And when you understand that a little, then you try for your own children, try to get something that is qualitatively better out of it for them. Also when that is really totally not PC, isn't it? Because it is going in the direction of everybody equal, and eh, we should all have the same chances in education and so on, and then you pull your own children out again. You say no, stop, we do the *Schülerläden*. Fact is however, the food there is better, it tastes better, the staff is

> always the same, they know the children and so on. While of course politically it is nice, when all have the same chances. But it is also the case that what is for everyone, often, at least here in Berlin where so little money is put into schools, is also the worse option. Well and that hurts, no?

She heard about other schools being unclean, especially in the restrooms, suggesting that different social classes had different standards about hygiene; what was apparently okay for lower class children was not for middle class children like her own, who would not use dirty restrooms:

> Then children do it, they don't go to the restrooms, see? They hardly drink anything and keep everything up just to not have to go to the restroom. That provokes illnesses, they get ill, they don't drink enough, get head aches and get constipated because they keep it up just to not have to go to the restrooms. There is not even toilet paper there. It was a recommendation by a neighbour … our children were not in school yet and she had said, that is nice there, we have looked at it, but as I said, I don't think the teaching is really better, that is all similar … [but with lunch] they sit with four or five at a table, they care about a table culture a little, so one of the staff sits with four, five children and that is not so canteen like.

With the transformation to *Ganztagschule*, the *Schülerläden* were disappearing, she noted:

> That is good too, of course it is, because then in the classrooms the kids are being sorted a little again, there are fewer, even though it is a regular common school, a common *Kreuzberg* school, there are few children with migration background, not at the school in total but in the classroom, because these *Schülerläden* have to be paid for … . We pay for it, for the *Ganztagsschulen* you don't have to pay. We pay for it that they get different lunches and that they have different staff, we have to pay all that too, but naturally that means, that is also a certain selection, that is clear, when you have little money to spend, then you won't do it.

However, that cultural capital may be the currency that defines group boundaries of classes and not the money one has, becomes clear when she continued that the organization of the segregated after-school programmes divided the children of parents who understand the value of good education and child development from those who do not:

> Where then someone with an academic degree, even when you get a child now as a student, then you may still say ah (*clipped with fingers*), that is what I allow myself now. Because you grasp it, don't you? You'll pay a smaller contribution because you get support from somewhere, then you pay like €40, but you may probably grasp, that your child should still go in the *Schülerladen.* And not

> everyone grasps that, so it is more of a matter of education. That is clear. For you [as an educated person] it will be important that your child is healthy, it will be important to you or you know that it is nicer when there is more staff, and you'll say, that €40, I got to go, do one cleaning job for that, that is *scheißegal* … .

Christine's son plays basketball at school; his school being overall 'disadvantaged' it qualified for an initiative of Berlin's professional basketball club. While she did not let her children eat the food from the canteen, she certainly took advantage of such initiatives.

Martha lived with her partner and two sons, nine and 16, in the *Swiss Quarter*. She had her own gardening firm, her husband worked for a major toy shop as an accountant. She moved there from another street in the area. She had first lived in *Kreuzberg*, then moved to *Lichterfelde* and briefly outwards to *Spandau*, which they did not like. They came back, but did not like to rent again as renting turned out more expensive than buying. They went to look at the area and their son immediately liked it – and it was okay for them too. They had simply driven by the area as they often went grocery shopping nearby, so were aware of it being built. Her youngest son does not go to the catchment area school, but to a school near where they used to live, as all the children of his kindergarten went there. Her older son goes to a *Realschule* in another district. There was an alternative nearby, but she did not like that school. Apparently they locked the gates during the school day so that the pupils could not leave the school yard, and it was said to be a place where children would wave knives at one another. School reputation mattered, in Martha's view, because future employers would raise their eyebrows if he had attended a school with a bad reputation. This shows that the agency of middle class parents to act in favour of what they saw as best for their children did not just depend on the needs they had defined for their children and the strategies they chose to ensure they were met, but also on the story-telling and creation of rumours and stereotypes about certain schools compared to others. Exchanging information about schools in kindergartens (which as we have seen tend to be already segregated) and in elementary schools when further education becomes a theme in the fifth and the sixth grade, is a crucial practice at PTA meetings, school bake-sales, school Christmas parties and at the school yard where parents wait to pick up their children. Rather than data of school performance, absenteeism, or school equipment, story-telling about schools, both positively and negatively, seems to easily acquire the status of 'information'. As in kindergartens and elementary schools homogeneous groups form and story-telling is an essential element of group formation, it is not hard to see how unintentionally and without anyone to be blamed (Blokland 2012), middle class practices of school choice become marginalizing and segregating in their consequences.

Conclusion

The exclusionary practices that we have discussed in the chapter are, of course, the result also of the specific cultural resources and durable engagements that middle class parents can put to work to avoid the institutions they do not see as desirable in order to realize their capabilities. While residential choice is a very obvious practice for secluding, we found that middle class parents have decisive expectations and images about the institutions, be it the kindergarten or the school that their children are going to attend. In order to reproduce social status our interviewees relied on durable engagements in the kindergartens and neighbourhoods in order to get the right information about the schools that fit them best. Here, we see how these residents of Berlin have actually the means to realize their own capabilities and to prepare these capabilities for their children. And although these interview partners did not talk explicitly about their fear of social contamination with regard to the students population, and did not argue they preferred more White homogeneous classrooms over ethnically very mixed schools, as we will see later, some other middle class residents in *Kreuzberg* who opted out of the catchment area did explicitly talk about race, and much more deliberately excluded their children from multi-cultural school settings.

We hence have seen that next to residential choice, school choice is an important practice through which middle class parents try to ensure what they consider to be the best for their children. Whereas they generally did believe that the urban society should be an integrated, multi-cultural one in which segregation ought to be avoided, in their own practices they created exclusions of people unlike themselves, and sometimes showed awareness of this ambivalence without seeing a possibility to do things differently. As Christine's story revealed most clearly, the shortcomings of the state institutions, in this case the after-school programme, made her go for an alternative. This indicated that these middle class parents expected more from the state than the state of Berlin was currently providing. Such structural factors in the choices of agents could, in theory, be tackled by policy and political decisions.

In the next chapter, we will look more closely at the practices through which middle class parents in *Kreuzberg* found schools for their children.

References

Atkinson, Rowland G. 2006. 'Padding the Bunker: Strategies of Middle-class Disaffiliation and Colonisation in the City'. *Urban Studies* 43 (4): 819–32.

———. 2008. 'The Flowing Enclave and the Misanthropy of Networked Affluence'. In *Networked Urbanism. Social Capital in the City*, edited by Talja V. Blokland and Michael Savage, 41–58. Aldershot, England; Burlington, VT: Ashgate.

Blokland, Talja V. 2012. 'Blaming Neither the Undeserving Poor Nor the Revanchist Middle Classes: A Relational Approach to Marginalization'. *Urban Geography* 33 (4): 488–507.

Bourdieu, Pierre. 1992. *The Logic of Practice*. Palo Alto, CA: Stanford University Press.

———. 2002. *Distinction. A Social Critique of the Judgement of Taste*. Cambridge, MA: Harvard University Press.

Butler, Tim. 2003. 'Living in the Bubble: Gentrification and Its 'Others' in North London'. *Urban Studies* 40 (12): 2469–86.

Gemeinnützige Hertie-Stiftung. 2009. *Die Hertie Berlin Studie 2009*. Hamburg: Hoffmann und Campe.

Small, Mario L. and Katherine S. Newman. 2001. 'Urban Poverty after The Truly Disadvantaged: The Rediscovery of the Family, the Neighborhood, and Culture'. *Annual Review of Sociology* 27 (1): 23–45.

Smith, Neil. 1996. *The New Urban Frontier: Gentrification and the Revanchist City*. London, New York: Routledge.

Van Eijk, Gwen and Talja V. Blokland. 2010. 'Do People Who Like Diversity Practice Diversity in Neighborhood Life? Neighborhood Use and the Social Networks of 'Diversity Seekers' in a Mixed Neighborhood in the Netherlands'. *Journal of Ethnic and Migration Studies* 36 (2): 313–32.

Watt, Paul. 2009. 'Living in an Oasis: Middle-class Disaffiliation and Selective Belonging in an English Suburb'. *Environment and Planning A* 41 (12): 2874–92.

Chapter 3

Cheating the System to Get the Best for One's Kids: Middle Class Practices and Racist Marginalization

Talja Blokland and Georg Große-Löscher

Introduction

As we have seen in the chapter of Giustozzi, Blokland and Freitag, the scarcity of urban resources and the wish of urban residents to secure resources for the reproduction of enhancement of their social position make housing and education a field of struggle that draws and reinforces boundaries between social groups. In many parts of the city, residential and school segregation coincide: the local school reflects the social and ethnic composition of the neighbourhood. In other areas, however, in particular those where gentrification is changing the social composition of the neighbourhoods, school segregation and residential segregation appear less of a one-to-one match. In principle, given a catchment area system, schools should be as segregated as neighbourhoods. However, German studies on school segregation demonstrate that especially in socially and ethnically heterogeneous neighbourhoods, the fixed catchment areas do not reflect the residential composition (Schulz 2001, 14–15; Noreisch 2007). These studies show that especially middle class residents seem to have issues with sending their children to schools with many poor or migrant children, so that German scholars have even spoken of an 'exodus' through sending children to other public or even private schools (Häußermann 2008, 343–4; Häußermann 2009, 96; Bauer and Häußermann 2009, 360; Kersten 2007, 51; Radtke 2004, 209 ff.; Häußermann et al. 2008, 40). These scholars argue that the elementary schools with many migrant children get to systemic dead ends in teaching, as too many children have language problems, have not been to a Kindergarten before entering school – which is voluntary in Germany – even though especially migrant children whose parents do not speak German at home profit from Kindergarten strongly (Kersten 2007, 51; Geißler and Weber-Menges 2008, 21). In connection to the chapters by Lewek and Schilling, we see here that general racist views about the deficiencies of immigrants reside in the moral orientations of mainstream society. Such forms of racism may not be located within the thoughts of individuals, who may believe that personally, they are not racist and racism is a matter of the (East Berlin or East German) narrow-minded uneducated 'other'. But their practices draw on racist assumptions about immigrants, and narratives about otherness are constructed in their reflections on their individual practices.

Such studies show, then, in addition to the sense of middle class families that we have discussed in the chapter of Giustozzi, Blokland and Freitag, that doing the best for one's children means careful school choice, not simply sending the child around the corner. Consequently school choice involves a desire and attempt to find the best (as when sending a child to a Montessori school, a bilingual Kindergarten, one with music as a special focus or a school with an integration concept).

The individual concern to give their own child, special and different from all others, the best possible in life, especially in the middle class families where motherhood has taken on its current symbolism as discussed in the chapter of Giustozzi, Blokland and Freitag, affects school segregation.

In the meantime, as we have also seen, parents in our interviews in *Lichterfelde* and *Kreuzberg* made remarks about what they believed to be weaknesses about the schools where their children did not go. Various reports have been published that confirm the overall idea that schools in disadvantaged neighbourhoods are struggling, because of the concentration of families with multiple difficulties, in health, economic or social situation. Schools in such areas have additional work beyond mere teaching, to 'compensate for deficits', which puts 'additional pressure' on the schools, as they are not equipped to do this (social) work, or so it is argued (Bundesamt für Bauwesen und Raumordnung 2004, 160; Meyer and Schulerei-Hartje 2003, 2). Analyses of available data (PISA 2000) show, moreover, that the more students of a migration background in a classroom, the lower the reading skills in that classroom at age 15, measured for the so-called *Hauptschule*, one of the secondary schools in the German system (Stanat 2006). Such rather alarming data show that, whether we like it or not, schools with a higher percentage of students of migration and lower class background do have more challenges to get their students to the same level as do schools in predominantly White middle class neighbourhoods. That does not make such schools bad places to learn at all, of course, as statistics generally measure school outcomes, not what students have learnt since they got into school. But it does mean that parents, like the middle class parents we have interviewed, who are very concerned with the social reproduction of their status *and* read the newspapers and other media in which such studies and their commentaries occur, may think twice before sending their children simply to the school down the road because the subtle difference between school performance measured as outcome or as process is not part of such discussions. And as we have seen in the chapter of Giustozzi, Blokland and Freitag, middle class parents in *Kreuzberg* certainly did not do that. Just like it was a standard practice to send the kids to school locally in *Lichterfelde*, without much reflection as the school was known to be 'good', it seemed a standard practice among the interview partners and their peers in *Kreuzberg* to *not simply* go to the catchment area school; if they did, this was a deliberate *choice*, it seemed. For some of our interview partners in *Lichterfelde*, their residential choices reflected mobility for the schools of prospective children (cf. Kersten 2007). Indeed, Berlin statistics suggest higher mobility for non-migrant families with children before the elementary school entrance year than for other categories (Große-Löscher 2011; Meyer 2013; Förste 2013).

This chapter, then, starts from the observation that White German children end up more often outside their catchment area schools than children of immigrants. In statistical analyses, Große-Löscher has found (2011) that *Kreuzberg* has schools attended by both more and less immigrant children than one would expect on the basis of the ethnic composition for school-aged children in the catchment area. This indicates very strongly that *Kreuzberg* shows processes of micro-segregation that are not residential or spatial per se, but of a social nature. Residents may rub shoulders with a wide variety of others in terms of ethnical, racial and class positions, durable engagements in educational institutions tend to be less crossing boundaries of ethnicity, race and class than one would statistically expect, because the White Germans (and we *presume*, based on our interviews, predominantly middle class) create their own islands. Here, then, we explore the strategies that White middle class parents in *Kreuzberg* who have successfully opted out of the catchment area school have employed to do so, as well as the stories they tell about these strategies: how did they come to their school choice, what were their arguments, and what exclusionary mechanisms, if any, can we find in their practices? Moreover, what is the role of their durable engagements or fluid encounters with others, both middle classes like themselves or people from other social positions, in such practices?[1]

The (since our research changing) German educational laws in the state of Berlin enable parents to apply with a 're-schooling request' (*Umschulungsantrag*[2]) for a different school than the school their children are allocated to by the catchment area. As the state of Berlin expects parents to send their children there where they are registered in the state administrative registry, registration in the catchment area of the preferred school is another, albeit not legal, option. Finally, parents can opt for a private school, attended by around 10 per cent of Berlin schoolchildren. These schools often have alternative educational concepts, are bilingual or confessional. Whereas she did not have precise enough data to establish where it would lie exactly, Noreisch (2007) argued on the basis of a Berlin study that elementary schools seemed to have a tipping point: beyond a certain proportion of children with a migration background in a school, German parents started to stay away, and segregation sharpened.

1 The interviews we have analysed in the earlier chapters had not been primarily focused on school choice. In this chapter, then, we draw on an additional eight in-depth interviews (conducted by Große-Löscher) with parents residing in *Kreuzberg* who avoided the catchment area. They were interviewed for Große-Löscher's MA Thesis '"... At last you want the best for your child". Elementary School Choice in Berlin-Kreuzberg' (Humboldt University Berlin, 2011).

2 It is a formal request for the relocation of the child's place of school enrolment.

The chapter of Giustozzi, Blokland and Freitag shows how middle class residents create islands in the city and exclude others from being part of these, not because of their bad intentions, but as an unintended consequence of their organization of resources (see also Blokland 2012). Also Radtke has pointed out that this sharp segregation cannot be explained by unwillingness on the side of immigrants to integrate: it is the exclusive behaviour of the non-migrant Germans who have the resources to realize their school choice that explains such segregation patterns (2004, 169). Among the families interviewed by Große-Löscher, we find examples of all possible strategies: registering with a fake address for the desired school, putting in an official application for a non-catchment area school and being successful, and seeking residence there where a desirable school can be found (except for the legal route of taking the board of education to court, or threatening to do so, which is also reported to happen in Berlin).

From Kindergarten to Elementary School: Using Ties

Whereas we established in Chapter 2 that parents used arguments about the need for stability for their children as a reason why they wanted their children to go to an elementary school where others from the kindergarten also went to, we see here that the kindergarten choice is especially important because it is then used as an access strategy for an elementary school. Parents use the kindergarten's connection to preferred schools to access places. They argue that friendships are important to their children who would be 'socially isolated' or not have 'stability' if they had to move to a school without their kindergarten peers.

Katharina, in her late thirties and married to a musician, is the mother of two children. She put in an official *Umschulungsantrag* because she knew that there was a strong tie between the kindergarten where her daughter went and the elementary school nearby. For years, there had been collaboration between the school and the kindergarten. The school was said to be keen to admit children from this preschool. The kindergarten pupils visited the school on its open day, and it was self-evident that these children would go there. More important than spatial proximity and existing ties between kindergarten and elementary school was, however, the presence of existing social ties: parents argued for a school that would enable their children to continue friendships formed in the kindergarten. These were small kindergartens that the parents had first carefully selected as the ideal social setting for the first years of socialization, and hence for the first socialization into friendships with children of parents with enough similarity to opt for the same kindergarten. The durable engagements of the children and their parents in kindergartens where parent involvement is high and expected from all, thus focus 'inwardly' with the exclusionary effect for those not in the same kindergarten. Isolde, 39 years of age with a university degree and mother of two children, registered on a fake address for one child and did an *Umschulungsantrag* for the second, and Ludwig, a 46-year-old artist who happened to live in the catchment area of the school that the kindergarten parents had identified as desirable, both talked about how kindergarten parents had discussed how they could 'keep the children together'. For Isolde, her divorce was an additional reason to bring up the stability argument:

> [My daughter] Julia had, and I think that is the same for many children, needed to be really flexible already in lots of ways because of the divorce of her parents, and ahm … I think that is why it was so important for me, that there was a continuity, a social continuity for Julia.

Not just the children but the parents also, connected within the kindergarten or who knew each other already. Parents commented that it was possibly more important for themselves to have some stability than it was for their children: children could form new ties quickly, but they had to find their daily routines in a chaotic, large city in which they had to juggle many responsibilities at once. As Richard Sennett (1998, 22) has argued, in an increasingly flexible labour market, it becomes more and more difficult to develop stable relationships, so that people are keen to use durable engagements to form such ties where the opportunities occur. They may enjoy the brief encounters of urban life in the big city, but *also* need durable engagements, both for their sense of belonging and security as well as for pragmatic reasons of driving children to school or free time activities together or other forms of practical support. So Emanuela, a teacher and single parent with one child at the end of her forties, commented that one 'naturally' in the kindergarten already searched ties to people whom one 'liked' being with, and that once established, such connections increased in importance, as one then wanted to stay together with 'those whom one already knows'. Ingeborg, a 32-year-old student and mother of two girls, reported too how in the first grade, the kindergarten parents had been a 'group of befriended parents':

> Actually it is like this, it all depends on the kindergarten, and then they become friends, and you become friends with the parents, and then, when these people are nice, then you feel like staying together with them and you also wish for your children to stay friends, and so on. Yeah I think that is really important.

Durable engagements with the kindergarten provided access to a resource, a false address, in two examples. Isolde found an address to register herself at one of the families from the kindergarten. Another mother made use of the increasingly common fact that children of separated parents increasingly have two households where they live part-time – but no formal proof of 'divorce' is necessary for parents to split up, nor does anyone seem surprised when they get together again:

> We had to eh … we had to change our residential registration. And we did not want to do this officially, we just wanted simply, eh … we knew, till that or that street address is the catchment area and eh … the kindergarten teacher of my daughter, he lived there, so we asked him: tell me, could we … my partner and

> my daughter, can they register at your address, like a second address, and eh ... that was okay for him. So that means my partner had registered there with my daughter, and then we have registered at the school, and then we were in the catchment area so they took us.

The Fear for Isolation: 'Othering' and its Consequences

That the number of immigrant children in the school played a role for parents became clear in all the interviews. Resourceful as these parents were, they accessed information of the department of education on statistics about the school populations, and used the percentage of non-German speaking households where the children lived as an indicator for 'quality'. That they did not even consider sending their children there was clear among the interview partners, as Ingeborg, who had one child at a private school and used a fake address to get the other one to a school she preferred, made clear: 'In any case the foreigner problem, that is in any case decisive. That is the case. Eh ... that is what one also looks at'.

Katharina turned the language issue into a cultural issue of 'otherness' and referred to optical differences that mattered in her view. When Katharina linked cultural difference to someone's appearance, she clearly generalized cultural traits of differences too big to be bridged to race and ethnicity, inferred through visual clues. While living the life of those seen as desirably cosmopolitan in the market cosmopolitanism that Lewek discussed in Chapter 1, her idea of otherness is clearly remote from lived cosmopolitanism:

> So I mean, when it says somehow 98 per cent, then it is clear, that there are classrooms there without any German children and of course then it often is ... non-German language at home does not necessarily mean that those all speak German badly, but it is already very likely and I also think, when everybody there is so different, only not one's own child, as the only one there, and as the only one who looks different, I think that would be a really tough starting point .... That one ... that the child is suddenly such an outsider. Simply really, because it looks different or it does different things at home.

The boundary that Katharina and Ingeborg drew was linked to an argument repeatedly expressed in the interviews, that parents feared the social isolation of their child in a group of 'others'. The remarkable assumption made was that immigrant children would not be willing or able to accept the 'German' children in their in-group – this makes one wonder to what extent these parents themselves would be open to cosmopolitanism beyond a mere tolerance of the everyday fluid encounters with those defined as 'others'. The parents were scared that their child would not connect to the 'others', not just because of possible language problems but also because of cultural differences, or negative experiences or stereotypical prejudices.

For Anne-Marriell, too, the question of social isolation was important. She pointed to expected behavioural and language problems when she talked about the catchment area school, a school that she avoided with a fake address and then for her second child by making use of the rule that siblings got preferred places:

> That school has a very bad reputation. So, and although it has a very good gym, I mean, that is not enough for me and yeah I don't know, I have only heard bad things about this school and also that a lot of children are very violent and that the majority speaks Turkish and my child does not speak Turkish.

Roswitha, mid-forties with a university degree, had her daughter in the catchment area school, that had a 'balanced' ethnic composition, but very nearby there was a school with more than 90 per cent immigrant children. She would not let her child attend that school:

> No, then I would have raised hell, I know eh … a girl, she first went there and then after a week came to our school. She had been the only German girl in the classroom and the everyday speech among the students was of course Turkish, so no, when out of 25, 24 learnt Turkish as their mother tongue, then it is not surprising and she had, also from the social aspects, she would not have had any connecting points, because she also did not attend a German-Turkish kindergarten, she would not have been able to join conversations, and then her mother went quite on the barricade. I would have done the same, no doubt about it. … That means a social isolation for the child.

The assumption that the one who is 'different' cannot socially integrate fits well with the argument of parents that we discussed above, that the social networks of the kindergarten needed to be continued in order to avoid the child being on its own: the new social setting for one's child should be able to integrate him or her so that children adjust quickly and happily go to school – even better, their own social network of friends should be brought into the school.

Two of the interviewed parents recalled experiences of social isolation. Isolde, who stressed that immigrant percentages in schools did not play a role for her, was unhappy with the school that her daughter attended because of problems with the teacher. Looking for an alternative, her daughter went for a probation day to another school:

> That was in a classroom where she then had been the only German girl and she was totally stressed. She has somehow said: "oho Mummy, so I mean … in my class also half of the children are speaking a different language, but in school all speak German and I have contact with them" and in that classroom it was like, that she had said: "they all speak a different language and I cannot get in at all". I think that was one of the reasons why for herself she had also said, I don't really want to go there.

So maybe the fear of parents was not always without reason – exclusion along lines of the construction of ethnic differences is not simply only a practice on the side of the White or the middle classes, after all. Thinking that ethnic differences are strong boundaries that are hard to overcome, notwithstanding all the cosmopolitanism rhetoric in Berlin, is hegemonic: not an individual narrative, but a meta-narrative to which not only White Germans are subjected. Of course one may also ask to what extent any child would feel integrated after one or two probation days in any school.

Emanuela, a teacher and single mother with her daughter in the catchment area school, was also thinking about changing schools. Her daughter went with the kindergarten-children to a school with over 70 per cent children classified as not having German as their native tongue; she had joined the other parents 'although with stomach cramps'. Her daughter went in the same class as two girls from the kindergarten and five girls from a Turkish migration background. One of the girls from the kindergarten had then emigrated, and the parents of the other girl now considered taking her out, too:

> then I would have to change schools too, that simply does not work, one German girl, who has contacts to the Turkish girls. They are super nice, but it is not a friendship in the real sense and that … well yeah therefore I still wonder whether in fifth or sixth grade maybe I should change schools.

Reference to stereotypical, presumed cultural differences explained why the Turkish girls could not be true friends:

> such friendships just don't happen, like between our girls, who invite each other over in the weekend, who have play dates in the afternoon, I take this child with me, my child goes over there, that rarely happens. They are after all extended families, where one joins the extended family in the afternoon and the weekends, there are smaller siblings there, and then the children get picked up form school and they are home or with friends or acquaintances, aunts, uncles, cousins. They really do not have any need for additional contacts. But we are nuclear families. One, two children, maybe sometimes three, that is where the children make appointments with each other, they go into clubs, one takes another child home, that is such a continuous exchange and the parents also meet, one exchanges information, invite one another and so on. They don't do that, or hardly ever.

The clear boundaries here are based on cultural generalizations about the 'other' and assumptions about homogeneity of an implicit 'us' versus 'them'. Those pupils don't fit with 'our' children, the parents seemed to say, so they wanted to keep 'their' children away from 'those': integration was impossible or even not desirable, and social isolation would, in their minds, naturally follow were their children to be exposed to too much 'otherness'. Stereotyping, the attachment of certain behavioural patterns to an ethnic or social group and drawing generalizations from such ascriptions, resulting in discriminatory practices of avoidance, became visible when parents commented on schools' mixture, as Emanuela did:

> When I enter [the school], once in a while, and see these Turkish and Arabic children, that are fighting there on the floor or I pick [my daughter] up at four and the assistant teacher is sitting there and cries because somehow every day they are fighting on the playground and always fights and always stress and always ... yeah then I get stomach pains.

Stereotyping sometimes resulted from personal experiences, sometimes from information processed from media, or from other parents – mostly from a combination of the three. It can hardly be differentiated whether stereotypes influenced the experiences, or were formed through the personal experiences. Katharina reported about an experience in the kindergarten that she thought did influence how she saw children with non-German mother tongue: their moral orientations produced practices in durable engagements that she would rather not have her daughter exposed to if there was not enough of a counterweight of people not 'like that':

> So, in the kindergarten we had such a mix ... and with the older children maybe, I don't know, about 60 per cent is non-German, but there are a few French, Spanish and Latin-Americans and then 40 to 50 per cent Turks. And that somehow still functions, or ... I think there, one can also ... well, at some point my daughter started like, a cross means you are dead and you are bad, and I think, you can still challenge this, when there is such a mixture, but if you then know that your child is the only one and the others come from those types of backgrounds, I think that is difficult somehow.

Katharina wanted to protect her child against challenges of her identity, and the Turkish speaking children were the problem here. The sign of the cross, the symbol of Christianity with whom Katharina identified herself, was seen negatively. This meant that Katharina worried about the norms and values she wanted her child to adhere to, and cutting her off from more than fluid encounters with the 'others' was a way to protect her. Ingeborg also tried to preserve the 'right' values: with one child in a school with 50 per cent non-German speaking children, she had decided to send the second daughter to a private school, motivated by the experiences she had had with her older daughter. In a very gendered society in which the labour participation of women is still lower than that of men, in which women are often criticized when they are working for being 'raven mothers', and in which household tasks are not at all shared equally, Ingeborg seemed to assume gender equality had already been achieved and she got quite offended by some of the gender images her daughter faced in school:

> I also believe that a healthy mixture is needed to somehow, oh God, that I say such a thing, that is really quite … but that some values are simply kept up, and that was for example with my older daughter, although she was in a very strong, really, I don't know, hum, more than half were German children with engaged parents … eh … and nevertheless it came to sayings eh … yeah … that boys from her class had said: "yeah, women are only there to clean and cook and have nothing to say at all". And that really upsets me, it really upsets me, because somehow those are values, for which many women have fought hard, so that one can say we are equal, we have the same rights in this country, and then it makes me incredibly angry, when someone arrives here and says something like that. I have then always tried to give my daughter arguments, what she should say in reply and so on, but I found that really … that I had to talk about that in the first place and think about it, that really made me angry … Or for example also, that it simply is the case – I don't want to talk in *clichés* all the time, but those are things that I have personally experienced – that often … I can only talk about Turkish parents now … that they are not as engaged as the Germans.

The part on women's rights reflects the moral orientation of the mother: women in Germany have fought for decades for their rights, so they should not be questioned by anyone and definitely not by someone from abroad. A clear boundary is drawn here between the moral orientation of the in-group, that are given universal validity, and those of others ('someone like that') who does not accept that orientation or even actively takes issue with it.

Statements like 'oh my God, that I really say something like that' or 'I don't want to talk in *clichés* all the time' point to the conflict between personal experiences and practices following from these and the other, cosmopolitan moral orientations one also adheres to. There is a conflict between beliefs in multiculturalism and open tolerance towards people with a migration background on the one hand and the concern about one's own child on the other. The parents in *Lichterfelde* whom we have met in Chapter 2 suffered less from this ambiguity, for the simple reason that they could be tolerant without having to worry about what such a moral orientation meant to their practices or their durable engagements or those of their children.

Ingeborg had sent her second child to a private school, but realized that this has exclusionary consequences:

> That is really totally hard, but it is … and that has nothing to do that these parents are xenophobic, but instead they want something good for their children and somehow don't see another, don't see another way …. Eh, that is a really bad and sad development and therefore you get these situations. Situations of achievement, and then you get a dual class society …. That's really sick, I think. One would have to change that, but how that should happen, I don't know either.

Aware of the debates on segregation and social mix in schools, the interviewed parents felt committed to mixture, but it has to be a mixture in balance. That is, the

German children should be the majority. When a tipping point was reached, they felt a responsibility to take care of their own children through finding them the school that did have a proper mixture. They were hence not overall racist about the presence of some pupils with a migration background. They did presume that these children were homogeneously different, a difference that was labelled if not negatively, at least as hampering the socialization and integration of their own sons and daughters.

Conclusion

From a macro-perspective the German, educated parents without a migration background form a group whose commonality in moral orientations, practices and durable engagements create boundaries between themselves and their children and other children with migration backgrounds. This symbolic boundary work (Lamont 1992; Lamont and Molnár 2002) creates an unspoken common sense that a high percentage of immigrant pupils is undesirable and contributes to a segregated school landscape. Following a picture of two concentric circles (Lamont 1992, 9), the schools with high immigrant percentages are outside of the second circle, from which one wants to turn oneself away and that are seen as 'bad' schools. The boundary work is connected to the kindergarten-networks, where similar patterns of exclusion occur and are generally shared by most parents.

In summary, then, this chapter has shown that the exclusion from ethnically mixed schools of children with a migration background is a marginalization that at least partly results from German middle class practice, whether intended or not. Focused on the best for their own children, internally orientated to the inner circle of the doughnut-shape processes of boundary work, they tended to opt out of the catchment area school when they believed that this school did not have an ideal mix. Out of fear for social isolation and therefore a stereotypical, homogenizing notion of cultural difference that cannot be bridged, discriminatory mechanisms that assume undesirable if not deviant behaviour on the side of immigrant children, and negative experiences that produce generalization through emulation (Tilly 1998) all produced categories of schools to go to and schools to avoid. Although the parents we have interviewed showed some reflexivity about the marginalization that their practices contributed to, eventually the interests, as they saw them, of their own children came first.

From the perspective of symbolic boundary work (Lamont 1992; Lamont and Molnár 2002), two causal mechanisms can be seen at work here. First, within the networks formed in the kindergarten, especially also among parents themselves, we see a passive, unintended process of exclusion in the desire of the parents from one kindergarten to keep their children together in elementary school. One cannot point to a simple racism in the heads of the parents to blame the middle classes for the fate of the marginalized, but it is clear that the focus on the in-group affects the capabilities – marginalizes those – of others. In the analyses of how parents dealt with schools with a large percentage of children with a migration background, we have seen that there is a much more active process of boundary work with its exclusionary consequences and the limitations on the capabilities of others: the efforts to realize resources to maximize the capabilities for one's own children, based on general hegemonic constructions of 'otherness', produce a segregated landscape of schools in which immigrants have to make do with the schools left by the middle classes at the margins. In doing so, they reinforce the existing urban inequalities that characterize the city relationally.

References

Bauer, Christine and Hartmut Häußermann. 2009. 'Ethnische Segregation in deutschen Schulen'. *Leviathan* (37): 353–66.

Blokland, Talja V. 2012. 'Blaming Neither the Undeserving Poor nor the Revanchist Middle Classes: A Relational Approach to Marginalization'. *Urban Geography* 33 (4): 488–507.

Bundesamt für Bauwesen und Raumordnung (eds). 2004. *Die Soziale Stadt. Ergebnisse der Zwischenevaluierung*. Berlin: Deutsches Institut für Urbanistik.

Förste, Daniel. 2013. 'Cheating the lottery. Correlations between a state regulated school access to high quality schooling and middle class school choice in Berlin'. Paper presented at the RC21 Conference in Berlin, 29–31 August 2013.

Geißler, Rainer and Sonja Weber-Menges. 2008. 'Migrantenkinder im Bildungssystem: doppelt benachteiligt'. *Aus Politik und Zeitgeschichte* (49): 14–22.

Große-Löscher, Georg. 2011. *'... At last you want the best for your child'. Elementary School Choice in Berlin-Kreuzberg*. MA Thesis, Humboldt University Berlin, unpublished.

Häußermann, Hartmut. 2008. 'Wohnen und Quartier. Ursachen sozialräumlicher Segregation'. In *Handbuch Armut und Soziale Ausgrenzung*, edited by Jürgen Boeckh, Ernst-Ulrich Huster and Hildegard Mogge-Grotjahn, 335–49. Wiesbaden: VS Verlag für Sozialwissenschaften.

———. 2009. 'Segregation von Migranten, Integration und Schule'. In *Einwanderungsgesellschaft Deutschland. Wege zu einer sozialen und gerechten Zukunft*, edited by Abteilung Wirtschafts- und Sozialpolitik der Friedrich Ebert Stiftung, 89–98. Bonn: Bonner Univeristätsbuch Druckerei.

Häußermann, Hartmut, Daniel Förste, Jan Dohnke and Patrick Hausmann. 2008. *Monitoring Soziale Stadtentwicklung 2008*. Berlin: Senatsverwaltung für Stadtentwicklung Berlin, Referat I A.

Kersten, Jens. 2007. 'Segregation in der Schule'. *Die Öffentliche Verwaltung* (2): 50–58.

Kristen, Cornelia. 2008. 'Primary School Choice and Ethnic School Segregation in German Elementary Schools'. *European Sociological Review* (24): 495–510.

Lamont, Michèle. 1992. *Money, Morals, and Manner. The Culture of the French and American upper-middle Class*. Chicago: University of Chicago Press.

Lamont, Michèle and Virág Molnár. 2002. 'The Study of Boundaries in the Social Sciences'. *Annual Review of Sociology* (28): 167–95.

Meyer, Maurice. 2013. *Der Einfluss von elterlicher Schulwahl auf das Wanderungsverhalten und schulische Segregation.* BA Thesis. Humboldt-Universität Berlin, unpublished.

Meyer, Ulrike and Ulla Kristina Schulerei-Hartje. 2003. 'Bildung im Stadtteil'. *Soziale Stadt Info* (12): 2–8.

Noreisch, Kathleen. 2007. 'School catchment area evasion: the case of Berlin, Germany'. *Journal of Education Policy* (22): 69–90.

Radtke, Frank-Olaf. 2004. 'Die Illusion der meritokratischen Schule. Lokale Konstellationen der Produktion von Ungleichheit im Erziehungssystem'. In *Migration, Integration, Bildung. Grundfragen und Problembereiche*, edited by Klaus J. Bade and Michael Bommes, 143–78. Bad Iburg: Grote Druck.

Schulz, Andreas. 2001. 'Schule im Brennpunkt. Was können Schulen beitragen gegen soziale Segregation?' In *Fachforum: Schule in sozialen Brennpunkten*, edited by Regiestelle E&C der Stiftung SPI and Sozialpädagogisches Institut Berlin, 11–18. Berlin.

Sennett, Richard. 1998. *Der flexible Mensch. Die Kultur des neuen Kapitalismus.* Frankfurt am Main/Wien: Büchergilde Gutenberg.

Stanat, Petra. 2006. 'Schulleistungen von Jugendlichen mit Migrationshintergrund. Die Rolle der Zusammensetzung der Schülerschaft'. In *Herkunftsbedingte Disparitäten im Bildungswesen: Differenzielle Bildungsprozesse und Probleme der Verteilungsgerechtigkeit*, edited by Jürgen Baumert, Petra Stanat and Rainer Watermann, 189–219. Wiesbaden: VS Verlag für Sozialwissenschaften.

Tilly, Charles. 1998. *Durable Inequality*. Berkeley: University of California Press.

Chapter 4
In the Interest of the Child: Gendered Practices of Middle Class Mothers

Carlotta Giustozzi

Introduction

Parents of young children often experience an extremely stressful period in their life, when care and parenting tasks coincide with the beginning of a career and the positioning in society. This period has been identified as the 'rush hour of life' (Bertram et al. 2006; Bittman and Wajcman 2000). In such a situation of shortage of time, families must find support. They can either try to rely on the extended family, public institutions, the market or on other forms of community. As we have argued in the introduction, the ways in which some people make their lives in the city inflict on the possibilities of others to turn resources into capabilities, as fluid interactions and durable engagements include and marginalize at the same time.

The previous two chapters have shown how middle class parents' accounts of their residential and school practices can be seen as their capabilities – having the right resources and putting them to use – to realize the best for their children. This chapter further discusses the inclusionary mechanisms resulting in this grouping together of privileged households, contributing to their segregation. Rather than just talking about families though, we focus on mothers and their gendered practices to secure resources for their families.

We examine the interplay of family and neighbourhood again in our two exemplary areas in the former western part of Berlin using our two times 20 interviews conducted there: the inner-city gentrified neighbourhood *Viktoriapark* in *Kreuzberg* where middle class families live in an otherwise ethnically and socially mixed district, and the *Swiss Quarter* in *Lichterfelde*, a newly built neighbourhood with mostly semi-detached family houses in the south-west of the city. It is important here that both neighbourhoods have clear physical borders, a distinct architecture and privately owned yet publicly accessible streets, and that our interview partners were mainly mothers with more than one child.

The interviews suggest that the respondent's family situation and their specific moral orientations on family life render a socially homogeneous neighbourhood a valuable resource. The demands of motherhood and of the 'modern' woman contribute to this. The spatial profit that they enjoy as their position and location match (cf. Bourdieu 1999) is inclusive and exclusive at the same time. While inclusive to others on the neighbourhood level, their practices marginalize the poor and ethnic minorities in other areas, reinforcing the workings of spatial profit.

We will first discuss the ambivalences of mothers generally and the historical development of the nuclear family and motherhood in Germany in particular as this development influences how family structure, and especially motherhood, structures urban space. The two neighbourhoods in Berlin then help us to understand the resourceful practices of mothers for their middle class families that segregate them from other Berliners. As we will see, middle class homogeneous neighbourhoods create the capability for middle class women to reconcile their roles as modern women and mothers. This highlights the gendered organization of urban space.

In this chapter, we thus argue that a set of social needs influences the residential practices of middle class families. In trying to address these needs, and to realize their capabilities as parents, workers and partners, these families opt for housing in neighbourhoods where they can create spatial profits.

Motherhood and Modern Womanhood

The social needs which make middle class parents opt for homogeneous neighbourhoods do not just result from a lack of time. Their construction as needs is culturally and historically shaped. Women showed anxieties over the possibilities to create a setting for their children where they could realize their capabilities and social positions could be reproduced. Different from their parents, current middle class mothers and fathers can no longer assume that their children will do at least as well as they did. Flexibilization of the labour market has affected the prospect of long-term, fixed contracts, and self-employment with all its risks has become more common. Globalization in the economy requires flexible, mobile workers. Increased educational attainments have intensified competition in the labour market. The next generation, hence, will face new challenges and parents are anxious about how to best prepare their children for this quickly changing context. The 'unsettling conditions' of the post-industrial city in a global economy seem to intensify 'cravings for security', as Stacey (1990, 260) writes. As Miller (2005, 61) argues, uncertainties and complexity require the production of biographical narratives that allow mothers to ascertain ontological security. In a society of risks, this reflects on their efforts to nurture their children into adults well-prepared to position themselves in the world. Not knowing what capabilities one may need for that tomorrow, they turn to intensive parenting.

Additionally, parents find themselves under pressure resulting from the structural changes of family life. In the course of the industrialization, family structures changed in two ways. First, there was a distinct shift from a multi-generational association, including domestic workers, to the nuclear family. To the degree that the married couple claimed its independence and autonomy from the patriarchal, extended family, the benefits due to the economic advantageous cooperation of a larger economic unit diminished (Bahrdt 1998, 72–3). As feminists in the 1960s and 1970s pointed out, women's responsibility to care for children created a sexual division of labour and subordinated women to a new form of patriarchy. Second, the separation of work and private life divided care tasks and paid labour into distinct spheres (ibid., 137) and created the apparent dichotomy of 'public' and 'private'. This affected the position of women, who were relegated as wives and mothers to the private sphere. Nurturing came to be seen as taking place in the private sphere (Everingham 1994, 21) and the nuclear family as an isolated, self-contained unit (ibid.). The increase of the welfare state regime has made mothers more dependent on the state, but also emancipated them somewhat from patriarchal communal life, as Everingham (ibid., 128) states following the feminist arguments of Nancy Fraser. With the increased individualization, secularization and mobility, urbanites have acquired freedom to define their social identities and 'do' community: this depends less on given categorizations and the organization of urban space and has become more of an individual, private choice (Blokland 2003). Such societal changes however also mean that traditional forms of family support are 'not necessarily readily available' anymore (Miller 2005, 89). The freedom of privatized community also comes with the necessity to actively organize such support. And although the family has been repositioned, mothering is still primary to women's identity and 'locates them in the private sphere'.

Moreover, structural changes of the labour market have led to a situation where one salary often is not sufficient. In addition to the female emancipatory struggle along with the outsourcing and mechanization of housework, this has changed the families in western European countries. The housewife is disappearing from the urban social landscape. Not only legally have women achieved equal rights. Their educational attainment[1] and career ambitions (see Rösler 2012, 108) show that the identity of modern women has changed over time and that their self-realization is no longer confined to the boundaries of home. New mothers show that paid work even gives them a possibility of 'regaining a sense of self' (Miller 2005, 109). Statistics show that women with higher education and a prestigious career are significantly more often childless or have only one child.[2] This indicates that balancing work and family life is still a demanding task. Whereas household arrangements have changed, ideologies of good mothering persist.

1 In Germany, the share of female students is about 48 per cent since the early 2000s (Statistisches Bundesamt 2011).

2 The Federal Statistical Office reports that more than 50 per cent of highly educated women have only one child or are childless. ThCombine and shorten!!r an– is ly sha shortage of time but t du mit MC-Orientierung?ially valuable for mothers.is is especially true for certain professions: 47 per cent of female artists, 41 per cent of the women with academic jobs and 39 per cent of those holding top management and consultancy positions are childless (Statistisches Bundesamt 2012).

The Persistence of Gendered Care Duties

Even though many care related tasks have been handed over to machines such as washing machines or are provided by the state, as in day-care centres, some services either cannot be outsourced due to scarcity and costs, or families prefer to perform them at home, as the moral orientation of their status group expects them to do so. As Miller (2005, 29) shows, authoritative knowledge, following Jordan and Davis-Floyd (1993) defined as specific sets of ideas about how events should take place and the structures and practices that support these, not because they are correct but because they count, constructs expectations of mothers' duties. In most of the cases, it falls upon women to perform the nurturing tasks.

Recent research on the labour division within the family in Germany and other European countries has shown that women still conduct the largest share of care and household tasks, whether they are in paid employment or not. The survey 'women's lives' by the Federal Centre for Health Education from 2002 (cf. Helfferich 2002) as well as the 'Gender and Generation Survey' from 2005 reveal that marital status and the number of children play an important role in determining the labour division among couples (cf. Wengler et al. 2008). Married women are more often solely responsible for the household and with every child living in the house, the division gets more asymmetrical (cf. Helfferich 2002, 96–8; Hennig et al. 2012 quoted in Rösler 2012, 109). Similarly, the more women engage in paid labour and the higher their salary the more equally distributed are the household tasks (Wengler et al. 2008, 53–8 quoted in Rösler 2012, 87). Correspondingly, women tend to reduce their working hours when they have children, especially when the partner's professional status is higher than their own (Helfferich 2002, 96–8).

Blossfeld and Hakim interpret the high proportion of German women working in part-time jobs as a manifestation of the persistence of the male bread-winner model (1997, 14 quoted in Rösler 2012, 104). The German fiscal system, a lack of adequate childcare facilities and the dominant cultural scripts (Willard 1988, 226 quoted in Miller 2005, 28) of assignments of duties (of care and support with schooling) to women intensify and institutionalize this pattern (Rösler 2012, 104; cf. Allmendinger 2010, 11). Here, then, the importance of the historical, social, cultural, political and moral construction of the institution of motherhood (Miller 2005, 3) for the organization of family life becomes evident, especially in western Germany, as comparative studies of European countries have shown (Rühling and Kassner 2007, 61 quoted in Rösler 2012, 89). The assumptions about nurturing as being instrumental to serve the child's objective needs, based on unsocialized love because motherhood is seen as biologically defined and as carried out in the private sphere (Everingham 1994, 21), are continuously reinforced.

Many mothers in our interviews reduced paid work to perform their family duties. From the socially constructed moral orientation of motherhood, they put their children first, and calculated costs and benefits from the perspective of the child, as did Anna, a 44-year-old lawyer and mother of three. She used to work in an office but since the birth of her children reduced her work hours and switched to a home office. With her family, Anna lived in a beautiful house with plain but stylish furniture and a small private garden. From the backside we could see many of the neighbours' houses and the garden directly led to the large shared semi-public playground with a sandbox and swings. At the time of the interview, she had just come back from picking up the children from school:

> My husband is often away on business. I don't have that much time and if I had to offer something I would have a lot of additional costs. Which means that I would have to work more to cover them. And this is why … I wanted it that way [to work from home]. I did so voluntarily. I don't have to. I wanted it.

Catherine, a 43-year-old sociologist with a PhD, was one of Anna's neighbours and lived in a similar house. With her five children, she was at home and could not see herself working in a regular workplace, as they lacked the family-oriented structure she would need. Instead, she had turned to children's theatre as an alternative to 'get out of the house', a job she could easily combine with her children and that turned out to be – notwithstanding its voluntary nature – important for her identity:

> This is one reason why I'm doing this, not one, not the only one, but it adds to it that at the moment … with five children I can forget to work in a proper, you know, established, conventional workplace no matter how friendly and accommodating the employer. It just wouldn't work … But the [children's theatre] is just ideal since I can entirely … it's my thing, I can do it as I want and even more when I want and I can, I don't have to act in accordance with anybody.

In a society where the reproduction of the family's social status is highly related to the performance within the educational field, families try to actively help their children navigate the system (Bahrdt 1998, 77). Good mothering now means intensive nurturing (Miller 2005, 55). Time once invested in washing and ironing is now spent supervising homework and cooperating with the school.

The mothers spent a lot of time on educational tasks. Susan, a 35-year-old insurance saleswoman living with her husband and son in a semi-detached, neat house in *Lichterfelde* where the curtain's colour matched the decoration of the kitchen, an orchid stood on the kitchen windowsill and the garden was lovingly cultivated, explained how she had to perform a multitude of educational tasks, for example to help her son for over an hour per day with learning cursive writing:

> Such things as cursive writing, that was completely homework, they didn't do that at school at all. That is something we [me and my son] had to do at home. And like that there are many things you just do at home. I mean, Max had to, one hour minimum sometimes two, since at the beginning he was – I mean he was five when he was enrolled, and also a boy. That was a challenge.

Other mothers too spent a big share of their time and energy in helping their children with school work. The German educational system assumes that homework is an important part of the learning process, and expects support from the family. The moral orientation of these mothers often suggested that there was more than just an ideology that this is what 'good mothers' do. Children seemed to be projects in which one would have to invest to reproduce their social status position in a time of risks and uncertainties about their futures. Child rearing and education became the primary tasks of women, whose primary roles were their roles as mothers: the 'unsettling conditions of postindustrial society' seemed, as Stacey (1990) put it, to have 'intensified the cravings for security'.

Motherhood in Western Germany

Despite the fact that women's legal positions changed over time, this now sentimentalized as 'traditional' (Stacey 1990, 255) role of the mother is deeply anchored in Germany's dominant cultural script and has a highly persistent character. Today, young women are widely encouraged to participate in the workforce and pursue an ambitious career. Nonetheless, recent survey findings show that more than half of the West German population believes that the professional life of a mother might be harmful to the child (Pfau-Effinger 2009, 122 quoted in Rösler 2012, 108). The ideal of a successful professional life and the challenge to satisfyingly combine it with motherhood creates a morally difficult situation for highly educated women. They might see themselves as either having wasted their investment in training or neglecting their children. The conflicting expectations of work and family are based on women's social integration through two contradictorily structured modes of socialization: one is the emotional, family and home oriented mode, the other consists of autonomy and social recognition through paid labour (Becker-Schmidt 2003, 14) and few questions are asked about autonomy of women who nurture: mothering is seldomly defined as more than an instrumental act of meeting children's needs and imposing normatively held beliefs and values. These two conflicting modes shape their social position and disposition. Furthermore, there is a strong, historically rooted conviction that only the biological mother can provide her children with what they need (Rösler 2012, 110), a perspective criticized by feminists (Miller 2005) but still dominant. Vinken (2007) in her book the 'dogma of the German Mother' traces the historical origins of the 'unbroken myth of motherhood' in Germany. Germans have historical reasons to be suspicious about leaving childcare to the state. According to Vinken, Germany's National Socialist past with its authoritarian child development norms has led to the credo that the state should under no circumstances interfere with the pedagogics of the family (Vinken 2007 quoted in Rösler 2012, 111). Additionally, many West Germans perceived the educational system of the GDR where children were cared for and educated in public institutions from a very early age as invading into private family life and repressing the freedom of development of the child (Vinken 2007, 51). Thus, the privacy and autonomy of the nuclear family and the agency of the parents on child related issues had to be protected, against the background of the experiences of totalitarian regimes.

We indeed found this preference among many of the interviewed mothers. Lucy, a 36-year-old mother of a two-year-old daughter, lived in a sunny apartment in *Kreuzberg* filled with books, art pieces and plants. At the time of the interview she was still working as a costume designer in a theatre for which she has to travel from one job to the next all over Germany. She was trying to switch to a more stable position in the Berlin fashion industry or to go into business for herself so she could have more time for her daughter and would maybe even be able to move to the countryside. While talking about sending ones children to kindergarten at an early age, she stated that it was incomprehensible to her how other parents in Berlin could 'give their children away' when they were still young:

> No, to me it is a little strange to hand your child over so quickly.

Similarly, Susan explained how she had managed to rearrange her work as an insurance agent around the needs of her son. She worked from home two days out of five since he was born:

> So, I work two days a week from home and only three at the office. Since the beginning, after giving birth to Max, I had the opportunity to work from home. That was perfect for me. ... Especially, since that way I can meet all of my child's needs. I'm always there when he comes home after school and then work a little in the evening. He just has no restrictions of any kind.

Taking children's needs as given, the assertion of women's own needs and interests becomes subordinate to those of their children (cf. Everingham 1994, 8). It becomes clear here that working was acceptable as long as the child did not have to adapt to a working mother, a perspective that other countries, like the Netherlands, have been leaving behind (Morée 1992). Modern women who are also mothers hence found themselves in a difficult situation of either the loss of financial autonomy and a professional identity if they decided to opt out of the labour force or emotional penalties when 'leaving their children behind', a guilt also indicated in other studies (Miller 2005, 55) especially among middle class women. Combining work and family is a challenge with little time for recreation and personal needs (Becker-Schmidt 2003, 14), even when women manage to assert these. Sometimes women experienced severe professional setbacks. Irene, a surgeon who divorced her abusive, drinking husband in *Lichterfelde* had to switch to a lower paid, much less prestigious job as a health insurance doctor, as the German day-care system was not at all geared to the irregular working hours of a surgeon. Institutionally as well as ideologically, there then is a continuous reinforcement of idealized notions of motherhood that 'fail to accommodate the diversity of experiences of mothering' (Miller 2005: 56). Mothers thus struggle with the mismatch of the 'modern' woman's position and the persisting 'traditional' construction of motherhood, particularly in middle class settings.

The residential practices of middle class families can be seen as one of the ways in which women seek to cope with this mismatch. The ideology of seeing motherhood as women's role first once they have children is institutionalized in many daily practices in kindergartens and schools. When women do work, they face the challenge of being 'good mothers', for example mothers who fulfil all the expectations of school events, make breakfast, help children with their daily homework and pick them up early. Every birthday celebrated in school needs a home-baked cake and arts projects as part of science education are presented as 'wonderful occasions' for mothers to bond with their children. Even where after-school programmes are officially available until 6 pm, school is over by half past one or two and the majority of the children have left by half past three in the afternoon. In kindergarten, those mothers who pick up their children at 5 pm find them often alone with the kindergarten teacher, who already has her coat on to rush home. In middle class settings like the parent-initiated kindergartens, the expectations are made very clear: a mother can be told when children delay in development or display undesired behaviour that she should 'work less'. It must be noted that such cultural practices are effectively sanctioned by mothers themselves as mechanisms of social control as their moral orientations include those who conform, and exclude those who deviate. Because of the cultural assumptions about the fulfilment of motherhood, it is hard to talk about difficult aspects of mothering, leading us to 'conceal what are normal experiences and reactions, and so perpetuate the old myths of motherhood' (Miller 2005, 7).

How can mothers meet all these claims, ensure they function well as employees and conform to the moral orientations about good motherhood, orientations they often have internalized and are so institutionalized that they have to be put into practice or they would fear that their child would be at a disadvantage? How do they do so in a situation of shortage of time and, even among middle classes, eventually insufficient financial resources since part-time work means part-time salary? The 'traditional' family model only survives to the extent that the image of an active, modern woman is integrated into the everyday environment of the nuclear family while leaving enough space for educational and emotional requirements of the children, or at least for representing to the outside world that their societally defined requirements are met.

The following section shows how the neighbourhood eases these challenges for middle class mothers and their families. Housing helps, because a fitting residential surrounding and vicinity of supportive neighbours with similar social positions and moral orientations are crucial resources. The family structure and dominant cultural script about motherhood are hence crucial for structuring urban space.

Reconciling Motherhood with Modern Women's Identity

As described by authors like Butler (cf. 2003; 2008) and Atkinson (cf. 2006; 2008), middle class families tend to create homogeneous islands in the city. We will show that this practice of 'insulation' helps them to cope with the demands on women as mothers.

Villages in the City

In both neighbourhoods, we can identify four practices of distancing from other social groups. First, the radius of everyday action of the residents is limited. Second, most distances beyond the borders of the extended neighbourhood are covered by car. Third, the actual occasions of fluid encounters with other social groups are restricted. Finally, almost all interviewees experienced their neighbourhood as a distinct unit in relation to the city.

Most interview partners stayed most of the time in the neighbourhood, using facilities in the vicinity and pointing to the localness of their social networks. Anna did all her errands in her *Kreuzberg* area:

> Here you can do all you need easily. … Everything one could think of, all kinds of supermarkets, smaller shops. And there is the covered market, too.

Similarly, Susan explained that she spends most of her time around her home in *Lichterfelde*:

> Most of the time I'm in my neighbourhood. So, when I go shopping I go to the *Schloßstraße*. Also when I meet my friends. So, everything is in the area. That's why.

The practice of staying in the protected, well-known area was linked to a feeling of safety and comfort. And when moving around, their strategy reflected their home centred daily activities: short distances were often covered by foot or by bike, but longer ones by car. Some respondents stated that they tried to avoid public transportation since they felt uncomfortable, especially when young and drunk people were also using it, as did Lucy, from *Kreuzberg*. She reported a feeling of uneasiness when travelling on public transport:

> For me it is often like that when riding the metro or local train that I don't feel comfortable.

As with our discussions of cosmopolitanism and schools, the residents of *Kreuzberg* again had to come to terms with diversity in a more direct way than the residents from *Lichterfelde*. Anna from *Kreuzberg* avoided specific places in the city:

> So, there are specific things I would probably avoid. Yes, I would be reluctant to stroll around at night at *Kottbusser Tor*, by myself! I wouldn't do that.

In contrast to public transport, all residents reported how safe they felt in their neighbourhoods where certain types of 'difficult people' were absent. In the description of her neighbourhood, Anna emphasized the absence of drug dealers and stated that *Kreuzberg* was at least as safe as a well-known middle class area outside of the inner-city ring:

> Well, I don't think it is less safe than somewhere else, like *Friedenau* or so. … There are no drug dealers around here or something like that. I haven't encountered that, in any case not here. Not in our corner, not even until the *Bergmannstraße*. They are somewhere else. I don't know that. (*laughing*) I don't go there.

Catherine compared her *Kreuzberg*-neighbourhood with other, more dangerous areas to highlight its safety:

> Well, here it is very controlled and there are, as far as I know, you can't compare it to these kind of areas in *Neukölln* where there is really gang warfare going on. There are no such things like that around here.

In *Lichterfelde*, where 'difficult areas' seemed further away, disadvantaged areas were hardly part of the mental maps of the interviewees. Here, not the experienced lack of safety at other sites informed the use of the city, but the principle that one would not venture into areas one did not know, or only knew from hearsay, was decisive. Women did not differ in this respect from men. Thomas, 49 years old, a professor at the nearby university and father of two sons was living in *Lichterfelde*. He described a vague feeling of uneasiness in other inner city districts:

> There are many areas in Berlin I don't actually know that well since we usually remain in the area. There are rather, in Berlin *Mitte* or if you are at night in *Kreuzberg* that you might think, it is just a little unsafe.

The literature on middle class spatial behaviour suggests an active act of withdrawal. Except for some of the interviewees who did withdraw after having had experiences in parts of the city where they did not feel safe, it goes too far to describe these spatial practices as withdrawal: places are being 'othered' and sometimes defined as unsafe by lack of knowledge and experiences, a lack of knowledge maintained by the absence of any need to venture into other areas.

Most residents of both areas described their neighbourhood as a little island in the city or as villages ('we always call this the little village', as Catherine from *Kreuzberg* said). Some of them extended this pattern to the city as a whole where they identified certain islands they knew and broader areas of unknown land which emphasized that daily life was centred around the home and the use of the city restricted to very specific sites. The *Kreuzberg* mother, Anna, only liked certain parts of the city, and stressed the diversity of the urban landscape and the geographical proximity of 'nice' and 'not nice' places:

> This is something that strikes me about Berlin. There are always specific islands in the city you like and just around the corner is an area you don't particularly like.

This is not to say that the women necessarily lived in the areas they had pictured for themselves. In *Lichterfelde*, Sandra, a 47-year-old separated mother of three, is surprised that she is really living in a neighbourhood that seems almost 'unreal' to her:

> Well, I would have never thought that I'd end up living in such a Lego-Land one day, and that it would be really great.

The island is above all a site of convenience for a mother seeking out the best living conditions for her children, as Susan described:

> Well, I think it is wonderful, it is incredibly calm. Even though there are many children around. … And it surely is great that you have all those playgrounds for the kids without them having to cross too many roads. Well, I think, yes, a small island in the middle of the city. That is not bad.

Not active withdrawal, but an inward orientation on their own neighbourhood as the best site for a family can be found in both areas.

Mothering Expectations and the Need for Resourceful Neighbourhoods

Not only the degree of insulation and the expectations of mothering that are culturally scripted for and by middle class family life were similar in *Kreuzberg* and *Lichterfelde*, but the interviewees also used their neighbourhood in a comparable way and stressed its convenience: they valued the various forms of neighbourly support, the nearby amenities and short distances to the city centre, as well as the cohesion and neighbourliness among the residents. Above all, they highlighted the importance of their living situation for their children with respect to autonomy, safety and a 'good' environment for family life. Women in *Lichterfelde* often talked about the quality of being able to let their children play outside 'unsupervised'. They actually let them play outside without their own mother's supervision because they assumed, and rightly so, that all neighbouring mothers would keep an eye on the street for their children just like they did for others. Ties to neighbours developed primarily through the children and were based on exchange of child-related support. Elisa, a 44-year-old mother of two who had long been working as a nurse and was now, as her children were getting older, going back to university to achieve a better position, explained:

> Well, through the kids, we are friendly with our neighbours living here on this side. Those just next to us, well, they have looked after our kids now and then if we had to go somewhere urgently. Or the kids often play outside. In these cases you can, I have done that several times, you can tell the neighbours that you won't be away for long, if they could keep an eye. And they do that.

Children played alone in sandboxes and rode their wooden balance bikes from the age of two; parents went shopping in the shopping precinct around the corner leaving their small children unattended; bikes and rollers laid around outside in the evening as everybody assumed they would not be stolen; parents told their older children that the neighbours would keep an eye on them when they had to go out in the evening. Mothers told other mothers about the whereabouts and mischief that their children were up to. Nothing remained unseen, everyone noticed everything, and a moral orientation of strict social control followed. The child-friendly environment was one of the most mentioned and described positive features of their respective neighbourhood and was often also part of the primary reasons for moving there. Collective child supervision enabled mothers to be relaxed. Many described the connecting with other neighbours through their children and the favours and support they could ask for. Package deliveries were taken in for each other, garden tools borrowed, pets and plants taken care of during vacations. Whereas evening quietness and shared hours of taking the children inside were agreed upon by mothers, the practice and moral orientation was that children come first, and that this was above all a child-friendly area. These beneficial features of 'intergenerational closure and neighbourly exchange' have also been identified by Sampson et al. (1999) indicating a possible universality of such alleviating factors: while oppressive in the social control and constantly reinforcing and legitimizing motherhood as dominant cultural script, such a setting also made family life easier.

Catherine, the *Kreuzberg* sociologist and mother of five, described the cohesion among the adults and the resulting 'independence' of the children. It went without saying that all parents supported each other:

> Well, we have distributed our keys more or less in a way that you don't know any longer who got one and who not and the kids are just coming and going anyway. … There is a bunch of kids around distributed over all apartments and then eventually they will come home in the evening and we, I, no, I don't worry about where they are, and I know that every family would immediately [take care of them]. Well it just happened the same evening you were there, that Lukas was hurt by Maria and then one neighbour brings him to me and takes care of him and would also drive him to the hospital and … well, there really is a lot of support, I would say. You don't have only one person but actually everyone.

Also in *Lichterfelde* mothers knew the neighbours' children, at least from their own block, since they freely went from house to house and garden to garden. But, and this is remarkably put here in the following statement, this trust in the other parents was based on shared moral orientations that ease the collective supervision. The children are only allowed to play within clear boundaries and all parents feel responsible for looking after them when something 'critical' happens, as Thomas, the professor from *Lichterfelde*, sketched:

> Well, it works, they are just not allowed to go beyond the big, well the one up here the *Altdorfer*- and the *Lausanner Straße*, these [streets] are virtually the borders, and in between there is the *Swiss Quarter* and the roads, well they – at least our kids – are allowed to use them and it is the same for the other families and you know the kids since … they are on the street all the time playing. … In this sense, the kids are very much protected here. And if something happens, once it happened that a car, a bike collided with a car. That was a pretty critical situation. There were all of a sudden a whole lot of parents and in that sense there really is a great deal of attention on what is happening.

In general, the collective supervision provided relatively young children with an amount of independence otherwise rarely practiced in the city (Butler presented similar findings for London, see Butler 2003, 2477). Whereas in disadvantaged areas mothers who let their small children play outside without supervision are criticized and many middle class parents in such neighbourhoods try to 'protect' their children by a high degree of organized leisure time and play dates with children of their parents' choosing, children in our areas had much more freedom to choose their own playmates and activities. Furthermore, most children were allowed to go to school by themselves and play outside all day long. Since the children generally went to the same schools, they could leave the house in the morning in a group and their mothers did not have to bring them, as Anna explained:

> Because, it is like, they go in a group. Well, Laura and Susanna, they also come back by themselves. Despite of once a week or like today, when Susanna has an appointment in the afternoon, in that case I pick them up. Apart from that they go by themselves.

This independence is not only confined to the boundaries of the neighbourhood but extended to nearby activities in biking distance as Susan from *Lichterfelde* described:

> Well, I, [we live here] especially for my son. He's got his school here and his friends and he can do everything by himself, whether by foot or by bike.

Susan explicitly stated that one of the reasons she lived here was her son's independence. Through their children's independence many mothers gained some freedom to do other things than child supervision while their children were in a safe environment, making the juggling of their many tasks a little easier. That said, as they still needed to be on stand-by, going out to work was not an option. The great attention for independence and 'autonomy' for children in a time of highly structured, institutionalized childhoods on the one hand and the craving for security on the other hand made such areas fitting locations to practice good mothering.

Additionally, an important aspect for many was the location of the neighbourhood: the connection to the city or to green spaces. People felt free to leave their 'island' when they wanted. The positive features of a small village could thus be combined with the anonymity of the city. This mix of village-like lifestyle and urbanity was what Catherine from *Kreuzberg* described as crucial for her to feel at ease with her living situation, pointing to her need to break away from the ascriptive definition of being a mother (Everingham 1994, 5):

> For me it is of course [important] to have the two options. Yes, I think I would die, if this really was the little village. We call it little village, and I really love it ... But well, I need this, me, you know? To plunge into the anonymity and have all possible options and just take my bike and get out of here and just be directly in the thick of it, this is vitally important to me. ... It, hm, is mutually dependent. I think that if I was locked in here I wouldn't see the fun of it.

Susan from *Lichterfelde* also mentioned the advantage of having short ways to relevant facilities and the city. She compared the location of her neighbourhood to other more suburban places outside of the city:

> I think it is just horrible, many friends of mine live in *Teltow* or *Kleinmachnow* [suburban towns], ... Especially the way to get to work, I find that awful. If it takes such a long time just to get to Berlin.

The described combination of closeness to the city and a possibility of family privacy in a home in a supportive neighbourhood seemed to function as a substitute for the extended family.

Many of the residents were not originally from Berlin and had few possibilities of support from extended family members. Even if they had nearby and supportive kin, the neighbourhood was more than just a simple place of residence. The mothers appreciated the community feeling and cohesion. In *Kreuzberg*, Catherine illustrated how the friendship among the neighbours led to cohesion, particularly among mothers who had to get along while their husbands worked:

> Well, I do know everyone here in the neighbourhood, also, partly as very good friends, a strong relationship. ... Here it is just a very strong cohesion, well, and everyone is in this same situation. The men work a lot and the women work too, but have to get along, in a manner of speaking.

Children could play outside freely because the environment was congruent with their parents' child rearing practices and their moral orientations about how one should live together in a neighbourhood.

Values regarding the upbringing of children could be realized in their neighbourhood, as Catherine illustrated:

> Well, for me this is a very, very ideal living situation, I think. And I think that this is also an ideal living condition for the children to grow up because they too have the two options. Especially the older ones, who make their way through the city independently and have the competences to do so. And at the same time there is a complete safety with their friends and they don't have to make appointments and I don't have to drive by car or bring them somewhere because they can do everything by themselves, well, that really is great.

The practical features of the neighbourhood offered mothers beyond the demands to care for their children some framework for self-realization, including some time for themselves, and company. They enjoyed a certain degree of freedom thanks to the watchful eyes of others, experienced solidarity among the other mothers and could help each other out. Catherine described her situation in a way that was characteristic for many interviewees:

> I am in that age where the truth of the matter is that you spend a whole lot of energy to actually keep things going.

A 'functioning' neighbourhood hence turned out to be a valuable resource. Therefore, it makes sense that families with young children seek these places and group together to support each other, as such contexts facilitate, relatively speaking, the capabilities of women to close or at least reduce the gap between the ideology of good mothering and their lived realities of being women.

These findings correspond with those of Karsten's (2003) study about families of gentrifiers in the Netherlands. She emphasized that mobility, especially of mothers, highly depends on the successful management of daily tasks (Karsten 2003, 2575). In this context, she identifies the neighbourhood as being a 'firm basis for social meetings and practical support'. Through the feeling of safety created by the many informal networks they provide an 'important quality … in relation to parental responsibilities' (ibid., 2582). The proximity of people similar in terms of class, gender and the stage in the life course enabled many forms of support that rendered the neighbourhood a valuable resource 'in the combination of work, care and leisure' (ibid., 2582).

Conclusion

Segregation does not simply mean that the poor and immigrants stay among their own. The specific housing strategies of middle class residents heavily contribute to segregation. This does not mean that the middle classes actively choose to turn away from the poor and the immigrants. We have seen that in two areas of Berlin, *Lichterfelde* and *Kreuzberg*, notwithstanding their different location in the city, residents lived in homogeneous settings with no durable engagements of few fluid encounters with other social groups. This homogeneity constituted a resource for these families characterized by their moral orientations on the dominant cultural script of mothering, where women did most of the nurturing. Especially for mothers the neighbourhood as a resource was crucial to combine their duties of motherhood with their images of themselves as modern women, with healthy lifestyles, leisure time for themselves and, sometimes, professional careers. Many of those who did not work turned to their children as projects that served their self-realization and focused on the reproduction of their own social status through intensive parenting.

The neighbourhood played an important role on various levels. Practical support through supervision of children and material exchanges, and emotional support of shared values and norms of child rearing contributed to the creation of a place where women could combine good parenting and a modern woman's lifestyle. Hence, the possibility to escape the island made this 'refuge that is more extensive and embracing than the home alone could ever be' (Atkinson 2006, 822) attractive to women preferring an urban environment over the ennui of traditional suburbia. Nonetheless, the neighbourhood as a resource also facilitated the continuation of the 'gender fate' and patriarchy. Moreover, the focus on one's own children's needs and the needs of the family produced an inward orientation on the neighbourhood, with exclusion as a result. The absence of a strong awareness of the rest of the city, the localness of the use of urban facilities, and the limited geographical scope of social networks of the mothers all contributed to the neighbourhood as a village or island. Effectively, this meant that these mothers avoided routes through the city – also shown in their preference for cars over public transport – for fluid encounters, let alone more durable engagements, with residents unlike themselves. Their energy was so focused on the family and their neighbourhood that to make their social capital accessible to others unlike themselves was not happening. It did not occur to them as something they might do, and the everyday contexts in which such transfers of capital would become the automatic consequence of everyday practices and fluid encounters simply did not happen. Segregation, then, was actively enhanced and reified by the residential choices and everyday practices of these mothers. Different from authors like Atkinson (cf. 2006), Butler (cf. 2003), Slater (cf. 2013) or Smith (cf. 1996), we hence do not see a decision on the part of the middle classes to organize their lives in such a way that contacts with people unlike themselves were avoided. In contrast, the way they organized their practices, and the fluid interactions and durable engagements that followed from these, created lives in which the 'other' was seldomly met, without the deliberate intention to make sure that this did not happen. Marginalization, then, occurred there where these families use their voice, political clout and social and cultural capital to ensure high quality institutions and living environments – privatized through home ownership and collectively owned commons – and as a consequence excluded others from these institutions and places. Their strong internal cohesion and mutual dependency for social support as well as the relative freedom in time and for self-realization when others supervised their children in a context of high social control, all contributed to a convenience that made these residents unreflective on the question what their spatial and social practices might mean to their fellow citizens who did not happen to be middle class. This lack of reflexivity, in a situation in which modern womanhood is a challenge of combining gendered mothering with the conception of the modern woman as the well cared for, healthy and working woman with a decent career or at least as one, when not with a career, who seriously raises her children as a project of social reproduction, is thus one of the essential aspects of contemporary urban marginalization. This gendered set of imaginations and expectations is a core seldomly taken seriously in urban studies, where scholars too quickly bash the middle class as intentionally keeping the poor out of their own circles.

References

Allmendinger, Jutta. 2010. *Verschenkte Potenziale? Lebensverläufe nichterwerbstätiger Frauen*. Frankfurt am Main: Campus-Verlag.

Atkinson, Rowland. 2006. 'Padding the Bunker: Strategies of Middle Class Disaffiliation and Colonisation in the City'. *Urban Studies* 43 (4): 819–32.

——— . 2008. 'The Flowing Enclave and the Misanthropy of Networked Affluence'. In *Networked Urbanism: Social Capital in the City*, edited by Talja V. Blokland and Michael Savage, 41–58. Aldershot, England; Burlington, VT: Ashgate.

Bahrdt, Hans Paul. 1998. *Die moderne Großstadt. Soziologische Überlegungen zum Städtebau*. Opladen: Leske + Budrich.

Becker-Schmidt, Regine. 2003. 'Zur doppelten Vergesellschaftung von Frauen. Soziologische Grundlegung, empirische Rekonstruktion'. *Gender Politik Online*. Accessed 12 June 2014. http://www.fu-berlin.de/sites/gpo/soz_eth/Geschlecht_als_Kategorie/Die_doppelte_Vergesellschaftung_von_Frauen/becker_schmidt_ohne.pdf.

Bertram, Hans et al. 2006. 7. *Familienbericht der Bundesregierung: Familie zwischen Flexibilität und Verlässlichkeit – Perspektiven für eine lebenslaufbezogene Familienpolitik*. Berlin: Bundesministerium für Familie, Senioren, Frauen und Jugend. Accessed 18 April 2014. http://www.bmfsfj.de/doku/Publikationen/familienbericht/download/familienbericht_gesamt.pdf.

Bittman, Michael and Judy Wajcman. 2000. 'The Rush Hour: The Character of Leisure Time and Gender Equity'. *Social Forces* 79 (1): 165–89.

Blokland, Talja V. 2003. *Urban Bonds*. Cambridge: Polity Press.

Blossfeld, Hans-Peter and Catherine Hakim. 1997. *Between Equalization and Marginalization. Women Working Part-time in Europe and the United States of America*. New York: Oxford University Press.

Bourdieu, Pierre. 1999. 'Site Effects'. In *The Weight of the World: Social Suffering in Contemporary Society*, edited by Pierre Bourdieu, Alain Accardo and Priscilla Parkhurst Ferguson, 123–9. Stanford: Stanford University Press.

Butler, Tim. 2003. 'Living in the Bubble: Gentrification and Its 'Others' in North London'. *Urban Studies* 40 (12): 2469–86.

———. 2008. 'Social Capital and the Formation of London's Middle Classes'. In *Networked Urbanism: Social Capital in the City*, edited by Talja V. Blokland and Michael Savage, 217–37. Aldershot, England; Burlington, VT: Ashgate.

Everingham, Christine. 1994. *Motherhood and Modernity*. Buckingham: Open University Press.

Helfferich, Cornelia. 2002. *Frauen Leben – eine Studie zu Lebensläufen und Familienplanung*. Forschung und Praxis der Sexualaufklärung und Familienplanung, Band 19. Köln: Bundeszentrale für gesundheitliche Aufklärung.

Hennig, Marina, Mareike Ebach, Stefan Stuth and Anna Erika Hägglund. 2012. 'Frauen zwischen Beruf und Familie – ein europäischer Vergleich'. In *Zeit, Geld, Infrastruktur – zur Zukunft der Familienpolitik*, edited by Hans Bertram and Martin Bujard, 291–319. Baden-Baden: Nomos.

Jordan, Brigitte and Robbie E. Davis-Floyd. 1993. *Birth in Four Cultures: A crosscultural investigation of Childbirth in Yucatan, Holland, Sweden and the United States*. 4th edition. Prospect Heights, IL: Waveland Press.

Karsten, Lia. 2003. 'Family Gentrifiers: Challenging the City as a Place Simultaneously to Build a Career and to Raise Children'. *Urban Studies* 40 (12): 2573–84.

Miller, Tina. 2005. *Making Sense of Motherhood: A Narrative Approach*. Cambridge: Cambridge University Press.

Morée, Marjolein. 1992. *Mijn kinderen hebben er niets van gemerkt: buitenshuis werkende moeders tussen 1950 en nu*. Utrecht: Van Arkel.

Pfau-Effinger, Birgit. 2009. 'Unterschiede in der Kinderbetreuung im Ländervergleich im Rahmen kultureller und familienpolitischer Kontextbedingungen'. In *Die Vielfalt der Familie. Tagungsband zum 3. Europäischen Fachkongress Familienforschung*, edited by Olaf Kapella, 113–32. Opladen: Budrich.

Rösler, Wiebke. 2012. *Strukturwandel und Fertilität. Wie die höhere Berufsbildung der Frau die Geburtenrate beeinflusst. Quantitative Analysen für Deutschland im Zeitverlauf des 'zweiten demographischen Übergangs'*. PhD thesis, Humboldt University of Berlin.

Rühling, Anneli and Karsten Kassner. 2007. *Familienpolitik aus der Gleichstellungsperspektive. Ein europäischer Vergleich.* Forum Politik und Gesellschaft. Berlin: Friedrich-Ebert-Stiftung.

Sampson, Robert J., Jeffrey D. Morenoff and Felton Earls. 1999. 'Beyond Social Capital: Spatial Dynamics of Collective Efficacy for Children'. *American Sociological Review* 64 (5): 633–60.

Slater, Tom. 2013. 'Your Life Chances Affect Where you Live: A Critique of the 'Cottage Industry' of Neighbourhood Effects Research'. *International Journal of Urban and Regional Research* 37 (2): 367–87.

Smith, Neil. 1996. *The New Urban Frontier. Gentrification and the Revanchist City*. London: Routledge.

Stacey, Judith. 1990. *Brave New Families: Stories of Domestic Upheaval in late Twentieth-Century America.* Berkeley: University of California Press.

Statistisches Bundesamt. 2011. 'Entwicklung des Studentinnenanteils in Deutschland seit 1908'. Accessed 10 February 2015. http://www.gesis.org/cews/informationsangebote/statistiken/blaettern/treffer/?qualificationvirtual=&selcat=Studienabschluss%3E%3E&qt1=Studienabschluss&browse=qualificationvirtual&order=_title%3C&switchto=&=&selres=,5#5.

Statistisches Bundesamt (Destatis). 2012. 'Geburten in Deutschland'. Accessed 11 September 2014. https://www.destatis.de/DE/Publikationen/Thematisch/Bevoelkerung/Bevoelkerungsbewegung/BroschuereGeburtenDeutschland0120007129004.pdf?__blob=publicationFile.

Vinken, Barbara. 2007. *Die deutsche Mutter. Der lange Schatten eines Mythos.* Frankfurt am Main: Fischer Taschenbuch Verlag.

Wengler, Annelene, Heike Trappe and Christian Schmitt. 2008. *Partnerschaftliche Arbeitsteilung und Elternschaft: Analysen zur Aufteilung von Hausarbeit und Elternaufgaben auf Basis des Generations and Gender Survey – Division of Labor in Partnerships and Parenthood: Analyses of the Division of Housework and Parental Tasks Based on the Generations and Gender Survey*. Wiesbaden: Bundesinstitut für Bevölkerungsforschung.

Willard, Ann. 1988. 'Cultural Scripts for Mothering'. In *Mapping the Moral Domain: A Contribution of Women's Thinking to Psychological Theory and Education*, edited by Carol Gilligan, Janie Victoria Ward and Jill MacLean Taylor, 225–43. London: Harvard University Press.

PART II:
Making the City Work: Dealing with Marginalization

Chapter 5
A Youth Club as a Site of Resources: A Girls' Alternative to School and Family

Imogen Feld

Introduction

Capabilities of urbanites to create lives and livelihoods depend not just on means and instruments, but also on whether one is able to do the things one values (permissions in the broad sense and recognition on a meta-level), as we said in the introduction. Whereas the previous chapters have shown how the middle classes make the city work and how their practices marginalize others, we will now turn to some of the groups at those margins and ask how they make the city work. In contrast to the 'gender fate' of mothers discussed in the previous chapter, as long as women are still girls they are seen as having better chances to achieve stable social positions in contemporary society than boys. Although currently adult women still earn less than men, work more often part-time and make fewer career steps on the ladder, most societal communities worry about boys from low-income households, not so much about girls. In Germany, girls are commonly perceived as the winners in the educational system (Legewie and DiPrete 2012). Even though girls seem to fare better in schools, definitely not all girls have an easy school life. Girls from migration families seem to lack the 'right' habitus to make the transition from school to vocational training (Schittenhelm and Granato 2004; Bednarz-Braun and Heß-Meining 2004; Granato 2006) and experience difficulties in defining a future (Schittenhelm 2008). One may hence wonder how they find ways to succeed not just in school, but maybe sometimes despite their school performances.

Practices in institutional settings, we stated in the introduction, may both include and marginalize. Girls with a migration background must realize capabilities at the intersection of gender, class and ethnicity. This chapter discusses how dispositions defined by this intersection and the connected practices of girls in the educational system and an after school institution shape their resources. In better neighbourhoods, the practices of middle class youngsters and their parents can create relatively 'safe' havens for segregated teenage years. Girls marginalized by middle class seclusion have to rely on streets that are relatively dominated by masculine behaviour (Anderson 1999) and often experienced as unsafe or inappropriate. Institutions that are imagined as less adequate and therefore avoided by middle class parents, and leisure time facilities that are publically funded and free for them to access, do not provide them with the same instruments to realize their capabilities as do private facilities such as sports clubs and music schools. What capabilities do such girls have to mould their future to their dreams? What resources can they create at school and leisure activities to cope with their experienced marginalization and how do different sites shape girls' possibilities?

We discuss how a group of girls with a migration background from poor families realize capabilities, by drawing on interviews and observations done in a girls-only youth club in a deprived Berlin neighbourhood frequented mostly by Syrian, Turkish and Kurdish girls from low-income families where the parents had little formal education.

We focus on girls in ninth and 10th grade, shortly before their transition to vocational training or further education, a crucial moment of choice on their way to the labour market (Palamidis and Schwarze 1989). Berlin has three secondary school tracks: the *Hauptschule*, *Realschule* and *Gymnasium*.[1] The least demanding *Hauptschule* provides a basic general education. The *Realschule* prepares for vocational training and university. The A-level equivalent (*Abitur*) at the *Gymnasium* provides access to universities. At the end of the 10th grade, students who do not attend the *Gymnasium* must choose either the vocational or the academic track.

School success is a known predictor for later achievements. It is also well known that educational success does not solely depend on intellectual capacities but also on resources which can be mobilized outside the school (Bourdieu 2001; Solga 2006; Solga 2011). Since family situations can both mitigate problems at school and intensify them, the family has a major influence on educational outcomes. As we will see, the girls club became an alternative institution to school and family, providing the girls with resources and a setting to realize their capabilities. However, depending on their social position, school situation and citizenship status, the girls differed in how they benefitted.

This chapter starts with a description of the young women's positions and engagement with their future, defined as the practices and moral orientations deployed to create a future in the city. Rather than seeing this engagement as an 'intentional act', we do, in a similar way then in our discussion of middle class parents' strategies of reproduction of cultural capital, see in the women's presentation of their 'future plans' their habitus 'at work', i.e. a practice informed by their dispositions and structural conditions (Bourdieu 1977). This then turns the idea of planning into a practice that we think tells us rather something about the social processes the actors are part of in the present than about their actual realization of a future livelihood. It isn't per se the (strategic) act of making plans that have to lead in a linear way to a specific goal, but comprise all sort of engagements with the game of the social fields they are involved in (Bourdieu 1994, 151–61; cf. 1977, 72–8) – although in the following case study, 'to have a plan' becomes the dominant and valorised formula to engage with the future,

1 Since 2010 a reform integrated the *Real-* and *Hauptschule* into an integrated secondary school. The girls in this study still attended specific school-forms.

as it reflects the 'illusio' of the field in which the girls are growing up (Bourdieu 1994, 151–61).

Our analysis shows that the girls' engagement with their own future in the city differs in function of their moral orientations and their available resources; what it also reflects is their use of the Girls club as a hub for fluid encounters and durable engagements, in short: to create capabilities there. We discuss first how the school and the educational field shape the girls' creation of capabilities, before we turn then to the club and the possibilities it offers. The conclusion discusses how in the marginalized position of these young women, the interconnectedness of the fields of school and leisure time create possibilities to take advantage of institutional resources.

Participation in the Context of Marginalization

In contemporary 'Global North' cities, like Berlin, employment status strongly influences the sense of inclusion of individuals and their scope of active participation – also in terms of voluntary and political engagement (see among others Bödeker 2012). Those who work in formal employment are most likely to enjoy their social and political citizenship (as in Marshall 2009) as usually measured. Therefore, success in school and in finding a satisfying future workplace strongly impacts one's future professional and civic life (Solga 2011; Traue 2010; Kupfer 2011).

All girls interviewed at the youth club were aware that their present decisions mattered a lot to their future professional life. They were determined to move to a working life, as they wanted to become independent and to set a good example for their own children later. They often aspired to be more successful than their parents. Such ideas refer to general moral orientations about responsible participative citizenship and gender and parental roles. The assumption to become a mother demonstrated that women who are not mothers are also subject to the cultural scripts of motherhood discussed in the last chapters (Miller 2005, 3).

Notwithstanding these similar moral orientations, the strategies the girls used to try and get there were very diverse. What we call in the following strategies is the set of practices that are deployed in order to realize the respective goals or imaginaries of the future lives that particular moral orientations (or aspirations in this case) imply. Strategies are then by no means only and always strategic in the sense of being conscientious, rational and intended. Rather, the development of strategies is informed by the actor's disposition and habitus. At the same time, the effectiveness of the individual strategies depends on the rules of the game that move the struggles in a specific social field in which the actor is about to invest. In this game, the agents don't necessarily have to make their moves public in order to win, but it is their incorporated knowledge how to play the game that makes them capable to make points, a knowledge that is tacit, 'infra-conscious' and 'infra-linguistic' (Bourdieu 1994, 154).

In our case, the effectiveness of the young girls' strategies in making a future in the city depended on the one hand on their disposition of their familial background in which they were born – and their position, composed of the socialization in the family, the school form they attended and their legal citizenship status. On the other hand, the effectiveness of their strategies was strongly influenced by the ways in which the girls were able to develop durable engagements at the girls club and create resources to help them realize their plans through that institution. But it is not only the exclusion from resourceful sites that results from their position of marginalization. The difficulties of developing effective strategies to engage with their future in the city is also linked to a lack of self-confidence in being able to mobilize resources to implement these strategies successfully (Grundmann 2010).

In the girls' engagement with their future in the city we see three patterns. Some young women had developed a quite exact plan of how to be successful in the labour market, and felt capable to actively plan their lives. Other girls were very insecure about their future as they felt restrained by their legal status or by not knowing which school degree they would be able to achieve. A third group had plans for their future but were unable to develop a practical, concrete strategy to realize them.

Most girls who were able to develop and formulate concrete strategies attended the *Gymnasium* or the *Realschule*. Güpse was 15 and attended the ninth grade of a *Gymnasium*. Her parents were born in Turkey. Her mother came to Germany as a child. She had graduated from secondary school and worked as a nurse. Her father had the highest Turkish secondary school degree and owned a bakery where Güpse sometimes helped out. She had always been good at school but was recently very tired of doing homework. She was being 'more relaxed' about school: she did not feel the urge to improve her grades as she was satisfied with her grades from last term. Güpse went to the girls club every day and called it her 'second home'. She had quite an exact idea of what she would like to do after school and how to achieve it:

> Well, it is because, I would like to migrate to Turkey. In Turkey, because I lived here in Germany and I would like to study German, I am also doing German for my A-levels. I think, as I can speak German well, and get good grades in German, in the subject German, so I can study it too. And then in Turkey [I can] become a German language teacher in a school, or I can work at a private school or be a private tutor in Turkey, then I will make good money there. Yeah, that's why.

Güpse reflected on her strengths such as her German language skills and analysed her options based upon concrete facts such as her corresponding school grades. Similarly, Seda chose an art major for the next school year to prepare for studying design. She was planning to move away from Berlin to study, as she understood that the popular universities in Berlin were hard to get into. Seda was attending the 10th grade of a *Gymnasium*. She was positively excited about her future.

Although she expected not to be able to stay in Berlin for her studies she focused on the positive aspects of moving out from home. Her parents were born in Turkey and had no school degree. Her mother worked as a hair stylist and her father as a craftsman. She went to the girls club nearly every day, spending her time in the homework-room learning, lending books or going to a 'beauty day' at the girls club during the school vacation. She attended an extra *MSA*[2] training on the weekend to prepare for the final MSA exams: aware of the limitations that the marginalized position of her parents meant to her, she organized the resources to get ahead within the youth club.

Hilal, a frank and talkative woman, also had sharp ideas about her future. She was a proud Muslim. She had decided to veil herself when she was 14, against the will of her family. She explained that this was the way she and her friends wanted to live their religion. She attended the ninth grade of a *Realschule*. Her mother was a cleaning lady and her father a production manager. Both parents were born in Turkey and were Kurdish. Hilal was planning to study social pedagogics and knew the requirements. To prepare herself she did an internship in a Kindergarten and was working hard at school to achieve her goal. Hilal's youth workers and peers described Hilal as the best student of her class.

Selcan also attended the ninth grade of a *Realschule*. She was Kurdish, born in Syria. At the time of the interview, Selcan had a permanent residency, for which she had had to fight with a lawyer. This procedure had been difficult: it had 'caused her headaches'. Her parents never attended school and were unemployed. Sometimes she did her homework at the girls club but mostly she just came for a chat. She wanted to become a police officer because she wanted to have an 'interesting' job, and interned with the police: 'I wanted, well, something else, not always like hairdresser or something like that. I wanted something different. Something where one says: "wow, that is a good job"'.

While these girls frequented the club regularly, 14-year-old Miriam, attending the ninth grade of a *Gymnasium* in a different district, only attended a weekly drawing course in the same building as the girls club. Miriam's parents were academics, born in Germany. She was not quite sure yet whether she wanted 'something practical or something where one earns more money'. She tried to find out what she would prefer by doing an internship as a carpenter. Miriam was thus able to acquire information to facilitate her decision, and was certainly supported more by her parents than were the other girls.

These girls had plans for their working life and strategies to realize them. Others, who also did not come to the club that often, seemed less secure. Most of these young women frequented the *Haupt-* or *Realschule* and lived in difficult circumstances. They were not able to plan ahead as their future was insecure, either because of their school results or their legal status.

2 *MSA – Mittlerer Schulabschluss*: In Berlin, at the end of grade 10, pupils are obliged to take an oral and written exam to receive a middle school degree, a precondition to either continue their education within the school or to apply for vocational training.

Betül was a shy 16-year-old girl in the ninth grade of a *Realschule*. She only went to the girls club to prepare for school when she really needed help. Her parents, Turkish, had no school degree. Her father was a housepainter and her mother at home. She was very nervous about her future as she worried about her grades. When she had difficulties understanding her teachers she tried to study after school by herself. Betül never attended any offers of the girls club other than the homework assistance. She often felt anxious about all the things she had to do for school. When she was younger she wanted to become a fashion designer but she had no idea how to achieve this: 'I don't know what I want to become, I wanted to become a fashion designer but I am confused about it. It totally is this thing, I mean, pressure. So I don't know'.

Betül felt a lot of pressure, as she did not know what the future would bring. Despite her interest in the fashion industry, she mentioned that she could imagine herself as a pharmaceutical assistant, as she had done an internship in a pharmacy. Especially her insecurity about the outcomes of her *MSA* exams prevented her from looking ahead.

Leyla's situation was similar. She had to leave the *Realschule* when she did not meet the school's expectations and was doing a special municipal training programme to achieve a basic degree and enter the labour market. She expressed the wish to receive an *MSA* degree to increase her labour market chances. The job offers presented to her at a job-fair that she visited did not attract her. All they offered was 'housekeeping', and the working life, for girls like Leyla, had to be distinctively different from their gendered duties at home:

> Ah, one can work in hotels, for example, or in kindergartens or restaurants, yes. ... Yes, that had not directly attracted me, to be quite honest. That is, well, like when I would have done that training, then I would have to do twice the work I am already doing at home. ... That is the same as I am doing at home, only that I would then practically have training in it. ... [At home] fortunately on Sundays I only have to dust, but well no, that had not really attracted me, to be honest ...

Leyla's parents were born in Syria and were unemployed. She went to the girls club regularly, mainly to use the Internet or chat with the youth workers. She had little contact with other girls. As she did not know which degree she would get, she could only state hopes, unable to develop more concrete plans. She felt miserable about her school change and regretted 'not studying enough' in the past. She was especially scared not to pass an MSA exam.

While Betül and Leyla faced insecurity about their school performance, Dilan, 18, Kurdish and born in Syria with illiterate parents, was constrained by her legal refugee status that allowed her only to attend vocational training of specific kinds. At the time of the interview, her family was legally tolerated in Germany and therefore, nobody of her family had a work permit. Dilan appeared bored in the interview talking about her future, and only expressed some enthusiasm when talking about Kurdish politics and festivities. She was usually around in the girls club, drinking tea with the youth workers. She was fed up with her situation, as all that she could do was wait, uncertain about her stay in Germany:

> That is hard. And therefore I don't know. I just don't know. I don't know exactly what I want to become. I can only do this apprenticeship, and that is what I will do now, two years to become a nurse assistant or ehh ... a social care assistant and then (*sighs*) then I will continue to educate myself, I guess.

Her insecure legal status kept her from creating further resources. More than anything, she hoped to get a German passport – all her future ideas depended on that to happen first. With her parents unfamiliar with the German society, no employment experiences there for themselves, and no knowledge of the Berlin educational system, Dilan had to rely on her own inventiveness to find people to support her and access information much more than some of the other girls. Dilan had problems at school with her teachers and peers. That further frustrated and demotivated her.

Some other girls did have ideas but lacked plans. Ronya, a 14-year-old girl attending the ninth grade of a *Realschule*, enjoyed spending her time in the club's internet-café with her friend Ece. They only rarely made use of the homework assistance. Her parents were both born in Turkey. Her mother was a housewife and her father worked as a production foreman. She had thoughts on her future, but little idea how to get there:

> I will, if I don't pass my MSA exams, when I will pass my exams, and my grades are really good, so that I can take A-levels, then I will take A-levels, or I go to the United States for a year, like do a year abroad, or when I don't pass the MSA, then I take time off.

Ronya wanted to be a social worker, but did not know how. She did not know what the degree of the *Realschule* would enable her to do. She merely said she would do what her friends did. When she had to do an internship, she worked in the firm where her father worked; while she hence could rely on a tie to get her a place for her internship, the internship itself was far removed from what she thought she would want to do later. In contrast to middle class professionals who could rely on their networks to find work experience places for their children, her father was, although slightly better positioned than some other parents, still not able to provide her with the resources that she had needed to pursue her own interests.

The different strategies that the girls hoped would help them implement their future plans underline the interconnection of their evaluation of their positioning and possibilities offered to create the resources needed to realize their plans.

Schools as Sites of Resources?

Ideally, schools provide pupils with the necessary skills to participate as adults in society and realize their capabilities in many ways (Schiffauer et al. 2002; Osler and Starkey 2005; Fend 2006). When asking the girls about what they expected to learn in school, they primarily thought about school as leading them to the labour market, not as a site that would prepare them for participation in a broader, also political and social sense.

Hilal, in the 10th grade of the *Realschule* and planning to continue to get her A-levels, mainly expected her school to provide the competences to successfully enter a working life:

> [School should prepare us] for life, for the second chapter of our life. There is one for the school, up to the 10th grade, that is all just general knowledge that one does to move on to the second chapter: then one decides about the job, for the working life. Or at least how I will choose, for A-levels, but up to 10th grade it is all about preparing us for [the working life].

Seda, attending the 10th grade of a *Gymnasium*, emphasized the relevance of the A-levels to succeed in the job market: 'I think it is very important, through A-levels, one sort of finds better places to work. That's what I think. I believe so. So when one has done A-levels, one arrives at a better place, that's what I think'.

As with Seda, many of the girls, independently of the school type they attended, stressed the importance of educational success for their future and the degree, especially an A-level, was valuable to them. Their positions of coming from relatively poor, relatively uneducated and hard-working parents or parents who were unemployed made them acutely aware of the need to find work, and make the best out of school to find work, as the working life was the first and foremost important road to a stable future. Only Miriam, who came from a middle class background, saw education as important for her development as an individual person: this idea of broad education rather than practical skills was not shared by the other girls.

While the girls' moral orientations on the working life were surprisingly similar, their everyday life at school, the practices they encountered, the resources they could mobilize and the strategies they could develop within the school differed to a great degree. While some reported a school climate characterized by sanctions, disorder and disciplinary measures in which they felt they could not learn, others managed to create resources that helped them develop their plans.

Hilal and Ronya attended different classes of the same *Realschule* and both described the atmosphere at school in a similar way, explaining how the teacher disciplined the pupils during class with sanctions. Ronya, who was in a class given extra support, believed they had put all the pupils who were 'misbehaving' there together. When she was asked how a good school should be, she said:

> I believe one should have a good connection to the teacher, that one can talk to him. And you should be able to joke a bit, so that one can have a laugh. But in our case it is like, when we laugh we get sent immediately [out of the classroom] or you get suspended. That sort of thing.

Making yourself heard is quickly defined as 'misbehaving', as the habitus that the schools expect is one of *certain* ways of making oneself heard. Good school behaviour is defined as quiet, not to interrupt lessons. Ronya's teachers were not waiting for active participation and interactions. Hilal described how she felt at school:

> Yeah this school is like a prison. You come ten seconds too late, after 8 a.m., you can't get in anymore. Then you have to wait for a whole hour. You get suspended for just about everything. Then [they hold] classroom conferences [about you] and all that stuff.

From the stories of these girls, it seems that the school was so involved in maintaining discipline and order, that there was little space left for creativity and individual development.

Recalling attempts by the pupils to change the regime of their school, which had been unsuccessful, Hilal felt that she could not change her situation and that most of her teachers did not listen to her, and did not recognize her needs. In contrast to the girls club, which they saw as theirs and as a place where they were allowed to be themselves and to belong, and where youth workers would listen to them and take their concerns and worries seriously, even though they could by far not always bring them solutions, these girls did not experience the school as a place of belongingness. They did not seem to think the teachers liked them – they certainly did not like their teachers. This negative relationship to their school implies that they would not primarily see their school as enabling and emancipating and a site of resources: rather, they seemed to have seen the school as confining, a necessary stage to get through to get skills for a working life.

Whereas Ronya and Hilal expressed their dissatisfaction with the school as an institution and its teachers, Betül, who attends the ninth grade of another *Realschule*, complained about the noise and misbehaving classmates who prevented her from following the lessons. Then, however, she too expressed her disappointment with the teachers, who did not act adequately:

> Those pupils at our school. Quite a few of them are very rude. They don't pay the rules any mind. They do whatever they want. For example, in our class, there are some, they are really loud, so once in a while you can't even participate in the lessons. But it all depends on the teacher. When the teacher does not say anything, they just go on and on. They are so impolite.

The chaos in the classroom made it at times very difficult for her to follow, as the teachers often seemed unable to create an atmosphere where she could concentrate and learn. Not to fall behind, Betül had to study a lot after school: 'When you notice that your teacher is not teaching you anything, or does whatever she wants to do, then you got to do it yourself. And not give up too easily'.

While she did not want to give up, Betül asked friends to help her or went to the girls club for homework support. Again, the school did not seem to be the site thought of as the place to find resources, but merely as the necessary institutional road to acquire skills. With no widely available alternative system like the GED-programs in the United States, only being a pupil in school can lead to a degree: sitting through the school days, even when one had to actually learn in other ways, was part of the road to a working life.

The girls going to the *Gymnasium* did not seem to have the same sort of problems. They were made aware of their relative elitist status, and teachers would connect school types to behaviours, implying that 'bad' behaviour had to be associated with '*Hauptschüler*': whereas students at the latter school type are represented in the media as unable but also unwilling to see the need for an education – a perspective not found among the girls interviewed here – and as not interested in doing well in school, coming from families popularly represented as 'far away from education' (*bildungsfern*), *Gymnasium* students by the very fact that they *chose* to go to a *Gymnasium* were expected to be self-motivated and well-behaved, as if motivation to learn and knowing the habitus that institutions like schools expect are linked one to one. The greater the distance between dispositions and positioning, or habitus, from the habitus that such schools expect, the more marginalization is likely to occur for students who may have the cognitive skills, but do not meet the social expectations of such institutions. In such instances, it becomes clear how the inclusion in a *Gymnasium* is not simply a matter of learning achievements in elementary schools and 'good grades', but also of being expected to 'do well' in a *Gymnasium* or be 'the *Gymnasium* type', as elementary schoolteachers in a middle class elementary school classified their students. Being self-motivated to learn *that what the teachers expect you to learn* is however not the same as being motivated to learn overall; the marginalization of children of lower educated parents, poor and unemployed immigrant parents, can be expected to take place, even when the children have excellent cognitive skills, there where the school expects them to take an interest in themes and topics, for example in classroom round-table conversations, that are fairly remote from their life-worlds. While Seda gave off the impression that *Gymnasien* were better able to provide environments suitable to learning, they also confirmed the stereotypes about other school types:

> So [our teacher] always says that, when he … those kind of things, when he enters the classroom, we should all be quiet. Also when the bell has not ringed yet, we should sit down and not be so loud. And when someone – this is always the case at school – when someone speaks the others should listen. And often

> it is like that, some just talk in between. Then he says, my God, you are on the *Gymnasium*, what is all that, and ehh … when the *Hauptschule* pupils do it, I would understand that, but you are on the *Gymnasium*, so that is what it is, really.

In Seda's account her teacher tried to use the 'bad' example of pupils of a *Hauptschule* to reinforce the symbolic border between the different school forms. Girls attending the *Gymnasium* were encouraged on various occasions to engage in extra-curricular activities. They hence expressed a care for their students beyond the classroom walls, which was not the case in the experiences of girls at the other schools. This taught them, implicitly, that they were entitled to resources to develop themselves in ways that were not available to the other girls.

The Girls Club as an Alternative Site of Resources

The girls club provides valuable resources to all girls independently of the school track they were attending. As a state-funded institution, it engaged youth workers who offered a wide array of programmes. As the place was for girls only, it was an especially important site for those girls who were not allowed to frequent mixed-sex places after school by their parents (statement by a youth worker). It aimed to empower young women through women-related social work instead of mixed-sex social work, which usually puts young men at the centre of the attention. The club provided homework supervision, computer and Internet classes and a café where the girls could meet and talk to youth workers or each other. Without membership cards or fees, the girls club provided a space where fluid encounters could gradually develop into durable engagements, or where existing engagements between the girls could be consolidated. For these girls who were living at home with many housekeeping or babysitting tasks, the club provided a space to socialize outside of the gaze of the immediate family, as Güpse explained:

> So when I am free I come here in the Girls club and chill out with my friends here. Or I do my homework when I have some. Prepare for school. Go home, eat, watch television, do the housekeeping, cook the food. That's it.

In the café's casual atmosphere the youth workers could gain the girls' confidence over time and help them with all sorts of problems. They often helped in applying for social assistance for school trips, getting a double citizenship or sometimes even helped the girls' mothers when they had problems with the social services department.

The club has a small library with novels and manuals to prepare for job applications and interviews. A diverse range of leisure activities included social media lessons and workshops in fashion design, theatre or music. In cooperation with another youth project, the girls club organized for the girls to work as assistants of the anti-conflict team at the 1st of May celebrations. This was an opportunity for fluid encounters with people they would otherwise never have met. The girls received a certificate for attending preparatory workshops. Young women from middle class settings usually have various kinds of voluntary and extra-curricular activities on their CV's. For the girls at the club, their position did not make this as common; the girls club filled a gap here that also the schools, except for the *Gymnasium*, did not.

In contrast to the mostly rigid school setting, participation in the club's activities was voluntary. Nonetheless, many girls went to the club on a regular basis. It was a fixed part of their lives; some, like Hilal, 'practically lived there'. Güpse had been coming to the club for over eight years and saw it as her 'second home'. They came to hang out, but also found the help they could not get in their families and that the schools assumed to be available to students: parental guidance with homework and school projects. From first grade onwards, Berlin children in most schools have short days in school and homework is common. Miriam, whose parents were academics, thought it self-evident that her mother would ask her about her homework and look over her writing assignments, for example. This situation increases the impact of positions on educational outcomes, obviously, and is one of the less visible forms of marginalization: where middle class parents spend much time helping their children at home, and teachers expect parents to do so, children with low educated parents or parents who do not speak German cannot keep up. Although some reforms are being made in elementary school (the *Ganztagsschule* mentioned in Chapter 2 with longer school days and no homework), the secondary schools lag behind in acknowledging the way in which expectations of the involvement of parents marginalize those with lower class and migration positions. Betül did not find help at home: 'My parents are, are, are … not good in German. Do you understand? My aunts can help but they don't have any time. That's why I come to the girls club'.

Seda described her difficulties at school after the transition from primary school to the *Gymnasium* as a motive to come to the club:

> I used to have real difficulties with homework. One day I even cried over it. Because in the seventh grade, it was so difficult, so to say. Elementary school was very easy, really. And then suddenly you are at the *Gymnasium*. And then you are suddenly failing your tests. You do not know what to do! Yeah. At first that was really tough. Then at first I haven't … . Then I asked my father once, how I should do my homework and all that, this way or that way. He could not really help me. But he tried somehow. Then my friend had said there was this sort of girls club, so that's when we came here.

With the homework assistance Seda improved her grades. But as the club consisted of more than homework assistance it became a place where girls with various needs and problems, wishes and interests could meet each other and interact and form new ties. As they made use of a variety of offers on a regular basis and over an extended time period, for many of the girls, the club was not just a place for fluid encounters but an institution where they established durable engagements. It became a site where they could discuss problems outside the educational field such as questions about civil rights, citizenship, social assistance and family issues. Especially for girls living in constraining family settings the club was a site where they could spend time unsupervised by family members and where they could develop and pursue individual interests and ideas.

Conclusion

Most girls frequenting the club were living in a poor neighbourhood, with parents with little formal education and marginalized positions. Many experienced their schools as outright hostile, or felt they could not meet the expectations the school had of them. The girls club became an important site to make up for the gaps left by families and schools. The club thus compensated for missing cultural capital of the family, helping them to overcome inherited 'handicaps' (Parkin 1983, 161). With the aid of extensive homework assistance and emotional support some girls were able to overcome their problems at school. Others could not profit as much as they faced insecurities due to familial or legal problems.

The girls' accounts illustrated that not all of them were equally capable of mobilizing and creating resources for their futures. Girls who were relatively successful at school participated in more activities at the club, used help where necessary and developed plans for their future. While creating the resources they needed, they enhanced their relative advantage. Girls with problems at school, those who attended the *Hauptschule* and had fewer resources available at home and school to start with, were also less active in the club. Nonetheless, the club played a crucial role for them, as it was a site where they received – through durable engagement with the other girls and the youth workers – resources to cope with their everyday lives. Moreover, the girls club provided them with a gendered space that respected them as individuals, allowed them to be full persons and treated them with the respect and recognition they did not necessarily feel they got in their classrooms and their neighbourhoods.

References

Anderson, Elijah. 1999. *Streetwise: Race, Class and Change in an Urban Community*. Chicago: Chicago University Press.

Bednarz-Braun, Iris and Ulrike Hess-Meining. 2004. *Migration, Ethnie und Geschlecht: Theorieansätze, Forschungsstand, Forschungsperspektiven.* Wiesbaden: VS Verlag für Sozialwissenschaften.

Bödeker, Sebastian. 2012. *Soziale Ungleichheit und politische Partizipation in Deutschland. Grenzen politischer Gleichheit in der Bürgergesellschaft.* OBS-Arbeitspapier 1. Frankfurt am Main: Otto-Brenner-Stiftung (OBS).

Bourdieu, Pierre. 1977. *Outline of a Theory of Practice.* Cambridge: Cambridge University Press.

———. 1994. *Raisons pratiques. Sur la théorie de l'action.* Paris: Seuil.

———. 2001. *Wie die Kultur zum Bauern kommt: Über Bildung, Schule und Politik.* Hamburg: VSA-Verlag.

Fend, Helmut. 2006. *Neue Theorie der Schule: Einführung in das Verstehen von Bildungssystemen.* Wiesbaden: VS Verlag für Sozialwissenschaften.

Granato, Mona. 2006. *Berufliche Bildung von Frauen.* Bonn: Bundesinstitut für Berufsbildung.

Grundmann, Matthias. 2010. 'Handlungsbefähigung – sozialisationstheoretische Perspektive'. In *Capabilities – Handlungsbefähigung in der Erziehungswissenschaft*, edited by Hans-Uwe Otto and Holger Ziegler, 131–41. Wiesbaden: VS Verlag für Sozialwissenschaften.

Kupfer, Antonia. 2011. 'Bildung und Erwerbsarbeit'. In *Bildungssoziologie*, edited by Antonia Kupfer, 181–94. Wiesbaden: VS Verlag für Sozialwissenschaften.

Legewie, Joscha and Thomas A. DiPrete. 2012. 'School Context and the Gender Gap in Educational Achievement'. *American Sociological Review* 77 (3): 463–85.

Marshall, T.H. 2009. 'Citizenship and Social Class'. In *Inequality and Society*, edited by Jeff Manza and Michael Sauder, 148–54. New York: W.W. Norton & Company.

Miller, Tina. 2005. *Making Sense of Motherhood: A Narrative Approach.* Cambridge: Cambridge University Press.

Osler, Audrey and Hugh Starkey. 2005. *Changing Citizenship. Democracy and Inclusion in Education.* New York: Open University Press.

Palamidis, Helene and Johannes Schwarze. 1989. 'Jugendliche beim Übergang in eine betriebliche Berufsausbildung und in die Erwerbstätigkeit'. *Mitteilungen aus der Arbeitsmarkt- und Berufsforschung* 22 (1): 114–24.

Parkin, Frank. 1983. 'Strategien sozialer Schließung und Klassenbildung'. *Soziale Welt, Sonderband* (2): 121–35.

Schiffauer, Werner, Gerd Baumann, Riva Kastoryano and Steven Vertovec. 2002. *Staat – Schule – Ethnizität. Politische Sozialisation von Immigratenkindern in vier europäischen Ländern.* Münster: Waxmann.

Schittenhelm, Karin. 2008. 'Statuspassagen junger Frauen zwischen Schule und Berufsausbildung im interkulturellen Vergleich'. In *Ausbildungsfähigkeit im Spannungsfeld zwischen Wissenschaft, Politik und Praxis*, edited by Elisabeth Schlemmer and Herbert Gerstberger, 55–68. Wiesbaden: VS Verlag für Sozialwissenschaften.

Schittenhelm, Karin and Mona Granato. 2004. '„Geschlecht" und „Ethnizität" als Kategorien der Jugendforschung? Junge Migrantinnen heute und die Differenzierung einer Lebensphase'. *Diskurs* (1): 59–66.

Solga, Heike. 2006. 'Meriokratie – die moderne Legitimation ungleicher Bildungschancen'. In *Soziale Ungleichheit. Klassische Texte zur*

Sozialstrukturanalyse, edited by Heike Solga, Justin Powell and Peter A. Berger, 63–72. Frankfurt am Main: Campus Verlag.

———. 2011. 'Bildungsarmut und Ausbildungslosigkeit in der Bildungs- und Wissensgesellschaft'. In *Lehrbuch der Bildungssoziologie*, edited by Rolf Becker, 411–48. Wiesbaden: VS Verlag für Sozialwissenschaften.

Traue, Boris. 2010. 'Kompetente Subjekte: Kompetenz als Bildungs- und Regierungsdispositiv im Postfordismus'. In *Soziologie der Kompetenz*, edited by Thomas Kurtz and Michaela Pfadenhauer, 49–67. Wiesbaden: VS Verlag für Sozialwissenschaften.

Chapter 6

Loving, Sharing and Engaging: Sub-Saharan Immigrants in a Pentecostal Church

Stephan Simon

Introduction

Practices, fluid encounters and durable engagements build the infrastructure in which actors develop resources. Durable engagements, or the 'knitting' of social infrastructure, require settings that provide a regular focus for contact. Such durable engagements within institutions are informed by moral orientations of what to expect from others.

Social capital literature has focused on how, through membership of social networks, resources can be accessed (Portes 1998). Church gatherings cannot be mapped as graphics of personal ties. As far as they produce social capital, it is much more through their 'doing community' that this is achieved. Community is done in practices and encounters and engagements of agents.[1] Encounters create shared symbols and norms and the collective maintenance of these encounters, turning them into engagements, reproduces a symbolic and normative order (Collins 1988, 189). We speak of engagements and not of ties, because the agents involved do not have to connect on a personal level. This chapter shows, first, how women in a Pentecostal church created resources through supporting other women and through contributing to the joint goal of being united and maintaining the 'love' among each other. Secondly, it demonstrates how through sharing, members transformed fluid encounters into durable engagements with new opportunities. Third, the chapter discusses how agents accumulate symbolic capital through community practices as a safeguard for future rewards.

As a community, the church is more than an aggregate of personal ties. Importantly, and different from what our common sense notion of institution suggests, this community is not a fixed phenomenon, but transitory and emerging through the interactions of agents (see Brint 2001, 7; Collins 1988, Chapter 6; 2004, 47–50; Goffman 2005). Through 'interaction rituals', a community as an assemblage of durable engagements emerges. Such interaction rituals consist of assembled agents, a mutual focus of attention, a shared mood and a barrier to outsiders (Collins 2004, 48). A common focus of attention – usually a symbol representing the group or an activity – and a common mood (for example joy or

1 For an overview of community concepts see Brint 2001.

sorrow) reinforce each other. If encounters build up to a mutual focus and to mutual emotions, then the participants experience group solidarity, emotional energy (for example confidence and enthusiasm) and experience the group symbols (ibid., 49). This process can be circular: rituals 'reassemble[s] the social structure' and the social structure 'loops back' into the interaction rituals (Collins 1988, 189). We will use this lens to have a closer look at the practices of women in the church.

Figure 6.1 Church window displaying a biblical scene
Source: Author, 2014

The Berlin African Pentecostal church where the research was conducted was founded in 2012. Shortly after the congregation was formed, the church members collectively raised a credit to purchase a former Catholic Church building. Since then, the building and the adjacent parish house serve as a religious centre and home for about 300 church members, consisting primarily of Sub-Saharan immigrants.

The church members vary greatly in nationality, education, profession and income. The majority of the church members consist of first generation Sub-Saharan immigrants and their families. Among them are cleaners, nurses, teachers, housewives, engineers, home health carers, industrial washers and embassy employees. Many of the church members have lived in Berlin between 10 and 15 years and their centre of life is in Berlin.

Making Encounters into Durable Engagements

Resources produced in the church sprang from active efforts of the church members to create a community and to make and maintain durable engagements out of fluid encounters. Such efforts, as we will see in this section, came with sets of expectations toward social behaviour, and differences over such expectations lead to subtle forms of exclusion.

Sharing

The church leaders and the pastor stimulated the church members to give to others and share what they have. Jesus Christ served as a role model, who gave to people although he did not have much himself. Jenny, in her forties and born in Ghana, now living with her German husband in Berlin and working as a geriatric nurse in the mobile elderly care, is a committed and old church member. She teaches the bible to other congregants, participates in the Ministry's Home cell in her neighbourhood and comes very regularly to the Sunday Mass to sing in the choir and listen to the sermon. In our conversation, she stressed: 'We share, because Jesus shares his love with us. He even gave himself all out'. Sharing can include praying for and with others, and giving materially: clothes, household items or money.

Susie was in her late 20s. Born in Kenya, she came to Germany about three years ago as an au-pair. During a subsequent voluntary year of social service in Berlin, she had a love affair with someone she met at a party. When Susie found out that she was pregnant, she found herself in a very precarious situation: the man whom she had met was unsure about whether he wanted to be with her. The pregnancy forced her to stop her voluntary work, which made her lose her residence permit and her medical insurance. Susie managed to solve these problems by hiring a lawyer, whom a fellow church member had recommended to her. She now lived alone with her newborn son in an apartment and received welfare. Susie met other women at the weekly evening prayer services and the women's prayer service. Having children, or being of the same age, provided a basis for small talk in fluid encounters. In such conversations, Susie learnt about the women's needs. Although she was not very close to them, she gave something, when they needed it:

> Not all of them are so close to me, but you just feel that you should give something. Because you see like there is this girl. She tells me, my daughter wants something, my daughter doesn't have enough clothes, the clothes she is having are getting small all the time. The situation that if somebody talks to you, you just know it's okay to give.

Through sharing with other mothers whom she met at the church, Susie's fluid encounters turned into durable engagements. Gouldner (1960, 171) calls this a starting mechanism:

> When internalized in both parties, the norm *obliges* the one who has first received a benefit to repay it at some time; it thus provides some realistic grounds for confidence, in the one who first parts with his valuables, that he will be repaid. Gifts establish a relationship of reciprocity.

Vanessa, a single woman in her 30s, who migrated to Berlin from Ghana to continue her business as a seller of jewellery and other care products and clothes accessories, maintained that Africans in general would always call the person who had given them something the next day to say thank you. Susie not only gave, but also received from other women in the church. This helped her to get by: 'It helps, for example when somebody gives you tights or a pullover in the winter. Or if somebody gives you something nice that you need at that moment'.

The belief that God will reward in the future that Susie gave something to others, brought her to share with other church members although she had few resources herself. This contrasts the finding that agents in precarious situations do not accept gifts because of fear of not being able to pay it back (Blokland and Noordhoff 2008, 113–15). In contrast to the participants in the study of Blokland and Nordhoff, these women had the church as a focus that eased the formation of a knitted set of engagements rather than a set of unrelated dyads. Returns hence did not have to be given by the receiving woman herself. She may not have been able to reciprocate, but someone else may. Accordingly, for Susie, giving to others was not merely a profane, but a sacred act:

> It's just love, showing love and us Christians we know that if you give, God will also give you, it does not mean that if you give money, God sometimes will not give you the money (*laughs*). Maybe you are looking for work, God will give you work, maybe you are looking for a child God will give you a child. It's also to show love to one another.

In brief, giving to others established a reciprocity-web of affiliations based on debt and credit, a web in which 'people should help those who have helped them, … and people should not injure those who have helped them' (Gouldner 1960, 171). Church members 'paid back' a present via calling, to thank, by telling others about it or by taking their own turn in giving. Rachel felt that when a woman gave a present to another woman, it 'brings them close together' and created love between them: 'Because of her giving to this woman, this woman loves this woman again. So they, I see them at church greeting each other "hello, how are you doing?", whereas before they did not used to do that'.

Engagement

Rachel had studied pedagogics and worked as a teacher in an international school, so she had a stable income. She lived together with her German husband and her three children. Rachel was the leader of the Women Ministry. Rachel was active in various ways in the church: she was always present at the weekly prayer service, she gave presents to many church members, and was known to be always friendly. She visited all the families in which a new child was born and was there when somebody needed spiritual counselling. She greeted newcomers, organized the groups within the women's ministry and was said to treat all women equally; and she brought jobs into the community. She felt confident in what she was doing and she was doing it with 'passion and love'. Rachel explained why the pastor and his wife had chosen her to become the women's leader:

> The pastor and his wife decided for me to be the leader for the women because of the love I have for the ministry, I love working with women and I have been in the women ministry for a long time even in Africa and I just love it. … Once you get the important thing is to love them, to love each other in truth, not lying.

Rachel saw herself as someone who loved the women in the church and wholeheartedly cared about their wellbeing: 'I pray for the women, I visit them, and I help them. I support women materially when I can or I organize somebody who helps them materially'. When a woman was sick, depressed or giving birth, she felt obliged to visit her and organized other women who accompanied her and bring gifts and money. In this way, Rachel tried to make the other person feel as comfortable as possible and to give her courage through praying together and counselling. Rachel's attempt to treat each church member equally meant that she avoided making close friends in the church. This would undermine her effort to be equally accessible for all women: 'I cannot say I have a best friend in the church. I try to avoid having that, because if people notice that I am very close to a person, some people start feeling rejected'. Rachel can be seen as what Collins calls 'the sociometric star', or 'the person who is always most intensely involved in the ritual interaction' (2004, 116). Through her practices, Rachel accumulated symbolic capital. She felt that her investments in the engagements with others paid off, 'so it's like the love that I have given is coming out back to me in double':

> A fresh example is when my son was born, I got so much (*laughs*). A lot of people came here to visit me and bring presents. And there are certain things I never bought for him, but they are just presents from the people that I have, you know, so, that alone is enough. … and I am still receiving presents. Like every Sunday there is a present for him.

For Rachel, the love she received confirmed the value of her work in the church and she also felt that receiving all that love was a sign from God, 'thank God for that. Yes, that is what it is'. Rachel's way of giving to the community brought her a social status that then led to more resources.

Figure 6.2 Offering scene during a service
Source: author, 2014

Markus, a German man in his early 40s, who had no migration history, has participated in church activities for several years. He said that church members appreciated the work and presence of certain church members very much, especially when they were viewed as devout and gentle. Markus was overwhelmed when he saw how many people were present at a church member's wedding:

> Interviewer: And you ask yourself how a person can have so many friends? Are these people who have only incidental contact with him?
> Markus: They just appreciate him and then they come. … In general, when someone is pious or believing, then the others in the church will notice that. The person will be more appreciated. Then more people will come at such occasions.

Devoutness was symbolic capital. Samantha, a woman in her 30s, loved her job as kindergarten teacher. Next to her work there, she engaged in evangelizing work for the church and took care of the newcomers in the church, whom she accompanied in their process of getting to know 'the word of God' better. Her work at the kindergarten and at the church were her main activities. She did not undertake much else. She was often surprised by unexpected gifts from church members, who she barely knew. 'One guy came and gave me 50 Euros, another guy bought me some stuff for my house. Some woman bought me some shopping over Christmas'. Interactional rituals hence led to symbolic capital, which often materialized in gifts.

Exclusions

Don't Get what they Need

Markus got introduced to the church through his wife who was born in Ghana. They have a two-year-old son. Markus studied computer informatics at university. As one of the few native Germans, one of his responsibilities was to synchronously translate the Sunday sermons of the pastor from English to German. Markus felt that the resources available in the church did not match his needs. Four years ago he suddenly lost his job at a software company, a time he described as 'rocky'. At the time, it was announced after the Sunday ceremony that a church member looked for workers for cleaning canteen kitchens in various hotels in Berlin: 'A deacon in the church is the head of a cleaning division for the canteen in a hotel. From time to time he needs people and so he hired me. And I did real African work. With that I mean the work that the guest workers do'. Markus distanced himself from the work that he got by describing it as 'African work' or 'work that the guest workers do'. It did not 'fit' to his previous status as a computer programmer with a university degree. He worked in the hotel for a very short time, and was happy when he was fired for 'inefficient' work. In Germany, people whose income is supplemented by welfare while working cannot quit their jobs without being sanctioned (the withdrawal of welfare payments for three months). As he was fired, this sanction did not apply to him. He therefore could attend training from the employment agency on new technologies in informatics. This training led to a stable job as a computer programmer for an Internet company. The church had not been able to help him further: '[The church members] definitively give practical help. But they only can give practical help, as far as I experienced, on the level on which they are, that is: guest worker. Here, well, you don't get far'.

Emilia had a similar story to tell. She did not find that the resources matched her aspirations, status and formal education. Emilia was a pastor's daughter. She was born in Germany and went to secondary school in Berlin. She recently finished her Master's degree in political economics. Emilia felt pressured by the church members to act according to the status of a pastor's daughter and to be a role model for 'Africans' in Germany: to be a good Christian, to get a prestigious job and to marry a pious and worthy member of the church. Emilia wanted to get ahead and to follow her father's middle class footsteps, who, before he became a pastor, graduated in political economics as well. But she feared that the social relations and social control ties within the church and its limited resources would prevent her from reaching that goal. She did not think that a man from the Berlin church community could meet her expectations:

> All the black men here for example, they want to become football stars or start a music career. I have seen that too often. There are also some that studied, but most of them speak French. In the long run that is not my thing. Also, the African

> men in the church are so much wanting to get married and so hyper-Christian. Praying for four hours and all those things.

Emilia hoped for a future husband who was educated and spoke English. She was irritated by the primary focus of many church members on religious activities and – in her view – overemphasis on their religiosity and of their engagement in church activities. Emilia believed that her future of a middle class life could be easier realized in Ghana, where she lived with her family for one year when she was sixteen. Later, she did an internship there, and had a boyfriend. In Ghana, she saw how friends and acquaintances established a livelihood and a family, and a decent standard of living. Moreover, she would be 'among one's kind'.

For Markus and Emilia, durable engagements to the church members felt as constraining. The available resources did not correspond with their needs and understanding of their social status. Both felt that the engagements could overwhelm and possibly impede realizing their capabilities elsewhere, not within an exclusive and demanding Afro-German community. Whereas they were not actively excluded, for them the 'love' and sharing did not create an experience of a positively inclusive community but rather one that kept them down and blocked new possibilities.

Loving Each Other and Growing Together

Rachel described the women of the church as very diverse, both in social status and emotionally or spiritually. Her primary goal as leader of the women ministry was to unite the women: 'it's through prayer and loving each other that is what brings the unity among the women'. Such practices or 'ritual interactions' (Collins 2004, 49) created a feeling of membership and reproduced group symbols. Practicing love and praying together created solidarity among the women. Shared prayers made them feel part of the women ministry.

Vivien was the previous leader of the Church's women ministry, and our main contact person in the beginning of our field visits. This energetic woman in her 30s lived with her husband, a deacon in the same congregation, and their two children in a central district of Berlin. She was thinking about beginning an apprenticeship as an educator, but struggled still with the required level of German. The church was her second home, as she spent most of her time there. In our conversation she agreed with Rachel: 'women we are one, united we stand … If we don't come together and be united, we cannot stand'.

Each year, the women organized the 'love feast' together. One day long, they came together to celebrate the love of God and the love among all women and the church members in general. Everyone was supposed to bring something to share for the buffet, and besides prayers, the women shared their wisdom about how to care for their husbands, their children and themselves. During these meetings, the men gathered separately to embellish and clean the church together.

While the 'love feast' was clearly thought to be an occasion to unite the women, it was also an event that conveyed social expectations. Vivien recalled a conversation during the love feast:

> Somebody was saying "oh, when I gave birth, nobody came there to visit me". ... So it's like this sister will say this. She has been in the church for maybe, let me see, ... four years, five years. Since she came, she never visited anyone, she never joined anything that we do, she always gives birth, she never goes to anybody's place. So, if you don't go to anybody's place, who do you expect to also come to your place?

As Vivien stated, this 'sister' felt neglected by the other women in the ministry. When she gave birth to her son, nobody, except the women leaders – who are obliged to visit all women when they give birth – visited her. She did not receive the resources that other women shared in the ministry: emotional support, care, love and prayer, as well as presents for the newborn. As Susie explained: 'with us Africans you cannot go to see a woman in the hospital or you cannot go to somebody's home without bringing something'. Being visited meant to get presents, be it money, pampers and food or clothes for the newborn. For some women in the church, besides being included and feeling accepted by other women, the community was materially important, especially for those who received welfare. Vivien applied this moral orientation to the woman who had not shown 'love' to others. She had not attended their activities regularly, not shown interest in their matters and not visited other women herself. Not respecting the moral orientation of loving each other, the woman was ignored and met with irritation by those who were emotionally deeply involved in the church, like Vivien. Indeed, as Collins noted, 'persons pumped up with feelings of group solidarity treat symbols with respect and defend them against the disrespect of outsiders, and even more, of renegade insiders' (2004, 49). Vivien connected the behaviour of the woman with the length of time that she had been a church member. For how long she had been a member, the woman did not 'grow'. Growing included the idea that with the years of church membership, the church members got to know the ministry better and increased their activities. As Rachel explained, 'the more years you grow in the church at least you try to interact with one or two people, three, four, five. Every year you are increasing on the number of interaction, because you are growing old. And you are getting to know the ministry more and more'.

Active church members could lose confidence that their efforts to invest in the community by giving love were worth their effort, Rachel said: 'They don't want to [continue to visit the person], because they feel like what they are investing they are not getting back'. Caring for others stood for caring for the community in general. Rachel believed that not caring for one another was a fundamental breach of a Christian moral orientation:

> God has commanded us to love each other and take care of each other. We are one another's keepers. That is the principle we have. And if I take care of my brother, the Bible says, when you do good to somebody, you are doing it to me. Because the Bible says we are created in God's image. And when I do a good thing to you, I am doing it to God.

In short, accessing resources within the women's ministry required the capability to focus on the major common group moral orientations and practices, the former of which include *love*, *growing* and *the love of God* – and to invest in upholding them. Certain institutions within the church served as foci in which group members practiced their love. These included *prayer*, *asking after each other's wellbeing* and *showing interest* in others' lives, *visiting* at certain occasions (birth, sickness), *gift giving* and *active participation* in activities of the women ministry.

Can't Give what is Expected

Women who were seen to deviate from the expectations within the community experienced a different and more straightforward set of practices of exclusions. They were said to not be 'loving' and 'growing'. Their situation shows that durable engagements demanded of agents that they conformed to certain norms and behaviours.

Christine was a 39-year-old mother of three children, aged two to seven years. She was born in Nigeria and has been a church member for five years. Christine had worked at the check-in desk of an airport, but she faced racism there and did not feel accepted by her colleagues. She got fired very quickly. Since she became a mother she had received welfare, but this was barely enough to go places with her children and husband. Christine felt dependent on state institutions. The church offered some activities that she was comfortable using: to worship and to sing in the choir. But she tried to stay independent of others. She could ask others for help with her children, but she was reluctant to do so. Others had their own problems, she said. She wanted to maintain control over her life, an independence already challenged by her state dependency. Blokland and Noordhoff call this a need for 'gendered independence' (2008, 113–15), in which women try to stay independent in order to keep control over their situation of dependence. She could, but would not ask church members for help:

> Yes, maybe in the church, but I don't know. The people that come to church have their own problems. For me, I don't burden people with my problems, no.

The ties in the church were there. Given the importance of showing 'love', she could easily ask church members for help looking after her children or to help her in other areas. But Christine refused to get indebted to other church members, afraid to not be able to pay it back. Different from Susie, who through her activities was strongly integrated in the community and could see reciprocity in a more general, not dyadic way, Christine saw gifts as creating debts that made her dependent on other individuals.

Andrew, 50 years of age, has lived in Germany for 25 years. Andrew was born in Nigeria. He was married and had two sons, one and two years old. Andrew's story is a story of struggles, conflicts with colleagues and racism. While working in a hotel where he was responsible for the work shift, his colleagues would not listen to him or accept his orders, and that he perceived as racist: 'Whites, you know. So, and you can see that in the job I used to be alone. They don't like to communicate with me. If I give orders they don't take my orders. They neglect my orders. They want to give me orders. Even if they are not trained'. Andrew's experiences with racism made him strive for independence. He withdrew himself from most collective activities in the church, except the Sunday ceremony. Andrew asked certain people in the church for help when he needed it directly, but avoided engaging in more than fluid encounters:

> I greet everybody "hi, hi, hi". We laugh together .... When the church finishes I enter my car and go. ... I go to church, because I love things about God and for me that church is where I go and ask for help from God. ... I am not somebody who goes permanent in the church because they say church is social, help is coming from [the church]. No. I like to do things in my own way and with my power.

Vanessa was a 45-year-old woman who described herself as someone who has always gone her own way and tried to be independent of welfare payments: 'My whole life I did not want to want the state to help me paying my apartment and my food'. Interviewer: 'You refused?' Vanessa: 'I fought myself, my whole life long'. Like Andrew, she wanted no support from the church either. Vanessa was self-employed. She sold cosmetic products to shops. She also sewed fancy hats that she sold to other people in the church. She was known in the church for her cheerfulness and chattiness. She liked especially to play and talk with the children in the church. Although she enjoyed being in the community, she sometimes seemed annoyed by the expectations. Once, Vanessa did not attend the Sunday ceremony, because she was tired from having been at a party the night before. In the evening, several church members called her, among them the pastor's wife, several deacons and people from the choir, where she sang. As she was supposed to have sung with the choir that day, there was commotion in the choir as they wondered where she was. She felt that the expectations made her justify herself. But Vanessa did not understand the commotion of the fellow church members. She stressed that she 'was unable to find any peace of mind' and 'could not hide'. Vanessa, too, then, saw turning to the church for support as interfering with her independence.

Conclusion

This chapter has shown how fluid encounters and durable engagements produce community, which does not exist before agents practice it (Jenkins 1996, 106). Encounters turn into engagements with the help of norms and symbols that refer to a moral orientation, which agents maintain through interaction rituals (Collins 2004, 48–9). Sharing is the main practice through which this transformation of social ties happens. To profit from the resources within the community that do emerge, agents must enter and maintain these engagements. The church provided a focus where they could be institutionalized.

We have seen that for women to get access to resources that derive from practices (like visiting when a woman gives birth) within the women ministry requires efforts to 'love', 'grow' and mutually care. Such practices excluded women who, in the eyes of others, did not get involved enough in the ministry. Community members who fully gave themselves to the church were able to access symbolic and material resources.

Church members faced difficulties to uphold durable engagements in two ways. Members like Markus and Emilia did not find those resources in the church that they needed, given their social status and aspirations. After Markus got a job in a hotel via a church member, he concluded that the type of information, for example on jobs, which one could get in the church helped to get along, but not to get ahead. Emilia, daughter of one of the church leaders, felt pressured by the church members to marry a church member, but could not find a man who met her expectations of good education and moderate religiosity within the church. Social capital literature generally argues (especially Putnam 2000), that institutions are important for the development of weak ties, that provide access to information. However, information alone (as for example on jobs) is not enough for realizing capabilities. The church hence provides resources, but a mismatch between available and needed information excludes certain members.

Exclusion also occurred when church members could not comply with the expected behaviour of durable church engagements. Christine, Vanessa and Andrew all had economically precarious positions. They tried to keep their independence while being in a situation of being dependent on welfare or having unstable working conditions. This makes durable engagements difficult. Christine did not ask other church members for support, because – as accepting implied one's readiness to give in the future – she avoided debt. Vanessa did things her own way all her life and refused to comply with expectations – as weekly church visits – and was rather without support than submitting to this social pressure.

This chapter then has shown how Sub-Saharan immigrants in marginalized social positions in the city have found their own ways of doing community and creating resources through the church, an institution that enhances the possibility to refer to moral orientations to create cohesion and mutual support. Yet such practices of community, with all their connotations of 'love' and solidarity, should not be romanticized: as in any institutions, here, too, expectations of behaviour and status hierarchies help hoarding opportunities within the community. Moreover, the structural marginalized position of the community members implied that the church provided access to resources, but not to get substantially ahead – they merely helped to subsist.

References

Blokland, Talja V. and Floris Noordhoff. 2008. 'The Weakness of Weak Ties: Social Capital to Get Ahead Among the Urban Poor in Rotterdam and Amsterdam'. In *Networked Urbanism: Social Capital in the City*, edited by Talja V. Blokland and Michael Savage, 105–25. Aldershot, England; Burlington, VT: Ashgate.

Brint, Steven. 2001. 'Gemeinschaft Revisited: A Critique and Reconstruction of the Community Concept'. *Sociological Theory* 19 (1): 1–23.

Collins, Randall. 1988. *Theoretical Sociology.* San Diego: Harcourt Brace Jovanovich.

———. 2004. *Interaction Ritual Chains.* Princeton Studies in Cultural Sociology. Princeton, NJ: Princeton University Press.

Goffman, Erving. 2005. *Interaction Ritual: Essays in Face-to-Face Behavior.* New Brunswick, NJ: Aldine Transaction.

Gouldner, Alwin W. 1960. 'The Norm of Reciprocity: A Preliminary Statement'. *American Sociological Review* 25 (2): 161–78.

Jenkins, Richard. 1996. *Social Identity*. London: Routledge.

Portes, Alejandro. 1998. 'Social Capital: Its Origins and Applications in Modern Sociology'. *Annual Review of Sociology* 24 (1): 1–24.

Putnam, Robert D. 2000. *Bowling Alone. The Collapse and Revival of American Community*. New York: Simon & Schuster.

Chapter 7
Social Ties and the Moral Orientation of Sharing: Information-Giving among Sub-Saharan Immigrants in Berlin

Rebecca Arbter

Introduction

For making a city like Berlin work for oneself, formal employment eases everything, or is maybe even essential, not in the least for immigrants who need to make a living in a city that is new to them (Bender and Seifert 2000; OECD 2007; Constant and Zimmermann 2009). Studies show that using networks of durable engagements for job searching is more effective than the use of state agencies (Granovetter 1974; Wegener 1991; Montgomery 1992; Bian 1997). The formal ways of job search through state agencies are little effective especially for immigrants due to, among other factors, discrimination in institutions and the labour market (see for example Wilp 2007; Hormel and Scherr 2010). The literature differentiates little between various groups of job seekers and seems to assume that for every ethnic group, immigrants or not, the labour market functions the same way and the same strategies will lead to success. Networks that are of relevance to White Americans, as they found jobs through these ties, are assumed to be effective, if not necessary, for others as well. The specificity of social life, sociability and moral orientations of specific groups are not taken into consideration.

What is more, the difference between strong and weak ties, in Granovetter's (1974) work a difference in the intensity of a tie, is conceptually mixed with bonds and bridges, where bonds are expected to form between members of the same ethnic groups and bridges to cross boundaries of ethnicity and sometimes class (Putnam 2000). It is argued that the strength of weak ties matters most for finding jobs and that hence members of one ethnic group depend on ties to other groups of a higher social status to be successful in finding a job. This argument contains various untested assumptions. If the city in the making, as Simone (2010) has argued, is a people's infrastructure where sociability takes many forms, it may well be that this modern, 'Global North' understanding of social ties is culturally hegemonic in the literature and conveys a Eurocentric way of thinking about sociability. This chapter explores the potential of this criticism by analysing the ties used by Sub-Saharan immigrants in Berlin to search and find jobs. This research did not include a full network analysis but did allow for the analyses of ties as the interviewees themselves named and classified them (see Blokland and Van Eijk 2007 and Blokland and Noordhoff 2008 for similar approaches). We conducted 40 qualitative interviews with Sub-Saharan immigrants[1] using a semi-structured questionnaire. The interviewees were found by visiting places like Afro-shops, cultural associations and two Pentecostal churches. Our research started from the assumption that Sub-Saharan immigrants as people of colour in Berlin are particularly affected by discrimination and exclusion from resources and places. This marginalization limits the capabilities of Sub-Saharan immigrants to get access to jobs, state support or apartments. As we were interested in people as infrastructure, we hence thought that Sub-Saharan immigrants would enable us to see some of the workings of making the city in a sharper way than with other groups: given their marginalization, there must exist alternative ways to get access to resources encapsulated in places and people. How, then, does one realize capabilities when not through mainstream channels? What role do social ties as alternative ways to access resources play?

We discuss in the following how fluid encounters became resources for interview partners in their search for jobs or other forms of support and focus particularly on the moral orientations that a possible willingness to share information (or not) with others could be linked to. First, we introduce the main theories on social capital and social ties and show how the Sub-Saharan immigrants in Berlin use ties in job searching. Second, we briefly discuss theories on exchange and gift-giving to address the question of the moral orientation of sharing information. It is not the aim of this chapter to generalize empirically on relations of Sub-Saharan immigrants or the nature of ties in general.

This chapter's main aim is to critically look at theories of ties, reflect on their Eurocentric nature, and discuss some of the fluid encounters that help people to achieve basic needs, encounters that 'Global North' urban studies have not paid much attention to so far. The plea for comparative urbanism and the comparative gesture includes the argument that comparative studies are not just a matter of comparing across regions and countries, but also of changing conceptual lenses. This chapter alters the dominant perspective by looking at a 'Global North' city like Berlin through the lens of urbanism of 'Global South' cities, where deals are made and engagements develop and dissolve in much more fluid and flexible ways than (statistical variable-led!) research in the 'Global North' has included in its analyses. Our purpose is not to point to 'cultural and ethnic differences', as if the 'Global South' simply comes to the 'North' through immigration. Rather, our argument is that the practices that we see most strongly and sharply among Sub-Saharan immigrants may also provide a conceptual lens refining our understandings of the role of fluid encounters for capabilities of all other urban residents. It is hence not that we claim that Sub-Saharan immigrants build relationships differently and are

1 Eighteen interviewees from Ghana, seven from Nigeria, five from Cameroon and one each from Togo, Tanzania, Ethiopia, Benin and Zambia.

'other'. Instead studying their ties opens up the opportunity to think about fluid encounters as resourceful in ways that the literature so far has not done.

Social Capital Theories and the Use of Social Ties among Sub-Saharan Immigrants in Berlin

Social Capital Theories and the Strength of Ties

Pierre Bourdieu's 'cultural anthropology of social reproduction' (Field 2003, 13) explains how social mobility works and social inequality is reproduced. Bourdieu developed a theory of different forms of capital (economic, cultural, social and symbolic capital) that can be transformed into one another (Bourdieu 1992). The amount of different forms of capital together produces and reproduces an interrelated class-specific habitus, defined as values and structures of thinking and behaviour that mark and symbolize social positions. Some people are able to climb in their social position through the use of capital and habitus while others are trapped within their milieu and lack the 'right' capital and habitus to be upwardly mobile (Bourdieu 1987, 277 ff.). Bourdieu defined social capital as 'the sum of resources, actual or virtual, that accrue to an individual or group by virtue of possessing a durable network of more or less institutionalized relationships of mutual acquaintance and recognition' (Bourdieu and Wacquant, 1992, 119).

James Coleman analyses social relations from a rather economic perspective, using the concept of human capital of which social capital is part (Coleman 1988, 95; Field 2003, 20 ff.; Van Eijk 2010, 57). He understands social relations as reciprocal and cooperative actions of exchange, aimed at maximizing individual profit. Social capital is defined by its function within different social entities that are characterized by common social structures and by its productivity (Coleman 1988, 96; Field 2003, 24). Moreover, Coleman states that 'most forms of social capital are created or destroyed as by-products of other activities': social capital is unconsciously produced in interactions (Coleman 1988, 118).

Coleman and Bourdieu represent only two perspectives on social capital on which there is a large debate (see Field 2003 for an overview). Their approaches stress social networks that might give access to different resources. Instead of measuring the amount of contacts of a person and what is exchanged with them, we focus on the processes and contexts in which social contacts develop and become resources to people. By highlighting the process of sociability itself rather than – as Bourdieu and Coleman do – the use and profit of social networks, we can learn how people create capabilities through social ties.

Mark Granovetter discusses how social capital works through differentiating between 'strong and weak ties' (Granovetter 1973, 1361). Weak ties have strength because they are far reaching and therefore give access to information that is not yet known through strong, namely family and kin, ties. Weak ties therefore provide people with more valuable social capital (ibid., 1361–2). Granovetter is defining a third kind of tie that he does not further elaborate. An absent tie is defined as 'the lack of any relationship and ties without substantial significance, such as "nodding" relationship between people living on the same street' (ibid., 1361). Those ties exist when there is either no relation between people at all or the relation is negligible and therefore, at least in theory, not important. Fischer (1982) describes such encounters as based on 'public familiarity' (60–62). They do not become visible in social networks, because the method tools used in networks research do not pick them up.

In his study on job searching methods in Boston, Granovetter found that most people get a job through their weak ties (for studies with similar findings see Wegener 1991; Montgomery 1992; Bian 1997). This argument cannot be generalized as only people with middle class income and positions were included in his research (Granovetter 1974, 143–4). However, it has taken a strong influence in the study of unemployment, where diverse social networks are believed to be essential.

Weak and strong ties are understood rather differently by those working within the framework of Robert Putnam. He used the concept of social capital to analyse the development of overall American society (Putnam 1995; Field 2003, 29–40). He differentiated social capital along the lines of bridging and bonding capital, which since then have come to be connected to weak and strong ties and accordingly fulfil different functions. Bridging social capital leads to more resources while bonding capital consists mostly of strong ties to kin and close friends that support homogenous identities (Putnam 2000; Field 2003, 32; Van Eijk 2010, 64). Briggs called weak ties those that make it possible to 'get ahead' while strong ties give support to 'get by' in everyday life (Briggs, 1998 quoted in Van Eijk 2010, 59).

Social capital and its impact on resources and social mobility has become the conceptual framework for public policy that promotes mixed neighbourhoods to support the development of more interclass and interethnic weak ties. The lack of social capital was identified as the source and cause of inequality and poverty (6 1997b, 1–2; Blokland 2003, 1–6; Van Eijk 2010).

This policy approach expects the poor to profit from the mere presence of people with higher social status and assumes that ties that help the poor 'to get ahead' develop automatically from physical proximity and will result in capabilities of the poor to reach desirable outcomes. However, these ideas of weak and strong ties or bonding and bridging social capital have been criticized in empirical research (see Blokland and Noordhoff 2008 on ties of urban poor in the Netherlands and Van Eijk 2010). Blokland and Noordhoff (2008) found that poor people did have weak ties, but that they did not use them because of a need to keep their personal independence. Weak ties are not only potential capital in that they give access to resources and make someone more capable to deal with specific problems but carry a higher risk and stronger expectations of reciprocity than strong ties do (ibid., 112–15). Moreover, the mere presence of different kinds of people in one place does not automatically result in relations between them if there are no 'meeting opportunities' (Van Eijk 2010, 89) or 'focus activities' (see Feld 1981) to develop ties. Van Eijk argues that the neighbourhood is not necessarily the space where most individual meeting opportunities are located (2010; see also Blokland 2003). In urban contexts many other settings and places offer locations with opportunities to meet, such as churches or sport clubs outside the own living area. Moreover, Van Eijk criticizes the generalization of the 'strength-of-weak-ties' argument for its implications that every weak tie is a bridge, which certainly is not the case (2010, 65 ff.).

What matters is not the strength of a tie, but why and how some ties function as bridges and thereby extend peoples capabilities while others do not (Leonard and Onyx 2003; Blokland and Noordhoff 2008, 111). Moreover, Blokland and Noordhoff have questioned the idea that ties have a fixed form rather than being located on a dynamic 'continuum' ranging from strong, weak to absent or fluid (2008, 119; see also Fischer 1982). This chapter further reveals the limitations of understanding ties as durable contacts in one's network. First, we use the concept of durable engagements and fluid encounters to look more precisely at how 'weak and absent ties' are developed and used to generate support or access information. This discussion not only pleads for taking weak ties more seriously, but also suggests that the idea that strong ties give support to get by and weak ties information to get ahead is too crude. Second, we argue that a closer look at moral orientations enables us to understand why people create and use social ties.

The Use of Ties in the Job Searching Process

The interview partners used different kinds of social ties and formal roads to search for a job. For some, formal institutions helped. Melanie, a 40-year-old Ghanaian woman living in Berlin since the early 1990s, worked as a cleaning lady in a hospital. She found her job through the state employment agency. Before that, she had been unemployed for about two years. Rob, 41 years old, born in Nigeria, although he had no formal qualifications, was self-employed in Africa for more than seven years. He was now working for a big fast food chain since about half a year. He found his job through a temporary employment company. But it had been a 'friend' whom he knew from the church and has worked there before who told him about it.

Some interview partners found jobs directly through close friends or durable engagements. Such ties were presented as kin, although they were often not literally kin in terms of the family tree, pointing to a moral orientation of mutual solidarity associated with the ideal of the family. Edem, a 40-year-old kitchen aid from Nigeria, found his job through a friend who was his 'brother':

> Edem: It was from my brother because he knows more, better.
> Interviewer: So the jobcentre told your brother and your brother told you, that way?
> Edem: Yeah, because I don't understand.

> Interviewer: So you went with him together? So he came with you?
> Edem: He came with me.
> Interviewer: Tell me about when you came to Berlin. You had your brother here?
> Edem: In Berlin. It's my friend but he's like my brother. I talk to him like my brother.
> Interviewer: And you knew him from Nigeria?
> Edem: I know him from Nigeria, yeah.

Edem's 'brother' personally took him to the restaurant where he now worked. Like a brother, a cousin, referring to a relative at some distance, could help, as in Samantha's case. Samantha was a 26-year-old student from Ghana who worked on the side:

> Let's say, how I got the job was through my cousin, who worked their already and they were looking for more employees, because I was actually looking for a side job and she said: 'Oh, they take you anyway there when you want to work there'. And then I said, it doesn't matter to me where I work now to begin with. The main thing is I do have a job. Because I got *Bafög* [public student loan] at that time already but at some point you realize that at the middle of the month the money from the student loan is gone. And then I said sometime you go travelling as well, yes, and then you need a little bit more money and anyway, I only wanted to work in a 400–Euro based job.
> Interviewer: That means you heard of it from a friend?
> Samantha: So I heard of it from my cousin, I work there since two years already, since March.

Both, Samantha and Edem constructed kinship ties to explain their finding of a job. To call someone a brother or a cousin was a way to create ties that provided legitimacy to reliance on their support without further expectations: kinship ties stretch and relax but rarely break. The substantive rationality that guides them derived from moral orientations that does not assume tit-for-tat.

Other interviewees found jobs through loosely connected friends and friends of friends or people who cannot be classified in categories like 'friends' or 'kin'. Here, places that offer meeting opportunities as the workplace, church or school were essential. Demba (49) from Ghana, who finished his university degree in Germany, got his current job in road construction planning after doing an internship with the company. His professor had built the initial bridge. Demba has been working for the same company for almost 20 years. His professor at the university knew the director of the company at the time and this was how he got to know about the internship that later became his job.

Charly (47) from Ghana, who now was a German citizen, worked for the British Army in Berlin until they withdrew in 1994. He became an employee of an African embassy in Berlin. He learnt about the job through a person from the church that already worked for the embassy. In one of their casual conversations at an encounter at the church he heard that the embassy would move from Bonn to Berlin in the near future and would be in need of staff. Charly was about to become unemployed as the company he worked for did not want to renew his contract. He sent in an open solicitation and then was contacted by the Embassy when they moved to Berlin. The person at the church that gave him the tip was not described as a friend, let alone a 'brother', but as someone he just casually and incidentally met at the church.

Rather than trying to classify these ties in our examples as either strong or weak, we think it makes sense to look at the context and regularity of interactions, and the use of these ties for the creation of capabilities. Our empirical examples show how ties can be *experienced* as strong ties (like a non-kin brother) or weak ties in terms of commitment and solidarity, but that durability, not frequency, matters. If one is to see them as strong ties in Granovetter's terms, then they provide more than support to get by.

Moreover, the findings contrast with the argument that people with low or no education lack the 'right' ties to help find a job (Granovetter 1973; 1974, 136–7; 6 1997a, 10 ff.). About half of the interview partners were low- or non-skilled workers, and yet many of them found jobs through weak ties. These Sub-Saharan immigrants did have ties that connected them to people who shared information and provided help to find a job. They were weak, strong and absent.

Rather than classifying them as weak or strong or absent, it may make sense to locate them on a continuum from fluid encounters to durable engagements. The accounts of Demba and Charly provide different examples of situations in which fluid encounters led to sharing information with a 'stranger' who might or might not be familiar, but happened to use the same public or semi-public places.

Fluid encounters can take place in institutions such as the church. Although most people knew each other by sight from seeing each other in mass, this did not imply that they automatically built personal ties. Simple presence in the same place does not create a tie but creates familiarity and possibly, but not necessarily, meeting opportunities (Fischer 1982, 60–62). If one was to apply a network generating research tool, these fellow church people would not show up in the ego's network. Their potential support is hence by and large neglected in social capital research that so often is based on the collection of such network data. In Charly's case, we have seen a fluid encounter between two persons. But durable engagement within the institution, the church, may provide access to information without any personal tie developing, which underscores why we think the concepts of encounters and engagements rather than ties can be promising. On a fieldwork visit, after Mass a man came to the front to tell people that his employer was looking for workers. Charly reported:

> Interviewer: Going to the job centre is one thing, but getting a good job is another. Are there sometimes opportunities that many people do not have?

> Charly: Yes and that's why church is so important. If somebody will know about a job, family or wife or a friend, they will announce [it] in the church. For example, last week, there was a job opportunity, someone came and announced it in the church. ... Berlin is big and information also goes out, somebody knows somebody. So they are looking for people at this place that has got information. So suppose a person was looking for a job, somebody will bring him to the church. They are looking for people to do this kind of job. Maybe, if someone has an idea or a certificate and someone announces a job. That at times is also how people got work.

Although we do not know if the announcement resulted in a successful job application for anyone in the end, everyone had the chance to address the man afterwards, even when he or she had never talked to him before. So durable engagements without personal ties seemed to matter. Other examples suggest that practical support was also frequently offered or asked for in the church. Interview partners described that you didn't have to know the person to give any kind of support, as discussed extensively in Simon's chapter.

An opportunity for encounters that were much more fluid was meeting someone in a shop or simply in the street. Many Sub-Saharan immigrants in Berlin developed a practice of greeting each other when passing in the street, even when not knowing each other as people of colour are few, this is practically possible. This practice created another meeting opportunity and made it easy to start a conversation and share information with people that one didn't know but identified as imagined 'brothers' or 'sisters' as they were all *Africans*. Melanie, who worked as a cleaning lady and was active in the women's group in church, described such a situation:

> Interviewer: I once asked somebody ... 'how do you know this person?' He said, 'Oh, you know he is African I just saw him on the street and we started talking'. Does this happen to you also?
> Melanie: Yeah. Sometimes when we are going, you are going shopping, you can meet somebody. '*Hallo, Guten Tag* [Hello]'. And he says, '*Guten Tag*' [Hello]. Then he starts talking to you, you cannot go when somebody is talking to you. You have to stand [still] [so] that you hear what he is saying. So you will stand there and you hear what he is saying and give the answer and he again, you talk again, you give the answer and before you move. Yeah it can happen (*laughing*). If you don't know that person, you have to. Yeah it happens anytime, it happens to me, it happens to me anytime. Somebody greets you, you see, you cannot go like that. If I am going to a shop and I meet you I will say 'Hello'. Some people are very friendly. Some people are friendly. So when they say you 'Hello', you, too, say 'Hello'. Then they start talking. You cannot go when somebody is talking to you ....

These fluid encounters can result in information exchange as they are guided by a notion of respect for strangers and an orientation of sharing as Africans in Berlin, possibly linked to the marginalization so many of them face. Meeting strangers coincidentally in a shop might then turn into friendship, as in the case of Jonas, another Ghanaian man, 40, who was a musician and worked at an embassy as a driver:

> Interviewer: And those friends, where do you know them from?
> Jonas: Yeah, I knew some from the church, and some we just met in shop, in a shop.
> Interviewer: In a shop?
> Jonas: Yeah, like shopping mall.
> Interviewer: Accidentally?
> Jonas: Accidentally, yeah. And we started talking, 'Oh where do you come from? I come from Ghana', this one says, 'I come from Nigeria', this one say, 'I'm a German'. You know, so the other one was married to a German. He's from Ghana, but he's married to a German.
> Interviewer: How did that happen? You just saw each other and talked?
> Jonas: I saw one and then the other one also came … We were shopping in a shop. They sell dresses. So, I took one dress and he says, 'Oh that's a nice dress!' and I say, 'Oh thank you' and it just started.

Parties and festivities, as when a child was baptized, a funeral or the celebration of Independence Days of African countries, also provided sites for occasional meetings with strangers. Different from German practices and moral orientations of celebrating such family events and public holidays, the Sub-Saharan immigrants in Berlin celebrated these as community events, with many participants, often not known to each other. Germans, in line with the privatization of community (Blokland 2003, Chapter 5), generally limit invitations of family events or celebrations of public holidays to their nuclear or extended family, strictly defined by family trees, and those whom they consider friends. The Sub-Saharan parties were announced and sometimes arranged by embassies, churches or ethnic associations. At baptism ceremonies or funerals, up to several hundred people could be attending who did not have to know the child who got baptized or the person who died personally, as Melanie described in the following field note:

> I asked Melanie how she got to know her friend Dina. Melanie explained that she knew this friend from a party where the birth of a child was celebrated. This was many years ago. They knew each other for many years now, and knew each other from Ghana. They met at a party years ago and then met again. Since then they have become close friends. Being asked how many people came to such parties, Melanie estimated about 500 or more visitors. I expressed my doubts about the fact that they could all know each other. If someone knew someone who knew the women, then he was invited – among them kin and friends and

> acquaintances, Melanie explained. I commented that in Germany such festivities were rather small and she replied that many people were invited at these kinds of parties. They would send invitation cards and the festivities would take place in big halls.

The festivities, substantially rationally oriented on religious ceremonies or the celebration of ethnicity, provide the opportunity to meet people and make contacts with people that one didn't know before. Given their ceremonial nature, it was easy for those coming from a similar ethnic background to join in the rituals, making participation easy and much easier than for example at a neighbourhood committee meeting or a PTA meeting at school, where the formal rules of behaviour are largely implicit and hard to get to know. Moreover, the shared ethnic background can be used as an assumption of mutual identification with the linked moral orientation of community, solidarity and sharing. These festivities hence provided settings where sharing or receiving information in fluid encounters could, coincidentally and unplanned, happen. Although there was no explicit job recruitment after a festivity mentioned, these convivial gatherings offered a dense room of meeting opportunities to make new contacts and share information on any issue. Absent ties thus can be turned into resources and hence, other than the mainstream 'Global North' literature on social capital suggests, offer social capital that might or might not be turned into profit, help or support that enhances a person's capability. These practices contrast with theories on social ties understood as strong or weak durable engagements and bridging and bonding capital in the way that Granovetter and Putnam define them. Whereas a clear classification of types of ties as either weak or strong may serve variable-driven statistical research, we see that everyday practices mould, change, enhance and shrink ties constantly. One may argue that the use of absent ties is a very specific phenomenon that is only found in the context of urban areas like Berlin. Simone, however, has abundantly shown that such fluid encounters play an important role in making opportunities in cities in the 'Global South' (cf. 2004; 2006; 2010). Work of McFarlane and Waibel (2012) on markets, second-hand car dealers and clothing traders in African cities confirm Simone's thesis. While density is a necessary precondition for the development of the subcultural (Fischer 1975) events that present meeting opportunities described here, and hence such fluid encounters may be more likely to occur in urban areas than elsewhere, the fact that they have not been studied extensively by social scientists interested in social capital may be the consequence of a Eurocentric lens more than that it is the result of something very peculiar going on in Berlin. 'Global North' urbanites may have foci such as childcare centres (Small 2009), school yards, doctors waiting rooms, churches, sport clubs and the like where such information transmission as a by-product of fluid encounters and meeting opportunities takes place (Soenen 2008 for example shows how stores for baby gear provide sources of information through the fluid encounters of pregnant women). The case of our Sub-Saharan interview partners points to the need to rethink the importance of absent ties as fluid encounters also in other urban contexts than 'Global South' cities. That information on jobs and other issues was shared among people who did not know each other before, and that fluid encounters possibly expanded their capabilities, shows that the differentiation of ties in only strong and weak ties, with a focus only on durable engagements, is not appropriate for analysing social capital – we found a moral orientation that differs from conventional exchange of information and support with social ties.

The Moral Orientation of Sharing: Reciprocity or Beneficence?

We have seen that fluid encounters can create opportunities to realize social capital and allow people – particularly those who are marginalized – to realize their capabilities to cope with everyday life. Moral orientations facilitate the sharing of information or support within fluid encounters. The question why people share is covered by theories of gift-exchange. After a brief summary of the main theories, we will track the moral orientations that the interview partners referred to when sharing information or getting access to information from others.

Gift Giving, Reciprocity and Beneficence

The analysis of exchange, especially of gift giving, is central to anthropological analyses of (archaic) societies (for an overview see Sherry 1983; Adloff and Mau 2005). Marcel Mauss (2011 [1954]) published one of the most famous analyses of gift giving. He argued that '[in] theory such gifts are voluntary but in fact they are given and repaid under obligation' (ibid., 1). Exchange is understood as the 'bases of social life' or any kind of relation between people (ibid., 2). Although Mauss does not use the term reciprocity to analyse the obligation to give, receive and repay, it is central to his arguments (ibid., 37 ff.). Gifts and exchange are understood as social phenomenon within an economy and moral system of reciprocity that is still valid in today's societies (ibid., 1, 63 ff.).

Similar to this approach, Parsons (1949) and Merton (1957) describe reciprocity as the main structuring principle of society (quoted in Gouldner 1984, 40 ff.). In contrast, Gouldner finds that not every exchange is complying with the norm of reciprocity. Some giving-behaviour is motivated and grounded in a norm of beneficence, the commitment to help the other person because he needs this help (see ibid., 147). The norm of beneficence does not include the expectation of a repayment and is motivated by the idea that someone who is in need should receive help without having to pay something back. A payback might occur later in time, but when the decision to help or give in a beneficial way is made, the potential payback is not the mere motivation to give (ibid., 118 ff.). The fluid encounters of Sub-Saharan immigrants in Berlin seem to be based on exactly such a moral orientation of beneficence when sharing information and support with 'strangers' – people they don't define as friends, semi-kin or kin relations but with whom they are familiar although they never spoke a word with them before. The next section will describe this mechanism in more detail.

Beneficial Exchange of Information Within Ethnic Boundaries

Agents can only act on the basis of the expectation of reciprocity when the engagement with someone else is durable. When meeting someone that one did not know before on the street, in a shop, a park or a bar, there is no guarantee that this person will be met again. In institutions like a church this is more likely, but nevertheless not guaranteed. The benefits of giving in terms of building a positive reputation that can be cashed-in in other settings also is not likely to apply when one simply meets in public space. This is more likely in a setting like the church, where giving may be motivated by the desire to create social credentials, which is, given the moral orientation institutionalized in the church, likely to find a fertile soil (see Chapter 6). Absent ties show that reciprocity is not always the leading moral principle of interactions. Instead some of the interview partners shared and exchanged information with people they did not know, although there was the risk of not receiving anything back from that person. Various interviewees describe a willingness to help others even when they did not know each other. Michael, a man in his fifties from Togo, who had been living in Germany for about 30 years and lived some years in Russia before that, was regularly helping different people of non-German but not necessarily African descent to deal with bureaucratic problems. He has translated documents and accompanied people to institutions. Since he has been offering this support for many years already, people knew through word of mouth that he could be found or contacted in or through an Afro-shop. With his counselling and support he was primarily helping people that had problems with institutions and did not speak German, as in a case where he helped a person after a car crash to communicate with police and the justice department. Moreover, there were people who needed help with translations of hiring contracts or documents for the immigration department. Asked why he gave this support Michael answered that 'this is everyday solidarity … that every African knows, that it pays off to help people. That is easy here, the one that searches for help, he asks, he is trusting you'. This 'everyday solidarity' is described as the motivation to help other 'Africans' that mostly are depending on asking for help within their ethnic community due to their lack of language skills in German.

For sharing information or support with someone, one does not have to have a durable relation. It can be seen as a beneficial act. Instead of expecting a repayment which would imply the beginning of a relation, respectively turning a fluid encounter into a durable engagement, there is little concern about if and how a gift or favour will be returned when sharing support or information with people who are seen as being from the same ethnical background. The moral orientation that facilitates support for people met in fluid encounters stems from their own migration experience during which especially the low-educated Sub-Saharan immigrants had to overcome precarious situations. Through these experiences they know that it is necessary to depend on information and practical support from any social encounter especially those of ethnic ties, if strong, weak or absent, durable or fluid (see Stack 1975).

Rob (41) experienced such ethnic support when first arriving in Germany from Nigeria more than 10 years ago. He travelled to Berlin by train and got the hint of a German woman on the train to ask another African person for help when arriving at the train station. He asked a man that turned out to be Nigerian as well and spoke the same language. This man let him stay at his accommodation and explained to him that he would need to go to an asylum camp and that he did not easily get a working permit. The support and information shared on the basis of the moral orientation of beneficence and ethnic solidarity as well as a shared experience of immigration becomes clear here.

After applying for asylum and spending years in an asylum seeker centre, a man from Sudan whom he met in the asylum camp before offered to help Rob when he would need a place to live in Berlin. Rob reported that when he came to Berlin, this Sudanese found him a little place, nearby *Frankfurter Tor*: 'He called me and I went I was staying with a family there in one small room'.

The willingness to help and support others in need can be clearly classified as beneficial behaviour. Here, the solidarity based on a shared ethnic category as well as experience of immigration is among the crucial driving forces for beneficence. Rachel pointed at this ethnic dimension of solidarity while explaining her beneficial behaviour in church:

> Because I am far from home, and when you find some people in the foreign land and you become close. You trust each other, you help each other. It's very interesting. And very nice. Then you feel at place. Because, I know in life, no one, we say in English, no one is an Island. You cannot live a life to say well I am Rachel I don't have my brother and sisters here, so, I don't need to have. But Africans mentality, we always want to bring ourselves together. Maybe you have seen that in the church. We want to bring ourselves together because we are far from home, so if I can find another Africans that, we understand each other, we like each other and we help each other. That is the best. Because there are certain things that you as a German you cannot understand. Me, my culture and your [the interviewer's] culture are totally different.

Rachel saw in a common ethnicity, seen as a 'sense of belonging, based on the belief in shared culture and common ancestry' (see Wimmer 2008, 973), the explanation for the moral orientation of beneficence. She described how Sub-Saharan immigrants saw themselves as a collective that had shared the common experience of being away from their own brothers and sisters in Africa. To survive as someone who was different and had a different culture made it necessary to develop a solidarity amongst Sub-Saharan immigrants. Moreover, she gave examples for the activation of ethnic boundaries in semi-kin ties as well as in fluid encounters:

> But in terms of African Society. There are things we have in common. Whether I come from Zambia, whether I come from Cameroun, we have some things which are common. That is, relationship. Keeping the relationship is very common among the African people. It doesn't matter where you come from. That's why I will be in the street I see an African I say 'Hallo!' And my husband: where do you know this person? No. I've seen it's an African guy or a man, a woman. (*laughing*). ... Why? Because we just want to say 'hello' and that is quite important. That is very common for African people.

This description is pointing at the ethnic solidarity and boundaries within social ties of Sub-Saharan immigrants and emphasizes that the frequency of a tie is not defining the strength of a tie nor does the fluid encounter with 'strangers', such as unknown others, from African descent avoid the enacting of beneficence as moral orientation.

Moreover, the discrimination in the labour market faced by Sub-Saharan immigrants is fostering the sharing of information on jobs in durable social networks and especially with fluid encounters. Facing massive problems when trying to access and maintain a position within the German labour market because of the devaluation of certificates, language barriers and discrimination makes alternative ways to get support and access to jobs necessary. This discrimination or barriers were less obvious, as in the case of Jamal (40, from Cameroon). He reported that the company he worked for wouldn't give permanent contracts but employed new workers after a year to avoid labour legislations. Interview partners also reported more explicit discriminations. Manu (46, from Cameroon) worked in cleaning and reported that he almost got fired after having being sick once. Working conditions are precarious and at the same time it is impossible to flee from it. Other experiences are those made within state institutions, especially with the job agencies, alien department and district office where 'the way they treat you, is so bad ... they frustrate you, they try to make you feel so bad, so that you go out of the system' (Jamal, 40, Cameroon).

These difficulties faced as an immigrant are common and shared knowledge in the heterogeneous group of Sub-Saharan immigrants that result in a moral orientation of beneficence: even if you don't share this destiny you, even though you are not akin, see the other as a 'brother' or 'sister' that one needs to help as one could be in his or her place.

To summarize, the majority of our interview partners explained their solidarity with beneficial behaviour instead of expecting reciprocity, and with the perspective to diminish the impact of barriers and discrimination in the labour market and to give help in fluid encounters to overcome precarious situations in various spheres of life. The discrimination and marginalization of Sub-Saharan immigrants makes a moral orientation of beneficence necessary to survive and is at the same time supported by an understanding of ethnic boundary and solidarity. This practice is especially strong where people have little more than fluid encounters, because both giving and receiving help there is void of future expectations. Accepting help offered in such a context as a way of general ethnic solidarity is also easier than it is to accept support within a context of a weak or strong tie as the moral orientation of reciprocity creates a debt that one day needs to be paid back, and the chance may be that the day of being able to repay will never come (see also Blokland and Noordhoff, 2008 on the rejection of support in weak and strong ties). Gratitude hence becomes instantaneous and without further consequences for an interpersonal relation in the future. This, then, is why fluid encounters can provide social capital and thereby expand capabilities that comes with very low costs. They therefore have a high return with little more investment than the, sometimes maybe humiliating, act on the side of the needing agent than to admit the need for help from unknown others. Whereas our data merely shows that beneficence is the moral orientation that rules such encounters, it must be pointed out that the chances for exploitation are looming large here too: human trafficking, prostitution and other modern forms of slavery in nightclubs, kebab houses and restaurants where newly arriving immigrants with no language skills and knowledge about the society where they have moved to get trapped in underpaid jobs in bad conditions, with no proper housing, no health care and no opportunities to improve their fate, result from the very same fluid encounters and the positive experiences described here. Nevertheless, ethnic boundaries make the costs low to try to enhance their own social position by using any social encounter to generate information or support needed. Trying to withdraw from poverty and precarious work doesn't turn out to be successful for most of the Sub-Saharan immigrants. We have shown that social ties are on the one hand more complex than Granovetter's approach of ties suggests but on the other hand having and using different social ties to access resources without insisting on the norm of reciprocity doesn't seem to grant upward social mobility. This is contradicting the thesis that certain ties make social upward mobility possible. Scholars have described this dilemma with the concept of 'network poverty' (6 1997a, 25), pointing to the lack of capital and resources in a broader and multi-layered sense. One could break this perspective down to the argument that the Sub-Saharan immigrants lack capital of various kinds – not only social capital – that makes integration to different social spheres difficult. Network poverty illustrates not simply that they lack resources and access in a variety of different fields but moreover that these are all interconnected and might push and pull, increase, diminish and exclude in the one or other field. The interwoven, complex and multiple lines along which poverty and precariousness can be pictured as a net of precarious situations, within which the group of Sub-Saharan immigrants analysed here is taking various positions.

Conclusion

This chapter critically looked at theories of ties and empirically showed that the classical triad of strong, weak and absent ties is not reflecting the important role of fluid encounters as well as the complexity of social interactions in general. We have seen that the interview partners found their jobs through the use of kin and semi-kin ties as well as fluid encounters. Especially the practice of using fluid encounters expands the idea of what social ties are and how they can function, an expansion that critiques the commonly used notion of social ties as durable engagements that can be measured with network tools. We showed that the common measurement of ties by intensity and frequency of social contacts does not reflect the complexity of social encounters. Generating information from a fluid encounter in church or simply by meeting someone on the street showed that the strength of a tie is not pictured in its duration or frequency. Instead fluid encounters can also be used to access resources and thus realize capabilities.

Moreover, we have seen that these fluid encounters are not based on a norm of reciprocity but reflect the moral orientation of beneficence. The common situation of marginalization due to discrimination of Sub-Saharan immigrants is building solidarity and ethnic boundaries that is reflected in the moral orientation of beneficence. Using fluid encounters as an alternative strategy to access the labour market or other resources and thereby coping with barriers as discrimination and devaluation of certificates only becomes possible through the entanglement of ethnic solidarity and beneficence used in social encounters. We showed as well that shops, churches and festivities are central places that create meeting opportunities that make the use of fluid encounters possible.

We hence described how fluid encounters work by bringing in a 'Global South' perspective on social ties. Our findings help us to understand how people create capabilities through social ties, not only the marginalized, but in general. This does not mean, however, that the immigrants from Sub-Saharan descent get ahead in Berlin. A situation of marginalization severely constrains the creation of capabilities. Although social theory is arguing that heterogeneous ties help to access resources, the Sub-Saharan immigrants interviewed in Berlin do so too. These practices do not help them to get ahead as they are located in a 'network poor' position. This then explains how a segregated network arises and upward mobility is not enhanced. If there are fluid encounters above all with people in a similar position, it is difficult to get access to settings that allow upward mobility. For the African interview partners, neither the heterogeneity of social ties nor the institutionalization of settings to access fluid encounters in forms of festivities and other practices helped them to get ahead.

References

Adloff, Frank and Steffen Mau. 2005. *Vom Geben und Nehmen. Zur Soziologie der Reziprozität.* Frankfurt am Main, New York: Campus Verlag.

Bender, Stefan and Wolfgang Seifert. 2000. 'Zur beruflichen und sozialen Integration der in Deutschland lebenden Ausländer'. In *Deutsche und Ausländer. Freunde, Fremde oder Feinde? Empirische Befunde und theoretische Erklärungen*, edited by Richard Alba, Peter Schmidt and Martina Wasmer, 55–91. Wiesbaden: Westdeutscher Verlag.

Bian, Yanjie. 1997. 'Bringing Strong Ties Back in. Indirect Ties, Network Bridges, and Job Searches in China'. *American Sociological Review* 62: 366–85.

Blokland, Talja V. 2003. *Urban Bonds. Social Relationship in an Inner City Neighbourhood*. Cambridge: Polity Press.

Blokland, Talja V. and Floris Noordhoff. 2008. 'The Weakness of Weak Ties: Social Capital to Get Ahead Among the Urban Poor in Rotterdam and Amsterdam'. In *Networked Urbanism: Social Capital in the City*, edited by Talja V. Blokland and Mike Savage. Aldershot, England; Burlington, VT: Ashgate.

Blokland, Talja V. and Gwen van Eijk. 2007. 'Poor People's Bridging Ties: An Exploration of Poor People's Networks in a Poverty Neighbourhood and a Mixed Neighbourhood in Rotterdam, the Netherlands'. Paper presented at the International Conference on Sustainable Urban Areas, Rotterdam, 2007.

Bourdieu, Pierre. 1987. *Die feinen Unterschiede. Kritik der gesellschaftlichen Urteilskraft*. Frankfurt am Main: Suhrkamp Verlag.

———. 1992. *Die verborgenen Mechanismen der Macht. Schriften zu Politik und Kultur 1*. Hamburg: VSA Verlag.

Bourdieu, Pierre and Loïc J.D. Wacquant. 1992. *An Invitation to Reflexive Sociology*. Cambridge: Polity Press.

Briggs, X. de Souza. 1998. 'Brown Kids in White Suburbs: Housing Mobility and the Many Faces of Social Capital'. *Housing Policy Debate* 9: 177–221.

Coleman, James S. 1988. 'Social Capital in the Creation of Human Capital'. In *American Journal of Sociology*, 94: 95–120.

Constant, Amelie F. and Klaus F. Zimmermann. 2009. 'Migration, Ethnicity and Economic Integration'. Working Paper No. 4620, Bonn: Institute for the Study of Labor.

Feld, Scott L. 1981. 'The Focused Organization of Social Ties'. *American Journal of Sociology* 86: 1015–35.

Field, John. 2003. *Social Capital*. London: Routledge.

Fischer, Claude S. 1975. 'Toward a Subcultural Theory of Urbanism'. *American Journal of Sociology* 80: 1319–41.

———. 1982. *To Dwell among Friends. Personal Networks in Town and City*. Chicago, London: The University of Chicago Press.

Gouldner, Alvin W. 1984. *Reziprozität und Autonomie. Ausgewählte Aufsätze*. Frankfurt am Main: Suhrkamp.

Granovetter, Mark S. 1973. 'The Strength of Weak Ties'. *American Journal of Sociology* 78: 1360–80.

———. 1974. *Getting A Job. A Study of Contacts and Careers*. Cambridge, MA: Harvard University Press.

Hormel, Ulrike and Albert Scherr. 2010. *Diskriminierung*. Wiesbaden: VS Verlag für Sozialwissenschaften.

Leonard, Rosemary and Jenny Onyx 2003. 'Networking through Loose and Strong Ties: An Australian Qualitative Study'. *International Journal of Voluntary and Nonprofit Organizations* 14 (2): 189–203.

McFarlane, Colin and Michael Waibel. 2012. *Urban Informalities. Reflections on the Formal and Informal*. Farnham: Ashgate.

Mauss, Marcel. 2011. *The Gift. Forms and Functions of Exchange in Archaic Societies*. Mansfield: Martino Publishing. Originally published as Marcel Mauss. *The Gift. Forms and Functions of Exchange in Archaic Societies*. Translated by W.D. Halls. (New York: W.W. Norton, 1954).

Merton, Robert K. 1957. *Social Theory and Social Structure*. Second Edition. Glencoe: Free Press.

Montgomery, James D. 1992. 'Job Search and Network Composition: Implications of the Strength-of-Weak-Ties-Hypothesis'. *American Sociological Review* 57: 586–96.

OECD. 2007. 'Labour Market Integration in Australia, Denmark, Germany and Sweden'. *Jobs for Immigrants* (1). Paris: OECD Publishing.

Parsons, Talcott. 1949. *Essays in Sociological Theory Pure and Applied*. Glencoe: Free Press.

Putnam, Robert D. 1995. 'Bowling Alone: America's Declining Social Capital'. *Journal of Democracy* 6 (1): 65–78.

———. 2000. *Bowling Alone. The Collapse and Revival of American Community*. New York: Simon & Schuster.

Sherry, John F. Jr. 1983. 'Gift Giving in Anthropological Perspective'. *Journal of Consumer Research* 10: 157–68.

Simone, AbdouMaliq. 2004. 'People as Infrastructure: Intersecting Fragments in Johannesburg'. *Public Culture* 16: 407–29.

———. 2006. 'Pirate Towns. Reworking Social and Symbolic Infrastructures in Johannesburg and Douala'. *Urban Studies* 43: 357–70.

———. 2010. *City Life from Jakarta to Dakar: Movements at the Crossroads*. Abingdon: Routledge.

Small, Mario L. 2009. *Unanticipated Gains*. New York: Oxford University Press.

Soenen, Ruth. 2008. *The kleine ontmoeten: Over het sociale karakter van de stad*. Antwerpen: Aksant.

Stack, Carol B. 1975. *All Our Kin: Strategies for Survival in a Black Community*. Illinois: Harper and Row.

Van Eijk, Gwen. 2010. *Unequal Networks. Spatial Segregation, Relationships and Inequality in the City*. Delft: Delft University Press.

Wegener, Bernd. 1991. 'Job Mobility and Social Ties: Social Resources, Prior Job, and Status Attainment'. *American Sociological Review* 56: 60–71.

Wilp, Markus. 2007. *Die Arbeitsmarktintegration von Zuwanderern in Deutschland und den Niederlanden. Hintergründe, aktuelle Entwicklungen und politische Maßnahmen*. Münster: Waxmann Verlag.

Wimmer, Andreas. 2008. 'The making and unmaking of ethnic boundaries: a multilevel process theory'. *American Journal of Sociology* 113 (4): 970–1022.

6, Perri. 1997a. *Social Exclusion: Time to be Optimistic.* London: Demos Collection 12.

———. 1997b. *Escaping Poverty. From Safety Nets to Networks of Opportunity.* London: Demos.

Chapter 8

The Square as Sanctuary: Finding Social Recognition among Urban Poor

Daniela Krüger

Introduction

Marginalization produces social fringes to the city. Fluid encounters with mainstream urbanites reinforce such social fringes when people cross the street to not pass a group of homeless, avoid sites where drug users congregate or ignore 'a beggar in the street and make sure their eyes don't meet'.[1] Hence, those at the social fringes meet at spatial fringes where they are safe from such humiliating encounters that reinforce structural marginalization. At *Leopoldplatz*, a public square in the disadvantaged district Berlin-*Wedding*, urban poor congregated and created such a sanctuary. Mostly unemployed and residing in Berlin, they came to the square to engage with each other and consume drugs and alcohol. They called and described themselves as a *scene*. From an outside gaze, however, their public gatherings are likely to be seen as an outcome of 'neighbourhood deterioration'. Understood as such, they evoke political actions of containment (Häußermann and Kapphan 2004, 214). In the case of *Leopoldplatz*, a programme for urban redevelopment, a square-wide ban on public alcohol consumption and an enhancement of police operations to prevent drug sales had been put in place. Together with a neoliberal national discourse on poverty as individual failure and immobility (see Lessenich 2009) it formed the multifaceted context that surrounded these urban poor (see Lamont and Mizrachi 2011). Here, the status of unemployment and public display of time, drugs and alcohol consumption imposed a negative image on people at *Leopoldplatz*.

In Goffman's words it added to a stigma, or a discrediting and incorporated attribute (1986, 3). However, the process of stigmatization does not only refer to physical characteristics, individual character or membership of certain social groups. Although neglected in Goffman's approach to stigma and its management, the neighbourhood that people live in or the places they are associated with can be as stigmatizing as the stigma of unemployment itself (see Wacquant 2007, 67). Yet the resourcefulness of the sanctuary, this public square and its design in a low-income district, is rendered invisible in such an approach. The square

1 Chapin Carpenter, Mary. 1994. 'Stones in the Road'. Compact disc. Columbia Nashville: Tristar.

is a site where shared experiences of unemployment, forms of addiction, a daily monotonous routine and territorial stigmatization were negotiated.

Physical proximity with people in similar social positions and the square itself produced a stigmatized setting where identity work got done. Here, fluid encounters and durable engagements built a social infrastructure that affected the capability to receive social recognition – a resource that is of importance when marginalization leaves people to have 'little to fall back on in their attempts to salvage the self other than their own identity construction efforts' (Snow and Anderson 1987, 1364). The square, then, became a site to exercise moral orientations through spatial practices and verbal accounts and fostered the construction of a personal identity and its recognition.

First, this chapter shows how people gathering at the square produced parochial realms in public, a practice that for Lofland (1998, 12) results in 'home territories' and helps finding daily routines and a common ground for actively engaging in community 'doing' (see Jenkins 1996; Blokland 2009). We then trace the recent history of the square to understand how the attachment of certain groups to the square and their practices of nostalgic conservation of their symbolic community helped them to create access to spatial resources. Here, the chapter zooms in on the perspective of a group at the square that identify themselves as *German drinkers.*[2] From the resourcefulness of the square we get to know different groups and the capabilities they have, given the resources for social recognition that the sanctuary produced to develop identities through symbolic boundary work. These practices must be placed in the historic specificity of the square. Since 2009, *Leopoldplatz* was part of a programme of the *Senate Department for Urban Development and the Environment* in Berlin that aimed to revalue and redevelop the square as a centre and showplace in Berlin-*Wedding* (see Senate Department for Urban Development and the Environment 2014). The Department and further programme-involved community and business agents identified the *scene* as an obstacle to the square's livelihood. It had no eye, as we will conclude, for the resourcefulness of encounters and engagements within the *scene* and for the square itself as a resource for constructing a personal identity at the social fringes of the city, which resulted from city-wide marginalization and to which beautification and urban redevelopment initiatives, hence, did not provide an adequate answer.

2 This chapter relies on original fieldwork by the author. The material was collected during two years of fieldwork including participant observation and structured and unstructured interviews with 35 participants in 2011 and 2012. The choice to put the *German drinkers* in focus is theoretically informed, as they have the best capabilities to do boundary work, but also results from this group being most accessible and open to participation in the field research.

Public Space and the Purpose of Social Congregation

Establishing 'Home Territories' Around Benches

Traditionally, ethnographic studies emphasize the importance of public places for social congregation and community building, attributing a broader meaning to them beyond the mere physical setting (Gans 1982; Snow and Anderson 1993; Whyte 1993; Liebow 2003; Wasserman and Clair 2010). They can be sites to enhance resourceful relationships. Soup kitchens, street corners, shops or public squares offer a physical platform to develop what Lofland (1998, 13) calls 'home territories'. Lofland (ibid., 70) describes a 'home territory' as a relationship to a space that is established by people who have 'intimate-secondary relationships with one another'. Generally speaking, Lofland deduces realms as socially constructed and physically bound but neither physically nor geographically rooted (ibid., 11). Hence, 'realms as social territories come into being only in actual physical space – in physical territories. However, whether any actual physical space contains a realm, and if so what type, is always a matter to be discovered empirically. The realm type (private, parochial, or public) is not defined by the physical space in which it is located but by the relational form that dominates within it' (ibid., 14). The *Leopoldplatz*, as a public square, is legally open for access to all (ibid., 8). Transitions from public to parochial realms may occur and are due to the fluidity of the types of relationships between persons which can be durable or more fleeting (see ibid.). The research participants at the square sometimes referred to their social congregation at *Leopoldplatz* as a *scene* in which 'everyone knows everyone' and revealed a notion of community. The same research participants, however, also used the term '*scene*' to simplify matters as opposed to a differentiated view on their social environment. In this sense, 'public familiarity' as Blokland and Savage put it (2008, 11; see also Blokland 2003) must be seen as context for encounters and engagements and not be confused with the actual content and type of social relationship. Hence, the shared public square does not necessarily constitute a community simply based on the physical proximity (see Blokland and Savage 2008) but can also be a site of differentiation and distancing.

During my first encounters people at the square presented the *scene* as a differentiated social environment with various types of social relationships. Herbert, a 60-year-old German, was a retired craftsman who regularly came to *Leopoldplatz*. He explained that there was 'one scene' at the square but it consisted of different groups. Gabriele, who was a 45-year-old unemployed German and a former heroin consumer, described the *scene* in more detail, pointing to the benches at the square (Figure 8.1):

> The first bench for example near the public toilet is basically occupied by foreigners. ... and none of us for example would stand there ... and you know there is this middle group where ... well different people sit, and so the last bench is occupied by, let me say 'the more reasonable people' who know how to behave, who watch out that nothing too bad happens.

Figure 8.1 Benches at the front square
Source: Author 2015

During conversations with people at the square, they constantly assigned benches and localities to certain groups, as a way of expressing the types of relationships they formed. Gabriele limited the benches to different groups, defining 'their' home territories. She assigned herself deliberately to the *third bench*, the bench where 'the more reasonable people' avoided contact with others and 'watched out'. Ingo, another 60-year-old German resident of the neighbourhood, was also associated with the last or *third bench* which he named the bench of the *German drinkers.*[3]

When Ingo, Gabriele and Herbert referred to their *third bench* they labelled themselves as the *reasonable drinkers* and the *German drinkers*. The other two benches were occupied by 'people who do drugs', with *Turks* or *hard-core drunkards* who, for them, formed the groups that misbehaved. Hence, their geographical imagination and resulting spatial practice were informed by moral orientations.

Though it was emphasized above that social territories are not physically rooted, this spatial practice of assigning benches shows that physical structure can encourage the transformation from public into parochial or even private realms when the density and the type of the relationships enable this (see Lofland 1998, 70). The transformation into a private realm was indicated by Nicole, an

3 The picture above shows the front square of *Leopoldplatz* in 2015 after a physical redevelopment. Still, the allocation of the benches on the right side and the spatial distance between the benches is comparable to the spatial structure in 2011 when interviews were conducted.

unemployed German who had moved to the neighbourhood a year ago. She was in her twenties and received a substitution treatment for a former drug addiction. When her mother, who was also a German neighbourhood resident, did not answer the door, she knew that she could find her at the square, most often accompanied by her mother's partner.

Benches like the ones in my field phase in 2011 provide the means to occupy public space to form 'home territories' (ibid., 12). People reproduced their group by coming and occupying their bench routinely, developing durable engagements and drawing symbolic boundaries around 'their territories'. Most of the research participants shared a position of unemployment which obviously had consequences for their day-time activities. Beyond daily medical consultations (in the case of participation in a substitution programme) and visits to public offices or social workers, the square had become a fundamental part in the daily routine, as Peter explained. He was in his fifties, a German resident of the neighbourhood and currently withdrawing from alcohol and drugs. Back then, when he was still consuming drugs and alcohol he considered himself a part of the *drinkers* at *Leopoldplatz*. During that time the square was integral to his daily activities:

> Every day I met the same people. I already got there at 10 am and had my [beer] bottle with me, drank 4 bottles, usually at 10 am. Most of the time I went home at 12 am, because, I just live over there. Well, I slept two or three hours, then I returned to the square at 4 or 5 pm in the evening, and drank again my bottle, and did this regularly for years.

Regular meetings with the same people at the square turn fluid encounters into durable engagements. These encounters can circle around routines and time structures. The activities that people follow at the square were 'esthetical' and 'interactional pleasures' that the public realm with its built environment and people populating it offers (Lofland 1998, 88). The research participants engaged predominantly in activities of 'talking', 'chatting', 'smoking', 'drinking' or, like Andreas formulated it, 'people-watching'. Andreas, who was unemployed and a 65-year-old German, referred to himself as a 'people-watcher'. Studying human beings in public was 'incredibly important' for him because he 'would not know what else to do'. The group of the *drinkers* served as 'family' for Peter. For Gabriele some of them became 'really close friends'. They then formed an interpersonal network (see Lofland 1998) for receiving help in administrative matters, or information on job opportunities and available apartments. Some people started romances. Others borrowed money from each other. Or as Peter put it: 'no one has ever starved at the square'. As the daily practices and durable engagements constitute 'home territories', they drew symbolic boundaries that help constituting a community (see Jenkins 1996). Symbolic boundaries are 'distinctions made by social actors to categorize objects, people, practices, and even time and space. They are tools by which individuals and groups struggle over and come to agree upon definitions of reality' (Lamont and Molnár 2002, 168).

Bordering as technique then, as Kusenbach (2009, 408) pointed out, is a specific example of symbolic boundary work that individuals employ to position themselves against the geographically, culturally and/or structurally distant other. At the square, although interview partners sat on benches in close proximity they still emphasized the spatial distance between their territories and that of others.

In turn, the group of the *drinkers* defended 'their turf'. Who gets to sit on which bench in order to follow activities was, as Peter explained, rarely a cause for conflicts since 'everyone knew who sits on which bench by habit'. Still, the following field note shows how Stefan, a mid-forty unemployed and homeless *German drinker*, reacted when their *third bench* was approached by a so called *pill addict*:

> A man comes up and sits down at the bench next to Gabriele. He looks tired and is constantly touching his face in a nervous manner. Stefan [standing at the bench, next to me] immediately says: "get lost!". While Gabriele is answering the man's request to start a conversation, Stefan repeats that he should "move or there will be trouble". The others [Gabriele and two other drinkers] try to calm Stefan down but he is already dragging the man from the bench and trying to take him to the ground. Stefan's bottle of beer is falling out of his trousers' back pocket. The man stands up and leaves. Stefan curses loudly about the "pill addict". Now I notice people from the second bench who observed what was happening and whisper with each other. Ingo, standing next to me, explains that although he does not know which kind of "pills" those people consume, he identifies their substance consumption by a blue discolouration around the mouth.

This form of territorialization where place becomes literally appropriated by Stefan who considered himself a *drinker* and prevented a consumer of *pills* to join their group shows how 'border areas' (Lofland 1998, 45) get negotiated. Since it is a legally openly accessible place it is not always clear for everyone what the attribution of groups to benches 'by habit' looks like. This 'boundary confusion' (ibid.) can lead to conflicts and, as in the example above, can reproduce the territory by enforcing the symbolic boundary (see Lamont and Molnár 2002). When the *drinkers* engaged in 'place-making' (Blokland 2008, 31) they indicated boundaries that had excluding effects for some, while for the *drinkers*, it helped restoring relationships within their group. This is crucial for identity work and establishing a symbolic community with considerable outward effects. Accordingly, other people referred to themselves as outsiders or *visitors* at the square and applied a spatial practice of avoiding the company of groups and stayed alone. Tobias, a forty-year-old German who casually met up with a friend at the square came from another gathering spot in Berlin-*Wedding*. He usually sat on benches behind the church that were distant to the front place where, for example, the *drinkers* resided:

> As said before, I'm not interested in the things that happen at the square. I always spent here only a short time. I'm not one of the people who gather at the benches at the front [square], who gather and build a bench, and see each other every day. That's what I had at the subway station [referring to another subway station and gathering spot in Berlin-*Wedding*]. We had that there. There were always the same people, 10, 12 people and we had great fun there. But not at *Leopoldplatz*.

Since he visited the square occasionally he had only fluid encounters with people at *Leopoldplatz* and acknowledged the symbolic dominance exercised by cohesive groups like the *drinkers* at the front square 'who build a bench'. Later in the interview he reflected on an occasion where he and his 'buddies' got cast out from a bench when one of the *drinkers* hit his face and he 'went down to the ground'. Tobias's self-description as an outsider at the square became manifest in experiences where he was getting involved in conflicts with more established groups. This had excluding consequences, as since then he did not like to spend time on the front square and avoided the company of others.

The *drinkers* dominated *their benches* which enhanced their capabilities on the front square – on the one hand, to develop a 'home territory' (Lofland 1998, 12) and on the other hand, to be visible and be able to engage in 'interactional pleasures' (ibid., 88). Similarly, Nicole explained that the square was important and helped her to overcome the feeling of 'being shut in at home'. Still she knew who her 'folks' were and where she was sitting down. Others referred to a group identity such as the *druggist* or referred to themselves as *drinkers* who 'do a bit of drugs' but sat separately from the *drinkers* of the *third bench*. Spatial practices of 'place-making' (Blokland 2008, 31) and literally appropriating it draw symbolic boundaries and enable distancing. This paragraph showed, then, how a public square functions as a resource for developing a social infrastructure of durable engagements within 'home territories' (Lofland 1998, 12) and more fluid encounters through distancing and enacting 'place-making' (Blokland 2008, 31). For Mitchell (Mitchell 1995, 125) congregation spots can be considered a 'haven' for urban poor, especially homeless, which is still not necessarily the same like a 'safe' home (see for a different argument Veness 1993). He rather assumes that public squares like *Leopoldplatz* can function as 'political space' where structural problems like homelessness become visible and get represented (Mitchell 1995, 125). In the case of *Leopoldplatz*, as we have seen, the access to the square is a resource of social recognition and 'interactional pleasures' (Lofland 1998, 88). It is given to those who can exercise dominance over a 'home territory' (ibid., 12) to foster durable engagement and thus to have the capabilities to produce visibility. Different to what Oldenburg and Brissett (1982, 271) concluded for 'third places' as parochial realms for 'pure sociability' *Leopoldplatz* is not a democratic space in which equality is produced – rather, social marginalization is taking place and affects people's capabilities, whether intended or not, by excluding others from realms and possibilities to locate themselves visibly.

In order to understand how 'home territories' (Lofland 1998, 12) and differentiations in the use of benches coincide with how people position themselves within the social environment of *Leopoldplatz* and a wider social setting we have to make a detour and understand how the symbolic communities developed. For this, we need to bring time back in. As places have histories, they are 'always already hybrid' (Massey 1995, 183; see also Lofland 1998; Blokland 2001; Blokland 2008) and are articulations of social relations. Places can therefore not be reduced to their present structure but rather rely on interpretations of the past. For *Leopoldplatz*, the next section follows the narratives of the place's past and its use for identity work for the self-assigned group of the *drinkers* of the *third bench*. This demonstrates how practices of symbolic boundary work at a public square affect the capability of social recognition.

Narratives About the Square's Development

The Dilemma of the Drinkers

Ethnographic studies have provided compassionate accounts of how people manage to create a sense of self-worth in situations of marginalization and material deprivation (Williams 1989; Snow and Anderson 1993; Liebow 1995; Anderson 2000; Newman 2000; Duneier 2001; Liebow 2003; see also Blokland 2012 for a discussion on methodology) but favoured an emphasis on an individualistic or ecology approach of the Chicago School. Instead, a relational approach helps to see identity work not as a psychological act but as evolving out of a social infrastructure that enables, whether intended or not, access to resources while excluding others. This paragraph thus applies a 'relational lens' (Blokland 2012, 503).

Groups of people spending much of their daily life on the square have existed for several decades already. The memories of those years, as Peter explained, informed current moral orientations:

> In the past, you would find only drinkers here and then it started at some point. Then they had a little marihuana with them and now there are all these junkies, this wasn't possible in the past. ... one can say there is a downside development since the junkies came in. In the past, when the drinkers stayed here it was actually a calm atmosphere. Okay, there were fights of course, but you can't compare it to today when people try to betray each other. It's not the same anymore. In the past we had a strong solidarity here. Today, everybody thinks of themselves first, how I can betray the other person and so on.

Peter described a development of the social environment on the square that he saw as purely negative caused by the growing numbers of drug consumers. With their arrival, the atmosphere had changed and the solidarity within the former *drinker's scene* vanished. For Gabriele, who knew the square and the *scene* for over a decade, the place 'lost in value because it became asocial and deteriorated'. She recalled her earlier years at the square as a 'peaceful time' with fewer conflicts and less police operations. In contrast, today there was more stealing and people 'shooting up heroin'. In her words, the place became 'shitty'. In this general tenor of nostalgia Herbert tuned in, emphasizing the peaceful times before the *junkies* and *Turks* came to the square. In addition, Batu, a 45-year-old Turkish immigrant, missed the times when 'elderly and normal families' visited the square.

While the interview partners referred to themselves as *drinkers*, they pointed to incidents that brought the *junkie crap*, as Batu termed it. For him, it was clear that a newly opened office for methadone distribution led to an increase in the drug trade. Peter and Herbert held the strategies of the Berlin police responsible. The police carried out 'cleansing' of *drug scenes* at two central train stations in Berlin, which led to more police operations in general. Since they all called themselves *drinkers* and therefore shared a group identity, they expressed similar views on the development of the square. Interview partners like Kathrin, a mid-forty, unemployed German, who came from the *scene* from the *Zoologischer Garten* in 2012, one of the Berlin *drug scenes* that underwent 'cleansing' of the police, said in contrast, that the *druggists* 'need a place to gather' and so she came with her friends Ulla and Sybille to *Leopoldplatz*. Kathrin and her friends were in their forties, unemployed and consumed either methadone or heroin and alcohol. They explained that the square still had a reputation for being 'calm', a site where gatherings were relatively speaking tolerated. Sybille said she was the 'last person that was led away in handcuffs' because she did not want to leave her *scene* at the *Zoologischer Garten*. These stories 'capture the dynamic dimensions of social relations, as groups compete in the production, diffusion, and institutionalization of alternative systems and principles of classifications' (Lamont and Molnár 2002, 168). The *drinkers* considered people arriving from other *scenes*, such as Sybille, as unpleasant newcomers. They, on the other hand, had a different story and different approach to such a development. The *druggists* from the *Zoologischer Garten* made their claim for social recognition for which they saw the square as a resource. Further, they made clear that the marginalization of the square was embedded in city-wide marginalization and its spatial dimensions. The changes that the *drinkers* held responsible for moral decline at the square strengthened the social cohesion within their group, encouraged by the nostalgic narratives that preserved their symbolic community.

Besides the changes in the social environment the square was undergoing a substantial redevelopment. Since 2009, a network of communal and municipal members worked on a plan to redevelop *Leopoldplatz*, to be completed in 2013. The plan included the removal of the benches that the *scene* occupied and was accompanied by measures such as a time-bound ban on alcohol, an increase in police operations and a new *staying area* assigned for the *scene* behind the church at the front square. Gabriele worried about an increase in conflicts and fights on the square since the *staying area* was meant to assemble people who 'don't fit together and don't want to be related to each other', she said. In this sense, the *drinkers* as the more established group at the square were not only being challenged by the mere appearance of new groups of users at the square but also by the structural changes of the locality itself. This was a threat to their 'home territories' (Lofland 1998, 12) and to its symbolic boundaries which Gabriele as a *drinker* expressed as an unease about being 'related' to people who may invade their parochial realm and affect their cohesion (see Elias and Scotson 1993). In the planning phase, the planning bureau and a collaborating social worker contacted the *scene* in order to 'develop together a square for everyone' (Müllerstraße-Aktiv 2013) which represented the slogan that accompanied the redevelopment. The plan included the opening of a so-called *Drinking Room* in early 2011. In 2012 the benches on the front square were removed and a *staying area* (Figure 8.2) was constructed to relocate the scene from the front square to the area behind the church.

When I visited the *Drinking Room* for the first time, the benches on the front square were not yet removed and the *staying area* was under construction. The room was located on a side road, next to the front square of *Leopoldplatz*. The local church co-funded the project providing the room in a side building of their

Figure 8.2 Staying area at *Leopoldplatz*
Source: Author, 2015

communal property and a social worker who offered consultation services and recruited volunteers from church members and the *German drinkers* from the *third bench*. For Stefan, a *German drinker*, the project offered him the opportunity to work his hours of community service. The social worker claimed to know everyone at the square and established relationships with the *drinkers* over years. Frank, a 50-year-old German, a co-founder of the room and also a member of the *drinkers*, prepared coffee while I sat next to Peter and Gabriele who played cards on a table and drank beer. Frank explained the relocation of several spots of Berlin's *drug scenes* to *Leopoldplatz* and Gabriele stepped in to emphasize how 'bad' things were. Peter considered himself as not being part of the *scene* anymore since he withdrew from alcohol and drugs. He avoided the groups at the square, but came frequently to the *Drinking Room* and even celebrated his birthday here. Gabriele said that she preferred being in the room over being at the square. Her 'acquaintances from the last bench', the *third bench*, visited the room as well. For the self-assigned *drinkers*, the *Drinking Room* became a refuge that enabled them to preserve their durable engagements within their group. They developed new routines such as having breakfast together, coffee during the day and playing cards. The room also served for the preservation of memories of deceased friends and former *drinkers* for whom a memorial got painted on one wall of the room. Peter explained that 'the core' of the *drinkers* had already passed away. Similarly Batu, who visited the room frequently for breakfast and then left for the square, described that 'most of the *drinkers* were already dead' and unfortunately 'got replaced by the *junkies*'. One day, the *drinkers* were informed that one of their acquaintances died days ago and started to arrange a memorial gathering at the *Drinking Room* after the funeral.

The excluding consequences of the development of 'home territories' in a public space that the first paragraph has shown (Lofland 1998, 12) can be retraced in the *Drinking Room*. Although the concept of the room was to be 'open', the *drinkers* Peter and Herbert said that their acquaintances with whom they engaged regularly, *German drinkers* who 'consumed a little bit of drugs or stronger liquor', felt unwelcome due to the rules which they both found obstructive. They felt that the sign at the entrance stating: 'Everyone is welcome that complies with the rules: no weapons, no violence, no drugs, no liquor. We are looking forward to seeing you' was excluding.

Peter and Herbert identified the *drinkers* from the *third bench*, Stefan and Frank as self-assigned heads over the institution, who would even 'throw people out' who did not conform to the rules. In 2012 I met Micha again who was 45 years old, unemployed and had recently been released from jail on probation. We met up in the *staying area* that had just opened after the benches on the front square had been removed. Micha was tall and slim. The description of Jane Jacob's 'public character' (1961, 70) suited him well since he kept in touch with a lot of people and was well informed about what went on at the square. Micha was not part of the *drinkers* group but he visited the *Drinking Room* 'whenever open'. He explained the unequal access to the *Drinking Room* to me. For him the room was 'not open to all' due to the commitment of the 'clique' including the self-assigned *drinkers* from the *third bench* who made it their 'spot' and 'took their self-confidence' out of it. Nicole, the young woman who moved to the neighbourhood a year ago, was casually visiting the room 'when there's barbecue' at the front court, otherwise she preferred the square over the room because the persons organizing the room 'weren't her people'.

Generally speaking, the *Drinking Room* was a resource that allowed the *drinkers* to sustain spatial borders (for the practice of bordering see Kusenbach 2009; see also Snow and Anderson 1993) and their relationships within their group of the *third bench*, especially since the benches had been removed and the new *staying area* had opened. As a consequence, the changes in their social environment and the physical structure of the square affected their capabilities. The *Drinking Room* became a resource to moderate the 'dilemma of the drinkers' that we identified in the changes that the interview participants emphasized. Through expressing what Snow and Anderson (1993, 219) term 'institutional embracement' they showed a considerable attachment to the room that was for Peter the last option he saw to keep in contact with his group. Here, they engaged not only but also nourished durably their symbolic community with nostalgic memories of deceased friends and the past of the square (see Blokland 2003; 2008). This form of 'place-making' (Blokland 2008, 31) did exclude others from the room. Although the room was 'open to all' or as Stefan puts it, everyone who was not coming to the room 'is either an idiot or takes drugs', the room's rules and gatekeeper who helped keeping the room working had excluding consequences that restored the resources of the *drinkers*. Apart from the square, the room became a positive marker since it was accepted by the police and the church who came for casual visits and gave financial support. Even journalists showed interest in the *Drinking Room* as a good practice model for social work. In contrast, the *staying area* became a focal point of police operations to prevent drug trading. The following paragraph shows, then, how the morally informed spatial practices affected capabilities for identity work.

Construction of a Decent Identity

'Junkie Crap' and its Consequences for the Drinkers

The practical use of space for identity work was expressed at the square in forms of symbolic boundary drawing that produced geographical distances and was achieved by occupying benches or the adjacent *Drinking Room*. Distancing at the square, however, as a spatial practice of place-bound identity work was morally informed. As the previous paragraph showed, the history of the social environment and the durable engagements within the group of the *drinkers* became a resource that affected their capabilities within the process of the square's restructuring while it had excluding consequences for others. Identity talk actively expressed association and distance (see Snow and Anderson 1987; 1993). Fluid encounters played an integral part in this practice, since most descriptions and labels that the interview partners used were based on their observations of people with whom they had only fleeting contact. Nonetheless, as Snow and Anderson (ibid.) have shown in their research on homeless people in Austin-Texas, the construction and avowal of personal identities can provide people at the social margins with dignity and self-worth (see also Lamont 2000). Their respondents engaged in identity talk and typically showed one of the following strategies: embracement, distancing and fictive story-telling (Snow and Anderson 1987; 1993). While the latter certainly derives out of personal and psychological motivation, embracement and distancing are relational strategies that can be seen, analytically spoken, as complementary. Following Jenkins's (1996) work on social identity, we trace people's negotiations between personal claims and outside attribution (see also Snow and Anderson 1993, 213; Lamont and Mizrachi 2011, 368).

In ethnographies such as 'Code of the Street' by Anderson (2000), 'Sidewalk' by Duneier (2001) or 'Between Good and Ghetto' by Jones (2010) moral life and decency come to play a crucial role for inner-city social life. The lines for embracement and distancing (see Snow and Anderson 1987; 1993; Kusenbach 2009), or the drawing of boundaries that produces group solidarity and emphasizes difference by constructing the 'other' (see Kusenbach 2009; Lamont and Mizrachi 2011) is delicate. But it allows one to find a position in a social setting and to distinguish between 'us' and 'them' (see Lamont and Molnár 2002; Lamont and Mizrachi 2011). Following Goffman (1986, 107) 'the stigmatized individual may exhibit identity ambivalence when he [sic] obtains a close sight of his [sic] own kind behaving in a stereotyped way'. After all, the stigmatized individual supports 'the norms of wider society' (ibid., 108) and expresses his/her identity ambivalence in strategies of boundary drawing. Distinguishing between 'decent' and 'street' (Anderson 2000), 'deserving' and 'undeserving' (Blokland 2008) or 'good' and 'ghetto' (Jones 2010) for Kusenbach (2009, 407) resembles a 'pecking order': 'The strategy of passing the stigma down the social pecking order to even more subordinate people serves to redraw the symbolic boundary between "good" and "bad". It elevates the moral decency of one's self and social group vis-à-vis others whom, to outsiders, might look similar yet are fundamentally less worthy'. The square and its social infrastructure provide a resourceful platform for drawing the delicate line between 'good' and 'bad'. Such morally informed claims reflect societal standards (see Goffman 1986, 108).

At *Leopoldplatz*, as we have seen, labels such as *drinker*, *druggist* or *junkie* differentiated between groups at the square. The labels were connected to practices that were evaluated as indecent such as the use of syringes for consuming heroin. It was not the use of heroin that was sold at the square in small balls or powder that the interview partner criticized, but the publicly visible *shooting up* of heroin with syringes, as Gabriele illustrated:

> I used to go home for this shit [consuming heroin] and didn't annoy other people with it, for me it is simply a matter of harassment when the public toilet opens after the 20 minutes have passed [the door opens automatically after 20 minutes] and they still haven't finished! That's disgusting! That's gross! And then they leave all their filth and that's what actually annoys us! When you cross Leo [*Leopoldplatz*] and see syringes laying [around].

When Gabriele consumed heroin she did it discreetly at home, as a matter of respect and decency. She detested the visibility of substance consumption. The aversion against the use of syringes among former heroin consumers went along with the repeated discovery of syringes at the main ground or the playground of the day nursery at *Leopoldplatz*. Among others, the self-assigned *drinkers* Peter, Gabriele and Batu told about syringes that had been hidden in the sandbox of the playground. They sometimes collected them and threw them away. Consequently, identity work, here, was closely linked to the interview partners' personal history of former drug use. When Goffman (1986, 48–50) points to the visibility of a stigma, this is what Peter and Gabriele might also have worried about. Withdrawal from drugs and alcohol as a correction of a stigma did not become visible in a social setting and on a square that was infamous for its drug trade (ibid.). Distancing themselves was therefore an important technique in order to verbally construct a personal identity that embraced the self-concept of being a decent person (see Snow and Anderson 1987; 1993; Kusenbach 2009). In this sense, the square functioned for Peter, as he put it, as 'therapy':

> Peter: This is like therapy here. When I feel sad I go to Leo [*Leopoldplatz*]. Then I observe what's going on, and then I feel better again and then I go home.
> Interviewer: How do you feel better then?
> Peter: Well, when I see how fucked up they are, that they don't get out of it, it's like a cycle and I, almost made it, and I am working on it every day. And when I see how they veg out there, are busy fighting each other and wet their pants. That's what keeps me upright.

In this statement, Peter showed that the confrontation with the people who consumed drugs at the square helped him to remember the 'cycle' of addiction. Consequently, the humorous and degrading depiction of the drug consumers enhanced his capability to approve his personal identity as a *straight person*. The 'straightness' to which some respondents referred was a common practice of identity work on the square. For example, self-assigned *drinkers* and former drug consumers Gabriele, Peter, Nicole and others frequently expressed how many years they had been *straight* and how much this status depended on their 'discipline' and 'strength of will'. In addition to accounts that showed one-dimensional indecent portraits of drug users that were used for identity work, Nicole, who had durable engagements within various groups at the square, had a more differentiated view on this issue:

> I don't like that either [used syringes at the square]. Well, I think if someone has a problem with it [addiction] then he [sic] should look for a private space where he [sic] can do it and then he [sic] can clean up afterwards and then it's fine. We might be addicted, or many are addicted but that doesn't make you an indecent person, doesn't it? Why? You still are human and you still have a conscience.

Consuming drugs for Nicole was not synonymous to indecent behaviour. This showed the difference in moral demands made at the square, depending on fluid or more durable relations.[4]

A further way for the group of the *drinkers* to emphasize their legitimate presence at the square and the deviance of the drug consumers was talk about police operations. Batu described that the police intervention forms and their visibility have changed over the years:

> In the past, you know?! A long time ago, seven or eight years ago, it was like, the first bench was occupied by alcoholics, you know?! Elderly people and so on. A lot of them are dead. Most of them are. And then the junkies came, you know?! They were not so many as today. Maybe ten a day. And back then the police never came, why should they?! Everybody stuck to his [sic] own business, and there you would find no syringes on the ground. … Everything was cool!

Since the *junkies* came to the square in larger numbers the visibility of police intervention had increased, according to Batu. Back in the days where the *drinkers* or, as he called them, *alcoholics* outnumbered other groups at the square, police intervention was not necessary, and people 'could do their thing'. Herbert explained the new forms of intervention such as expulsion from the square or identity card controls by a change in the legal status of the square as a 'high crime area'. For a certain period the day nursery even employed a private security company and there had been a general ban on alcohol between 2009 and 2010 which was partly still in force.[5] Nicole thought the police focused 'mainly on people who deal with drugs'. For Gabriele the increased police presence at the square made her uneasy at first, until the police noticed 'who they are' and that they 'try to keep things calm around the square'. Although she sympathized with the police to a certain degree she noted that she could not work with them openly because she was 'not tired of life'. Conflicts within the *scene* or the expectation of revenge between groups kept her from reporting crime to the police and refer to tendencies of self-regulation. As Duneier (2001, 95) and Anderson (2000) have noted, self-regulation and the formation of 'codes of the street' prioritize the community's internal logic over the legal order.

All in all, the respondents showed verbal and practical strategies to confirm their decency and showed their support of society's moral standards, a form of 'ideological embracement' (Snow and Anderson 1993, 221). The square and its social infrastructure became a resource for developing a personal identity with self-worth. As Becker states, 'the degree to which an act will be treated as deviant

4 Further conflicts evolved at the square around the consumption of strong alcohol of a group called *hardcore drunkards* by the *drinkers*, the occupation of the public toilet, incidents of public urinating and issues about garbage (see Duneier 2001 for issues on public urinating and logic field constraints).

5 The ban applies to the front square, which is property of the local church.

depends on who commits the act and who feels he [sic] has been harmed by it' (Becker 1997, 12). When former or discreet drug consumers felt harassed by the sight of syringes or public consumption they tended to detest and denounce those acts and the people conducting them while they, on the other side, had justifications for their actions. Fluid encounters and stories about them supported the identity work for groups like the *drinkers*. Forms of symbolic boundary work concentrated on issues of consumption and behaviour. Snow and Anderson (1993, 215) found comparable practices among the homeless in their study and called this form of symbolic boundary drawing 'associational distancing', while Kusenbach applied the term 'fencing' (2009, 413). Both concepts indicate a practice of distancing for which the reference to a certain behaviour and moral character of the 'other' is fundamental. Referring to themselves as *drinkers* thereby seems to be an act of 'normalizing' matters (see Kusenbach 2009, 421) since drinking beer or wine, more than drinking stronger liquor, is a socially widely accepted practice.

Conclusion

The square can be seen as sanctuary at the social and spatial fringes of society. It offers a platform for a social infrastructure and thus enables access to resources. In order to hoard and access resources there is differentiation even at a small-scale space of a square. Indeed, the drawing of symbolic boundaries (see Lamont and Molnár 2002) exemplifies a social process that can apply to larger social settings as well. Social marginalization does not only become visible here, but it gets negotiated and reproduced. It is thus a sanctuary from marginalization in the sense that social gatherings produce a visibility and a claim for 'spatial justice' (Yiftachel, Goldhaber and Nuriel 2009, 121) connected by Merrifield (1996) to social recognition: 'Indeed, the visibility of all different sorts of characters in public spaces – poor and rich alike – challenges everybody, forces people to react, is one step towards affirming difference, demanding just deserts, voicing complaints and social grievances' (ibid., 120).

A relational approach helps to understand negotiations that may work less audible and visible than for non-marginalized other social groups but shows how people at the social fringes make a life in the city. To use a 'relational lens' (see Blokland 2012) to pursue the dynamic of social life on a square may appear banal – but it shows that the construction of a personal identity is deeply socially rooted and that changes in the social and physical environment affect people, but do not affect them all in the same way. Those changes initiate manoeuvres that do not follow a fixed path. Following Sen (2005), the same set of means such as the square provides a different set of possibilities to different people.

To make the square work for the research participants and bring their capabilities to function, as we have seen, depended on their social infrastructure of durable engagements and fluid encounters at *Leopoldplatz*. More precisely, established groups like the *drinkers* dominated the front square until 2011 by producing 'home territories' for 'interactional pleasure' (Lofland 1998, 12) and visibility, which gave them spatial profit (see Bourdieu 1999). Mediated through their durable engagement with the square and a social worker they had the capability to monopolize, then, the access to a social project (see Lamont and Molnár 2002) called the *Drinking Room*. When the benches at the front square got removed in 2012 the room became their sanctuary, where they preserved their symbolic community. But since the square is always 'in the making' (Simone 2010, 3), too, it stores histories and changes according to its social environment (see Massey 1995; Blokland 2001; Blokland 2008). Paying attention to the claims made by the self-assigned *druggist* and *visitors* from different *scenes* in Berlin who 'need a place to stay' and came to *Leopoldplatz* because it was still comparably 'calm' hint at marginalization as a process that becomes tangible at the square. The spatial exclusion by police operations at one part of the city and programmes of urban redevelopment changed the social environment and physical structure at *Leopoldplatz*. Both factors constructed a changing context that was again affecting people's capabilities at those social fringes for negotiating unemployment, substance consumption or an otherwise socially isolated life. Social recognition is a resource for those who are socially marginalized (see Oldenburg and Brissett 1982; Snow and Anderson 1993; Mitchell 1995; Merrifield 1996). But ambivalence about their social surrounding remained central to the research participants, since they were aware of, and reproduced, social stigmatization. An example related to that were two women I met during my research who explained how uneasy they felt about spending time at the square labelling themselves 'bad women' for spending time at the square and drinking beer publicly. This indicates subtle exclusions and stigmatization that had been enforced by men at the square and are the result of the reproduction of gendered stereotypes.

To conclude, there is variation in the labels people attributed to 'others' and used to evaluate behaviour to create decency for themselves and their kind, but those lines appeared thin. Verbal techniques of identity work coincided, as we have seen, often with spatial practices that tended to be excluding. Although benches stood in close proximity of a few metres those symbolic boundaries were a mediation or expression of something more crucial. When Kusenbach (2009) investigated stigma work of people living in so called 'trailer parks' she identified strategies which allowed the stigma carriers to distance themselves from the stigma and in this sense to cope with their situation. People employ practices that allow them to pass the stigma on to those whom, in their view, it really belongs (see ibid.). It is a way to position one's self in society actively and gain recognition for it (see Blokland 2012). In this sense, the *drinkers'* emphasis on their own decency apart from the *junkies*, may not be an attempt to appear as 'paragons of morality' (Wacquant 2002) but to negotiate their position within the social setting at the square and the social relations they found there – and from there, to symbolically negotiate their position within the city at large.

References

Anderson, Elijah. 2000. *Code of the Street: Decency, Violence, and the Moral Life of the Inner City*. New York: W.W. Norton.

Becker, Howard S. 1997. *Outsiders: Studies in Sociology of Deviance*. New York: Free Press.

Blokland, Talja V. 2001. 'Bricks, Mortar, Memories: Neighborhood and Networks in Collective Acts of Remembering'. *International Journal of Urban and Regional Research* 25: 268–83.

———. 2003. *Urban Bonds: Social Relationships in an Inner City Neighbourhood*. Cambridge: Polity Press.

———. 2008. "You Got to Remember you Live in Public Housing': Place-Making in an American Housing Project'. *Housing, Theory and Society* 25: 31–46.

———. 2009. 'Celebrating Local Histories and Defining Neighbourhood Communities: Place-Making in a Gentrified Neighbourhood'. *Urban Studies* 46: 1593–610.

———. 2012. 'Blaming neither the Undeserving Poor nor the Revanchist Middle Classes: A Relational Approach to Marginalization'. *Urban Geography* 33: 488–507.

Blokland, Talja V. and Michael Savage. 2008. *Networked Urbanism: Social Capital in the City*. Aldershot, England; Burlington, VT: Ashgate.

Bourdieu, Pierre. 1999. 'Site Effects'. In *The Weight of the World: Social Suffering in Contemporary Society*, edited by Pierre Bourdieu, Alain Accardo and Priscilla P. Ferguson, 123–9. Stanford: Stanford University Press.

Duneier, Mitchell. 2001. *Sidewalk*. New York: Farrar, Straus and Giroux.

Elias, Norbert and John L. Scotson. 1993. *Etablierte und Außenseiter*. Frankfurt am Main: Suhrkamp.

Gans, Herbert J. 1982. *The Urban Villagers: Group and Class in the Life of Italian-Americans*. New York: Free Press.

Goffman, Erving. 1986. *Stigma: Notes on the Management of Spoiled Identity*. New York: Simon & Schuster.

Häußermann, Hartmut and Andreas Kapphan. 2004. 'Berlin: Ausgrenzungsprozesse in einer europäischen Stadt'. In *An den Rändern der Städte: Armut und Ausgrenzung*, edited by Hartmut Häußermann, Martin Kronauer and Walter Siebel, 203–34. Frankfurt am Main: Suhrkamp.

Jacobs, Jane. 1961. *The Death and Life of Great American Cities*. New York: Vintage Books.

Jenkins, Richard. 1996. *Social Identity*. London, New York: Routledge.

Jones, Nikki. 2010. *Between Good and Ghetto: African American Girls and Inner City Violence*. New Brunswick: Rutgers University Press.

Kusenbach, Margarethe. 2009. 'Salvaging Decency: Mobile Home Residents' Strategies of Managing the Stigma of 'Trailer' Living'. *Qualitative Sociology* 32: 399–428.

Lamont, Michèle. 2000. *The Dignity of Working Men: Morality and the Boundaries of Race, Class, and Immigration*. New York: Russell Sage Foundation.

Lamont, Michèle and Nissim Mizrachi. 2011. 'Ordinary People Doing Extraordinary Things: Responses to Stigmatization in Comparative Perspective'. *Ethnic and Racial Studies* 35: 365–81.

Lamont, Michèle and Virág Molnár. 2002. 'The Study of Boundaries in the Social Sciences'. *Annual Review of Sociology* 28: 167–95.

Lessenich, Stephan. 2009. 'Krise des Sozialen?' *Aus Politik und Zeitgeschichte* 52: 28–34. Accessed 20 February 2014. http://www.bpb.de/apuz/31512/krise-des-sozialen?p=all.

Liebow, Elliot. 1995. *Tell them who I am: The Lives of Homeless Women*. New York: Penguin Books.

———. 2003. *Tally's Corner: A Study of Negro Streetcorner Men*. Lanham: Rowman & Littlefield.

Lofland, Lyn H. 1998. *The Public Realm: Exploring the City's Quintessential Social Territory*. Hawthorne: Aldine de Gruyter.

Massey, Doreen. 1995. 'Places and their Past'. *History Workshop Journal* 39: 182–92.

Merrifield, Andy. 1996. 'Public Space: Integration and Exclusion in Urban Life'. *City* 1: 57–72.

Mitchell, Don. 1995. 'The End of Public Space? People's Park, Definitions of the Public, and Democracy'. *Annals of the Association of American Geographers* 85: 108–33.

Müllerstraße-Aktiv. 2013. 'Projekte: Leopoldplatz'. Accessed 5 May 2014. http://www.muellerstrasse-aktiv.de/projekte/leopoldplatz/.

Newman, Katherine S. 2000. *No Shame in My Game: The Working Poor in the Inner City*. New York: Vintage Books.

Oldenburg, Ramon and Dennis Brissett. 1982. 'The Third Place'. *Qualitative Sociology* 5: 265–84.

Sen, Amartya. 2005. 'Human Rights and Capabilities'. *Journal of Human Development* 6: 151–66.

Senate Department for Urban Development and the Environment. 2014. 'Stadterneuerung Mitte: Sanierungsgebiet Mitte Müllerstraße'. Accessed 18 July 2014. http://www.stadtentwicklung.berlin.de/staedtebau/foerderprogramme/stadterneuerung/de/muellerstrasse/index.shtml.

Simone, AbdouMaliq. 2010. *City Life from Jakarta to Dakar: Movements at the Crossroads*. New York: Routledge.

Snow, David A. and Leon Anderson. 1987. 'Identity Work Among the Homeless: The Verbal Construction and Avowal of Personal Identities'. *American Journal of Sociology* 92: 1336–71.

———. 1993. *Down on their Luck: A Study of Homeless Street People*. Berkeley: University of California Press.

Veness, April R. 1993. 'Neither Homed nor Homeless: Contested Definitions and the Personal Worlds of the Poor'. *Political Geography* 12: 319–40.

Wacquant, Loïc. 2002. 'Scrutinizing the Street: Poverty, Morality, and the Pitfalls of Urban Ethnography'. *American Journal of Sociology* 107: 1468–532.

———. 2007. 'Territorial Stigmatization in the Age of Advanced Marginality'. *Thesis Eleven* 91: 66–77.

Wasserman, Jason. A. and Jeffrey M. Clair. 2010. 'Housing Patterns of Homeless People: The Ecology of the Street in the Era of Urban Renewal'. *Journal of Contemporary Ethnography* 40: 71–101.

Whyte, William F. 1993. *Street Corner Society: The Social Structure of an Italian Slum.* Chicago, London: The University of Chicago Press.

Williams, Terry M. 1989. *The Cocaine Kids: The Inside Story of a Teenage Drug Ring.* Reading, MA: Addison-Wesley Pub. Co.

Yiftachel, Oren, Ravit Goldhaber and Roy Nuriel. 2009. 'Urban Justice and Recognition: Affirmation and Hostility in Beer Sheva'. In *Searching for the Just City*, edited by Peter Marcuse, James Connolly, Johannes Novy, Ingrid Olivo, Cuz Potter and Justin Steil, 120–43. Abingdon: Routledge.

Chapter 9
Holding on to Faith: Religion as Resource to Create Capabilities in the Face of Institutional Discrimination

Hannah Schilling

Introduction

Religious settings enable durable engagements, as they function as foci for repeated interactions. We ask how religious practice is used as a resource to become capable, in the sense of Sen (2005), in a position of marginalization. Urban scholars like Mike Davis (2006) have expressed concern over religious practices of the urban marginalized and see them as new signs of a 'culture of poverty' – poor people are more likely to embrace ideologies that lead to fundamentalism, as they are living in anomic conditions without law and order for 'orientation' (Davis 2006 quoted in Bayat 2007, 580). This diagnosis is in particular applied to highly politicized religious movements (cf. Mousseau 2011; Davis 2006; Bayat 2007). This chapter challenges this position. It discusses the use of religious beliefs and membership of a religious congregation to confront everyday challenges in the city.

Taking *religiosity as a social practice* allows seeing religion beyond its function as a source of identity and belonging. Scholarship on religion and immigration predominantly discusses religious congregations from the perspective of their role for acculturation or socio-cultural integration (see Cadge and Ecklund 2007 for a historical overview), and more recently as nodes of belonging in transnational networks (Levitt 2003; Ebaugh and Chafetz 2002). Studying religiosity as practice embeds it in the social environment as well as in individual trajectories. Schäfer applied a 'habitus analysis' to reconstruct the beliefs of religious actors within the context of their experiences and within a framework of social competition and functional differentiation (2013, 14). He built on the work of Max Weber who saw religious beliefs as structuring and structured by social practice and social positions (see Weber 2006 [1934]; cf. Bienfait 2011). But an analysis of religiosity as a reflection of socio-demographic inequalities and as practice that shapes and is shaped by social differentiation needs to be complemented by a less inflexible perspective on cultural practices performed by actors. Rather than seeing religion as a substantial identity composed of a holistic theological ethic, it can be understood as a set of practices that are used for knitting social relationships relative to a given context and a resource for the actor's creation of capabilities. Speaking with Lamont and Small, religion then functions as an element of the actor's toolkit or set of practices, beliefs and attitudes (Lamont and Small 2008, 81–3), something that Michèle Lamont termed as 'repertoire' (Lamont and Lareau 1988; Lamont and Small 2008), by drawing on Ann Swidler's approach on culture (1986). Here, as elements of repertoires, religious beliefs are put into use in the construction of strategies of actions (cf. Lamont and Fleming 2005) and more precisely, can become, as we will argue, resources for creating capabilities. At the same time, this then means to account for the heterogeneity and ambivalences in the actor's repertoires, and calls for a relational perspective on religion: the way of deploying religious moral orientations is informed by the dynamics of the social contexts and borne by connections of all kinds (cf. Nagel 2010 for a relational perspective on migration and religion). In other words, religiosity has the potential to become a 'practice of informal life' (Bayat 2007) that enables fluid encounters and creates opportunities for durable engagements, when formal urban structures do not work for people or even against them (cf. Simone 2010).

We explore this argument further through a study in a Pentecostal church in the south of Berlin. For two years, around 150 people regularly attend the Mass in a former Catholic church. Nearly all of them are immigrants that left Ghana, Nigeria, Uganda or Zambia to make a living in Europe. During six months, we participated at the church's Sunday Mass and other activities and conducted 20 semi-structured interviews with church members. Our interviews and conversations at participant observations reveal the difficulties they had to face as new residents, but marginalized citizens, in Berlin.

In the following, we discuss how the participation in a Pentecostal church can become a resource for Sub-Saharan immigrants who face specific processes of marginalization in the city. First, we describe the immigrants' experiences in institutional settings as their particular space to manoeuvre in the face of marginalization. The second part of the chapter presents three different strategies of using religious practice to realize capabilities in such a context. These are, first, the use of religion as a source for moral orientation that allows them to open up to fluid encounters, second the investment of religiosity as cultural capital to get recognized in Berlin and, third, the benefits from a social infrastructure that the church offers its members, a place to which religiosity is a first entry card to creating resources.

Processes of Marginalization in Institutional Settings

In this section, we describe the processes, explicit and subtle, through which the Sub-Saharan immigrants that attend the church are pushed out of resourceful settings, not always because of anyone's intentions, but because the mechanisms in place and the various forms of capital that are required to make these settings work for oneself are effectively keeping them out and pushing them to the edges of especially the labour market. We look at processes in urban institutional settings where these newcomers negotiate their access to citizenship rights, and the related entitlement to access the labour and housing markets, with bureaucrats. Michael Lipsky (1980) stressed the importance of discretionary space to distribute resources by street level bureaucrats such as teachers, employers, state administrators and policemen. He points to their space of manoeuvre in determining the nature, amount and quality of benefits and sanctions to their clients. The scarcity of resources together with the ambiguity or complexity of rules and role models explain how 'institutions produce inequalities': the working conditions lead the agents to differentiate structurally between their clients and to redistribute their resources unequally (Sala Pala 2013, 53). Hence, institutions become crucial 'actors' in processes of marginalization.

Three forms of marginalization in institutional settings were central to our interview partners: the construction of the undeserving stranger who is a priori suspicious, the denial of resources on the basis of non-deservingness and the lack of recognition of cultural resources as cultural capital.

Becoming the Suspicious 'Other'

Hillary was a student in her early 20s. After receiving her bachelor in Ghana, she came to study in Germany for a Master's degree in Consumer Sciences. The renowned International German Academic Exchange Service supported her stay in Germany. The scholarship gave her the formal entitlement to come to Germany and benefit from Berlin's educational institutions. However, on her way to Berlin, she was confronted with the distrust of the agents who processed her visa application. To obtain the visa, she needed a written official invitation from a German and a statement of commitment to cover any eventual costs she might not be able to cover. Moreover, she needed to explain the relation to her sponsor. Hillary's uncle, residing in Germany, became her sponsor. In the application process, however, she was challenged:

> Interviewer: Could you describe the visa problems more? What kind of problems did you have?
> Hillary: I don't know. Actually I think they were trying to find out whether I knew my sponsor. It's actually my uncle. So they were trying to find out whether I knew my uncle. Whether he really was my uncle. Whether I knew his family. So they kind of interviewed me twice, can you imagine? Has somebody ever been interviewed twice?

The embassy got in contact with her for a first time and Hillary went for the interview. But then they called her again, demanding another interview, in which they interviewed her as if they had never asked her anything before about her sponsor. This 'double-checking' delayed the entire bureaucratic process of Hillary's visa application. As a consequence, the moment Hillary needed the visa in order to leave Ghana in time to begin the academic year in Berlin passed. The embassy in Ghana then declined her a visa, stating that she was too late for her studies. Only because Hillary contacted the university in Berlin again to confirm her registration there, the state administration in Accra finally handed her the visa. She started weeks too late in the academic year. This made her start at the university difficult and also complicated her search for accommodation. When she arrived, the university students housing office had already given all well located apartments to those who arrived earlier. She now stayed far away from the university, in one of the outer suburbs.

This confrontation with suspicious street level bureaucrats not only characterized the moment of entering the country, but also coloured Hillary's experiences of everyday life in the city. Hillary often used public transport, and as a student, she held a monthly ticket, included in her registration at the university. It was a personalized ticket, and only valid together with the person's ID. One day, Hillary was checked in the subway. She had to pay a fee, although she had her student ticket with her. 'Because I didn't have my passport, they considered it as if I didn't have my ticket and they billed me with €40', Hillary explained. She complained that it was not fair because normally when they looked at the student ticket it was sufficient to have just that. And the controller checked the other people in the subway and he did not ask them for the identity card. After all, she 'didn't take her passport around all day!'

The controller's request for her identity card was 'in line with the law', as the student ticket is officially only valid together with an ID – but 'strangely enough', Hillary was the only person that had to prove her identity. This special treatment shows the subtle distrust of street level bureaucrats like the ticket controller towards visible strangers. It is discriminatory not in the sense that the controller did something legally wrong, but because it put Hillary in the role of someone with fraudulent intentions, which can be seen as a practice of racial profiling (cf. Friedrich and Mohrfeldt 2012). Such differential treatment based on race happens in the space of manoeuvre that street level bureaucrats have in their everyday routines. It is an opaque space, as legal frameworks and rules of law cannot touch it. Such practices are part of a process that constructs the immigrant as 'stranger', a generalized 'other' who is a priori incomplete and has no integrity (Sayad 1999, 401).

Demba, 40 years old, another Ghanaian member of the church, recently bought a duplex in the south of Berlin to live there with his wife and three children. He felt he became the 'public outcast' when his neighbour told everyone in the neighbourhood how 'indebted' he was – debts that were in fact instalment payments for electricity. Actually, Demba was paying far more of the electricity bill that he and his neighbour decided to share when both started to construct the duplex some months ago. As he was not as fluent in German as his German neighbour, Demba explained, his neighbour became the official contracting partner with the electricity company. This gave him the possibility to then decide that he would rather use the electricity alone. Demba had to lay new cables, causing him additional costs. He interpreted the story as 'one of the things that happen in Germany, that one has to struggle with', and instead of becoming angry, he had to 'forget about it'.

This construction of the suspicious 'other', a priori supposed to be 'fraudulent' and 'immoral', is the basis and legitimation for labelling some to be 'undeserving' of resources, with marginalization as a result, as we will see below.

The Denial of Resources on the Basis of Non-Deservingness

Christine was a young mother who grew up in Nigeria and decided to leave the country to find work and a better life. Her dream was to live in the United States, but for now, she stayed in Germany, as it was too difficult to get a visa for the US. She had lived in Berlin for 10 years. When she arrived, she successfully passed a qualification training to become a security guard at one of the airports of Berlin. The city had two airports at the moment of our research, one in *Schönefeld* in the south of Berlin, and one in the northern part of the city, in *Tegel*, which was about to be closed in the near future. Christine worked at the airport *Schönefeld* for some months, but then was fired. Since then, she lived on unemployment benefits and became a mother of two children.

Soon after Christine began working for the security company at the airport in the south, her supervisor wanted her to switch to the airport in the north of the city, far away from Christine's residency in the south. Christine refused because of the distance. Shortly after, her supervisor demanded her to take working shifts from six to nine in the morning, and then again from two to three or four in the afternoon. When she refused the supervisor's schedule of shift work, Christine was threatened to get fired 'without reasons', as Christine put it. At the last moment, her chief decided to keep her, but transferred her to the *Tegel* airport after all. Christine described her contact with colleagues there as difficult:

> They were strange, these people. They didn't speak to me; they didn't want to have a lot of contact with me. If you speak to them, they make a funny face, so that you are thinking by yourself – hugh, where am I here? What kind of people are these?

She explained their reaction as being induced by her skin colour: 'All these different people, they have their own ideas and opinions, and some of them are just asking by themselves: Oh, there is a Black woman coming, why?'

After some months, Christine eventually did get fired. Again, there were 'no reasons' – except for a report that stated Christine's 'inappropriate social behaviour'. She was described as a loner who didn't speak with her colleagues, and didn't share anything about her private life. The employees' union representative didn't defend her case, and Christine lost her job.

In Christine's story, several dynamics in the end led to her dismissal. First, her employer organized her working schedule in a way that put Christine each time in a more vulnerable working condition – either she had to take the burden of long work-trips and the prospect of redundancy, as the *Tegel* airport in the north was about to be closed, or she got working shifts that broke up her day in the most inefficient way possible, in particular because it was a one-hour trip to arrive at the airport. Second, Christine's protest against being pushed out of her work didn't bring the desired outcome. On the contrary, she ended where she never wanted to work. Although she could speak up, as a member of a racialized minority in Germany, her relative power position at work made her incapable to protest effectively. This was related to her difficulties to get into contact with her working colleagues due to 'mobbing' and intentional alienation of the 'Black woman'. Marginalized at work, she could not draw on the social capital of other employees, represented by the union, at the moment of her dismissal – nobody spoke up to make her stay. In the end, it was the discretionary space of her employer to decide on the duty roster – here, he had to make the choice who to put at which shift and locality. Apparently, Christine was not on his top list of employees whom he tried to keep in his team. As some of the security guards, however, had to take shifts at the *Tegel* airport and had to be flexibly present for the rush hours spread out over the day, the employer seemed to choose those employees who were least likely to build coalitions with other colleagues and oppose the employer.

Jenny told similar experiences. She was in her 40s, born in Ghana and now married to a German who had lived in the same neighbourhood all his life. She managed to do an apprenticeship as a geriatric nurse through an employment agency. However, Jenny then was denied classes for her driving licence, although it was part of the contract:

> I was doing a professional training to become a nurse. And in my class I was the only one who didn't take driving lessons to get the licence. And I went back to tell the woman who is responsible for me at the jobcentre that everybody is doing the apprenticeship together with classes to obtain a driver licence. And so why I can't do it, too? And she told me: No, go. When you finish this class I will let you do one more level. With the driver license included. So that's what the woman told me. And so when I finished that first course I went to Africa for seven weeks and came back and she said 'No'. She personally, intentionally didn't want to give the driver license classes to me, because I was the only Black woman there. They give it to everybody, but the woman refused it to me.

Among the thirty classmates, Jenny was the only one not to get the driving licence, although she had the same entitlement as her classmates. As explanation for this denial, Jenny brought up her ascribed otherness as a 'Black' woman. Until today, Jenny didn't get a driving licence, which would be an improvement of her employment prospects as a nurse, especially as she wanted to continue working in the mobile home care service for the elderly.

These stories show the church members' marginalized position in the labour market as the consequence of the employers, colleagues and street level bureaucrats' choices of resource allocation, driven by the stigmatization of 'Black women' as undeserving. In both cases, the women had the means to contest the denial or withdrawal of resources – they had the formal entitlement and the skills to claim their rights (i.e. they addressed the problem to the street level bureaucrats). However, their minority position (Guillaumin 1972, 119–28) made it difficult to build alliances with other colleagues and to get heard by those who decided on the distribution of jobs, training and working shifts. This, then, hampered, in Sen's terminology, their capabilities to achieve valuable combinations of human functioning (Sen 2005, 151).

Lacking the Institutional Recognition of Resources

Rob's experience exemplifies a quite different process, that of the non-recognition of his capital in the German institutional context. The young father Rob left Nigeria, where he was born, with a six-years school degree, to travel the West African Coast. He learnt to run his own business in the Benin Republic for over seven years. However, he could not validate this experience into a professional qualification in the German labour market. He lacked the formal certificate that would validate his professional training as institutional cultural capital, in form of a job qualification. When he arrived in Germany, he did not get a residence permit and thus wasn't allowed to work. Friends here and there helped him survive, but he was far from earning a living. After having married a Nigerian woman, enabling him to become a legal resident in Berlin, he started to work as an unskilled worker at a fast-food chain in Berlin. He was hired through a temporary employment agency and thus only got short-time contracts, followed by periods of unemployment. Consequently, even though he had the skills to work as a self-entrepreneur, as he learnt to 'make business' and trade goods, he could not buy a small snack shop, as he had tried, and become officially a retailer in Berlin:

> I tried (to do my own business). If you want to do that, they will say bring this paper and the other paper. I had an appointment with one of my friends who is a retailer here. He is selling snacks. He wanted to close his takeaway, so I tried to buy it from him. But he said I should bring my bank statement, my passport, my working contract, my *Schufa*[1] document. So I took all of these documents to the landlord of the takeaway and the lady there called me back and she said my salary is too poor and that they can't give me the place. That is what I was saying before: that here it is difficult, because of this *Amt Amt Amt* [bureaucracy, bureaucracy, bureaucracy]. It's difficult for people to become self-employed. … But in Africa or I think in America as well, it is different: If you want to be

1 German society for the securing of loans, an organization that checks people's credit worthiness.

> self-employed, you can just be it on your own. Nobody will ask you how you become self-employed!

Rob's economic situation hindered him to work as the owner of a snack shop in Berlin. He could not transform his skills into cultural capital in the German labour market, and therefore could not transform them into economic resources. Moreover, for several months, he lacked the formal entitlement to work, slowing down the accumulation of economic capital and making it even more difficult to begin validating his cultural capital in the form of a professional qualification, i.e. through starting an apprenticeship.

The devaluation of resources, the stigmatization of the newcomer as immoral and not trustworthy, and hence the denial of resources as an undeserving 'other' and the consequences of relative power position in organizations marginalized these Sub-Saharan immigrants. These church members became a minority of *strangers* in the city, where they were not only a minority in numbers, but also a minority with regard to their power to make claims and their capacity to access resources (cf. Guillaumin 1972, 119–28). They were positioned as a group of 'strangers' in that they were legally and symbolically treated as 'immigrants' from elsewhere. This particular status was used to create their 'undeservingness' in institutional settings.

More generally, the examples showed how 'racism' worked not as intentional acts of some, but as an institutional setting, as Mark Terkessidis puts it: 'Racism is an institutional assemblage, that makes it possible to bind the hands of people in order to blame them afterwards for not using their hands' (2004, 107, author's translation).

Religiosity as Social Practice to Realize Capabilities

As we have seen, institutional settings are crucial sites for marginalization. In the following, we discuss how people use religiosity to create space to manoeuvre again and realize capabilities. We will show how Sub-Saharan immigrants use their membership of the Pentecostal ministry for their daily life struggles.

Opening up for Fluid Encounters

A key moment in the marginalization is the suspicion that the church members are met with in their everyday life in the city, practiced by street level bureaucrats to legitimate the denial of resources. Religiosity can then be used as a source of moral orientations that enables continuing to connect in fluid encounters with street level bureaucrats or other strangers. Jenny, who did the apprenticeship as a geriatric nurse, did so:

> So [things like the refusal of the driving licence training] just happen. … You have to work on yourself first. I worked on my heart. I want to be open, sometimes people will hate you, but you will forget their hate. … You know, one thing about Christians is that we take things easy. … So if somebody hates you, you forget it and go on with your life. That is Christianity. You understand. So we are still nice with [the agent in the job centre]. When I see her in her red jeans, I say to her that she looks good, and she answers kindly '*Dankeschön*' [Thank you] (*Jenny imitates the case worker's voice*).

'Being Christian' meant to Jenny to be polite and open for new encounters with the street level bureaucrat who refused collaboration. More generally speaking, Jenny's moral orientation was to practice openness and politeness, no matter what hate she encountered. This became a way to deal with her marginalized position that allowed her to remain open to potential future resources that spring from fluid encounters. Accounts from other church members confirmed this. The pastor Ilya saw the practice of prayer as a way to virtually transform a living environment that was potentially harmful to him:

> There is one particular place [in my neighbourhood] that is known for the neo-Nazis' gatherings. Almost daily, they come together there at the station. But until now, nothing happened. And in in so far as it concerns me, I think, with prayers you can also change things there. One knows that neo-Nazis are xenophobic, but God protects us and until now nothing happened. And we pray for them, that they recognize the truth in life, that they realize that foreigners are human being as everyone else and that it isn't worth [it] to fight them.

Prayers can become a practice to handle people and places that threaten actors' 'ontological security', or their confidence and trust in the world around them (Giddens 1990, quoted in Noble 2005, 113). Even if the neo-Nazis' presence could not be changed and continued to shape the church member's position as marginalized in the city, religious practice helped to overcome a paralysis of fear and discomfort. Feeling comfortable is a very basic enabling condition for the capacity to act (see Noble 2005), and more precisely, for being capable of opening up for fluid encounters and durable engagements. This became clear in Arthur's story. He integrated his religious belief into his experiences with mobility and practice in Berlin. Arthur is in his forties. He migrated from Uganda to Germany and was for a long time detained as an asylum seeker in the outskirts of Berlin. Finally, he was recognized as a refugee and allowed to begin to work and earn his own money as a custodian in a public school. Arthur assured that he did not fear encounters with strangers anymore when moving around in the city, as he had 'his Jesus'. Jesus was accompanying him and protecting. Why should he 'be afraid of a human being?', he asked. Deriving confidence from his belief he was empowered to continue visiting other asylum seekers in detention centres that were situated in the former eastern outskirts of Berlin that he described as 'uncomfortable' zones of the city, for its imagined and experienced xenophobia, discussed in Lewek's chapter. Through his visits to the detention centres, Arthur created opportunities for fluid encounters that the detainees could use to obtain information and support in their struggle to get access to the city.

Thus, these examples show how religiosity served as moral orientation to remain open to fluid encounters in the city, even though one experienced harm and mistrust in contacts with strangers in institutional settings and the public realm.

Validating Resources to Become Capable in Berlin

At the beginning of the chapter, we showed that the church member's marginalized positions stem partly from the difficulty to make capacities recognized by state and labour market institutions. Such barriers require the development of alternative strategies to turn capacities into capabilities – following Erel (2010), immigrants create mechanisms of mobilizing and validating cultural practices corresponding to the new living environment. We hence have to consider how different resources are made to work to become capabilities, rather than to simply assess whether the person's means and instruments fit or don't fit in a given context, as if both context and means are given.

We will see how the church member's turn their religiosity into cultural capital that brings them recognition and citizenship rights in the new living context of Berlin. We describe two processes essential to turning resources into capabilities. One the one hand, we will discuss conversion of cultural resources into economic or social resources (see Bourdieu 1983). On the other hand, we show how religiosity gets validated and becomes symbolic capital. The term validation indicates how certain capacities bring actors social recognition (symbolic capital) in a given context – and become an enabling resource to them (cf. Yiftachel, Godlhaber and Nuriel 2009; and Bourdieu 2000 on symbolic capital).

Mary met her husband in Hamburg in the Pentecostal church there. They were both from Ghana and residents in Germany for about 20 years. In the ministry, everyone called Mary *Mama*, expressing the symbolic status of respect she enjoyed within the congregation. Before starting church festivities such as the women's feast, everyone waited for her to take a seat and say the prayer. The women greeted her with respect and devotion. In contrast, when we met Mary for the interview, we found ourselves with a shy lady, who was cautious to choose the right words. Her everyday life in Berlin was very bound to the activities of the church. It led her to various sites in the city, for distributing missionary leaflets in one of the Berlin parks or for visiting church members in case of illness or birth. Besides, she left the interactions with the German institutions to her husband – 'because of the language, you know' – and had few activities or professional engagements in Berlin. However, as head of a women's group in the ministry, she socialized with the Catholic women's group of the neighbourhood, frequented by old German ladies. They used the rooms of the ministry once a week and were invited to a programme led by Mary, as the field notes on a conversation with the pastor documented:

> The pastor described very enthusiastically: The German women came also to this program. It was great: they enjoyed it so much! One woman even said that she has never heard such a good thing and that she was really enlightened. And normally Germans, they stay only one hour or something but this time they stayed the whole time of the program! Because they liked it so much!

We see that Mary's religious practice was an expertise that the German participants valued. It was a capacity that she could use to get 'affirmative recognition' (Yiftachel, Godlhaber and Nuriel 2009, 126), in a context where the same group of people, the old German ladies, had been rather hostile to the Pentecostal congregation when they moved into 'their church and neighbourhood'. Her religious expertise allowed Mary to build bridges. And it nourished her self-esteem. The way she spoke about her role as a Christian in Germany reflected the construction of a positive self-identity, fed by this affirmative recognition she experienced:

> Mary: I wish that all may come to Christ. I wish that all may, and also should know Jesus. So that is what I pray every day, in my free time, I am praying to God, save, save the Germans. That Germans come to knowledge of Christ. …
> Interviewer (*later on*): I am impressed. I can imagine that this is hard sometimes, to talk with all those people who have problems.
> Mary: You have to. It's the gift. … To help humanity. The Germans, the American, the British, they came to Africa to help us. So now, we have to pray in the gospel for them.

Thus, Mary could turn her religiosity into cultural capital as it facilitated fluid encounters with strangers. Moreover, she validated her religiosity as symbolic capital that gave her a legitimation for her presence in Germany – that is, in her eyes, the need to help the Germans to come to Jesus Christ.

Pastor Ilya grew up in Ghana and came to Germany with a student residence permit in order to finish his studies in Economics. Living in Hamburg, he got into the Pentecostal community of Ghanaian immigrants and became 'African Pastor', certificated after participation in an African Theological Training of the Hamburg Missionary Academy. When he finished his studies in Economics, the immigration laws obliged him to leave the country.

At that moment, he could make his activities as a pastor valuable to become a German citizen. When he logged a complaint against the decision of the Immigration Department in Germany, pastor Ilya attracted the attention of the German Protestant Church and German political parties. The fact that the religious *and* the political forces came together and supported pastor Ilya's and the Missionary Academies struggle, shows how (Christian) religion and state are intertwined in Germany: the church is an important political force and voice in the public (cf. Amir-Moazami 2007). In this specific context pastor Ilya could validate his religiosity:

> The Protestant Church in Germany has played an important role. … At that time, I helped people in Hamburg who were in prison. [… The church said] since I was a great help there, they fought for me and after a year Miss *Van Felt* and Doctor *Eichhorn* – they were both one of the important people in the body of the Protestant Church … – they wrote me a letter, that I had to go to the German embassy in Accra. And they [the Protestant church] bought us our tickets back to Germany, for the whole family.

In the end, pastor Ilya and his family could come back to Germany. They received not only financial support, but also benefited from symbolic capital in the form of a letter from the German Protestant Church to convince the German state institutions to let them come to Germany.

Both stories showed how religiosity as a cultural practice got recognized: in the first example in face-to face interactions with neighbours of the church, in the second as it got validated as symbolic capital that legitimated the acquisition of German citizenship. Hence, religious practices created opportunities for these church members to achieve a legitimation to stay, symbolically, but sometimes even legally. These opportunities depended much on the specific national context that the pastor and his wife referred to. The particular cultural practice of a Christian religiosity got recognized as symbolic capital by the key theological figure. Many of the evangelical rituals are similar to Christianity, the main religion practiced in Germany. The institution of a German citizenship historically included Christianity as one of the cultural elements that defined the belongingness to a German nationhood. Up to today the Catholic and Protestant churches benefit from some privileges from the state and assume responsibility in public education and ethical questions in politics and society (cf. Amir-Moazami 2007; König 2003). The mobilizing and validating of resources to make them become capabilities thus depended on the opportunity structure in which the agents were situated.

The Church's Infrastructure for Fluid Encounters

The beginning of the chapter showed how church members were pushed to the margins or even out of the formal labour market. In this situation, the membership of a faith-based organization can give access to an infrastructure that offers opportunities for organizing livelihood beyond formal institutions. With infrastructure, we refer to the routinized activities and venues and the availability of spaces to meet after, before and outside the official events:

> [In the church, emerged a space of …] conjunction of heterogeneous activities, modes of production, and institutional forms constitutes highly mobile and provisional possibilities for how people live and make things, how they use the urban environment and collaborate with one another. The specific operations and scopes of these conjunctions are constantly negotiated and depend on the particular histories, understandings, networks, styles, and inclinations of the

> actors involved. ... These conjunctions become a coherent platform for social transaction and livelihood (Simone 2004, 410).

What specific operations, durable engagements and brief encounters, or, in other words, what time and context-specific infrastructure developed then under the umbrella of the Pentecostal ministry?

At our first visit at the ICC, we got to know Vanessa: her dark skinned face heavily made up, with a grandiose hat in leopard skin style, her nails polished, a nice costume and high heels, she approached us, smiling brightly. She talked with us expressively and gave us a personal business card. She told us immediately that she made her own hats – if we wouldn't like to buy one? And with the same quickness she passed by at the table where Vivien, introduced to us at the church over a cup of tea, was seated and then disappeared into the crowd of people standing around the parish building. In the interview a few months later, she confirmed this casual presence at the church. As a saleswoman, she sold cosmetics, hats and other items. She travelled around a lot to do her business. She therefore could not take the expectations of the church community too seriously. But once in a while she appeared at the venues of the ministry – one day she brought her big suitcase full of 'products' that she wanted to sell in 'African shops'. In order to get things done in the city, she relied on the fluid encounters made possible during the gathering of the ministry or other events where Ghanaians or other people, mostly foreigners, came together. Her marginalization from formal institutions was not preventing her from realizing her capabilities:

> I don't rely on the German state. I didn't let the German state interfere in my life so far, that he pays me food or rent. I have struggled on my own, my whole life long. I pay the rent and I have my food. That's why I went my own way. That's why I didn't work with my papers [legally]. That's why, until now, I didn't get my German passport. ... I searched my way. And ... it was so good for me. And I was so happy. I have money, I get money, I travel so much!

Vanessa used the church as a platform for her activities as an entrepreneur who did her business with products she brought from West-African countries to Berlin or the other way round. The church offered the physical and technical infrastructure to meet: heating, rooms, snacks and a mass of people that come to the church. This created opportunities for fluid encounters at a very low cost, i.e. without the need to spend money or energy to organize the rent of a room or to use other semi-public spaces like bars or restaurants where one needs to consume and spend money in order to have the right to use the space.

Maison's professional trajectory and life planning for the future confirmed such a use of the church as an infrastructure: Maison had a degree in engineering from a Berlin university. After finishing his doctorate, he decided to leave his university job. He reported his uneasiness about rigid work-contracts that hindered him to live a life 'in mobility':

> That's the idea: it wasn't as simple as that. I had a lot of offers from the employment agency. ... I could become an employee at an enterprise. But this would have meant to stay here at least three or four years. And we didn't want that. And this is when I said I will do something more flexible.

Maison became a coach for families who wished for their children to come to study in Berlin. The church became the node that connected Maison with his potential clients:

> Interviewer: You said that sometimes people who are still in Africa contact you. How does that happen? From where do you know these people?
> Maison: Sometimes also from here, from the church. As I am almost since nine years here in the church, a lot of people know me. And they know that I am a scientist, and I went through the system, I wrote my Master thesis here, I did my PhD. ... So I am an expert in the area [in which] I am coaching.

Maison could use the presence of people in the church for whom his experience was valuable knowledge to build up a professional career. Hence, he made the fluid encounters there work for him to achieve 'valuable combinations of human functionings' (cf. Sen 2005, 151) – a profession that fitted with his expectations and needs to manage a transnational life that demanded flexibility and mobility.

Maison and Vanessa are representative of other church members who found ways to not lock themselves into fixed commitments with each other. They passed goods and money with minimal regulation within a globalized urban network, engaging in self-entrepreneurial transnational transactions (cf. Simone 2001). Both stories show how the Pentecostal ministry ICC served for some members as a social and material infrastructure where they could manage their life at the margins in Berlin – it was adapted to the travelling of people, and their state of preparedness to come and go. It created new spaces to manoeuvre where formal institutions did not work for them. The examples depict the members' 'trying to balance the need to maintain some functional sense of local "rootedness" while at the same time gaining access to opportunities that are more transnational, even global, in scope' (Simone 2001, 36). And this was not restricted to the most dispossessed in the church, but also worked for people with higher and lower class positions.

Conclusion

Marginalization is the process of exclusion from resourceful settings. This chapter aimed to understand how marginalized people create new opportunities for achieving valuable sets of human functioning (cf. Sen 2005, 151). It showed how people used their religious practices as a resource that could be actualized to become a capability.

We saw that most of the church members had difficulties accessing the resources of state institutions and the formal labour market, either because they lacked the formal entitlements or they suffered from the street level bureaucrat's discretionary space to distribute resources, as it was used to their disadvantage. As a racialized minority of *strangers* in Berlin, the church members often could not mobilize alliances within the institutional settings and in their neighbourhood to make effective claims on resources. Last, but not least, the church member's ontological security was fragile, as street level bureaucrats and some groups of Berlin residents treated them as fraudulent and illegitimate urbanites.

This situation demanded specific practices in order to create capabilities: the validation of cultural resources as cultural capital, the recognition of one's legitimate presence and the re-creation of comfort in the public realm. But it also demanded spaces where fluid encounters and durable engagements could offer resources that institutional settings denied them access to.

Under these conditions, religiosity became a resource that allowed realization and creation of capabilities. Our analysis showed that religiosity was practiced as a moral orientation that encouraged openness to fluid encounters in a context of discomfort and experiences of discrimination. In other situations, religiosity became a cultural resource that was validated as cultural capital to obtain German citizenship or simply the social recognition as a religious expert. Moreover, the individual religiosity could become an entrance card to a religious congregation that served as a social infrastructure which people could use for their specific transactions and missions to organize their livelihood in a transnational context.

Bringing together processes of marginalization and the use of religiosity as social practice sheds a new light on the way religiosity is linked to racist marginalization and a 'culture of poverty'. Religiosity is not a pure ideology, attached to an individual identity and the individual's social position and habitus, nor is racism a problem of a few extremists. Rather, as this chapter showed, religiosity can become a tool that is used in relation to a specific context of marginalization in a way that cannot be confined to a stable set of theological ethics (cf. Simone 2010). And once again, our discussion of institutional marginalization showed that racism can only be conceptualized through including the institutionalized mechanisms that lead to the marginalization of new residents in the city.

Even if the membership of a church gives access to a social infrastructure and the use of religiosity as moral orientation and cultural resource helps to gain recognition and the capacity to act in the urban space, compensation strategies against marginalization have their limits. They give the members of the International Christian Church the capacity to act and to realize capabilities in their daily struggle for survival. Any opportunities to get ahead, however, are still written in the stars – they require fundamental institutional changes.

References

Amir-Moazami, Schirin. 2007. *Politisierte Religion. Der Kopftuchstreit in Deutschland und Frankreich*. Bielefeld: Transcript Verlag.

Bayat, Asef. 2007. 'Radical Religion and the Habitus of the Dispossessed: Does Islamic Militancy Have an Urban Ecology?' *International Journal of Urban and Regional Research* 31 (3): 579–90.

Bienfait, Agathe. 2011. 'Klassen, Schichten, Religionen. Über die sozialstrukturellen Grenzen religiöser Individualisierung'. In *Religionen verstehen*, edited by Agathe Bienfait, 196–218. Wiesbaden: VS Verlag für Sozialwissenschaften.

Bourdieu, Pierre. 1983. 'Ökonomisches Kapital, kulturelles Kapital, soziales Kapital'. In *Soziale Ungleichheiten*. Soziale Welt, Sonderband 2, edited by Reinhardt Kreckel, 183–98. Göttingen: Schwartz.

———. 2000. *Pascalian Meditations*. Cambridge: Polity Press.

Cadge, Wendy and Elaine H. Ecklund. 2007. 'Immigration and Religion'. *Annual Review of Sociology* 33 (1): 359–79.

Davis, Mike. 2006. *Planet of Slums*. London/New York: Verso.

Ebaugh, Helen R. and Janet S. Chafetz. 2002. *Religion Across Borders: Transnational Immigrant Networks*. Walnut Creek, CA: AltaMira.

Erel, Umut. 2010. 'Migrating Cultural Capital: Bourdieu in Migration Studies'. *Sociology* 44 (4): 642–60.

Friedrich, Sebastian and Johanna Mohrfeldt. 'Alltägliche Ausnahmefälle. Zu institutionellem Rassismus bei der Polizei und der Praxis des 'Racial Profiling''. *Antirassistische Zeitschrift* 61: 27–9.

German Embassy Accra. 2012. 'Requirements for Student Visa'. Accessed 18 July 2014. http://ic.daad.de/imperia/md/content/informationszentren/icaccra/13_merkblatt_studentenvisum_de_dld.pdf.

Giddens, Anthony. 1990. *The Consequences of Modernity*. Cambridge: Polity.

Guillaumin, Colette. 1972. *L'Idéologie Raciste. Genèse et Langage Actuel*. Paris: Editions Moutons.

König, Matthias. 2003. *Staatsbürgerschaft und Religiöse Pluralität in Post-Nationalen Konstellationen. Zum institutionellen Wandel europäischer Religionspolitik. Am Beispiel der Inkorporation muslimischer Immigranten in Großbritannien, Frankreich und Deutschland*. Philipps-Universität Marburg: Inauguraldissertation.

Lamont, Michèle and Annette Lareau. 1988. 'Cultural Capital. Allusions, Gaps and Glissandos in Recent Theoretical Developments'. *Sociological Theory* 6: 153–68.

Lamont, Michèle and Crystal M. Fleming. 2005. 'Everyday Antiracism. Competence and Religion in the Cultural Repertoire of the African American Elite'. *Du Bois Review* 2 (1): 29–43.

Lamont, Michèle and Mario L. Small. 2008. 'How Culture Matters. Enriching Our Understanding of Poverty'. In *The Colors of Poverty. Why Racial and Ethnic*

Disparities Persist, edited by Ann Linn and David Harris, 76–102. New York: Russell Sage Foundation.

Levitt, Peggy. 2003. 'You Know, Abraham was Really the First Immigrant. Religion and Transnational Migration'. *International Migration Review* 37 (3): 847–73.

Lipsky, Michael. 1980. *Street-Level Bureaucracy. Dilemmas of the Individual in Public Services*. New York: Sage.

Mousseau, Michael. 2011. 'Urban Poverty and Support for Islamist Terror: Survey Results of Muslims in Fourteen Countries'. *Journal of Peace Research* 48 (1): 35–47.

Nagel, Alexander-Kenneth. 2010. 'Vom Paradigma zum Pragma: Religion und Migration in relationaler Perspektive'. *Sociologia Internationalis* 48 (2): 221–46.

Noble, Greg. 2005. 'The Discomfort of Strangers: Racism, Incivility and Ontological Security in a Relaxed and Comfortable Nation'. *Journal of Intercultural Studies* 26 (1–2): 107–20.

Sala Pala, Valerie. 2013. *Discriminations ethniques. Les politiques du logement social en France et au Royaume-Uni*. Rennes: Presses Universitaires de Rennes.

Sayad, Abdelmalek. 1999. *La double absence. Des illusions de l'émigré aux souffrances de l'immigré*. Paris: Editions du Seuil.

Schäfer, Heinrich. 2013. 'Power, Powerlessness and the Holy Spirit'. *German Research: Magazine of the Deutsche Forschungsgemeinschaft* 35 (1): 12–15.

Sen, Amartya. 2005. 'Human Rights and Capabilities'. *Journal of Human Development* 6 (2): 151–66.

Simone, AbdouMaliq. 2001. 'On the Worlding of African Cities'. *African Studies Review* 44 (2): 15–41.

———. 2004. 'People as Infrastructure: Intersecting Fragments in Johannesburg'. *Public Culture* 16 (3): 407–29.

———. 2010. 'Reaching a Larger World. Muslim Youth and Expanding Circuits of Operation'. In *Being Young and Muslim. New Cultural Politics in the Global South and North*, edited by Linda Herrera and Asef Bayat, 145–59. Oxford and New York: Oxford University Press.

Swidler, Ann. 1986. 'Culture in Action. Symbols and Strategies'. *American Sociological Review* 51 (2): 273–86.

Terkessidis, Mark. 2004. *Die Banalität des Russismus: Migranten zweiter Generation entwickeln eine neue Perspektive*. Bielefeld: Transcript.

Weber, Max. 2006. *Der Geist des Kapitalismus*. Edited by Dirk Kaesler. Second edition. Beck'sche Reihe. München: C.H. Beck. Originally Published as Max Weber. *Die Protestantische Ethik und der 'Geist des Kapitalismus'*. Tübingen: J.C.B. Mohr, 1934.

Yiftachel, Oren, Ravit Godlhaber and Roy Nuriel. 2009. 'Urban Justice and Recognition. Affirmation and Hostility in Beer Sheva'. In *Searching for the Just City. Debates in Urban Theory and Practice*, edited by Peter Marcuse,

James Connolly, Johannes Novy, Ingrid Olivo, Cuz Potter and Justin Steil, 120–43. New York: Routledge.

Conclusion

Talja Blokland

The city in the making is relational, dynamic and in continuous change. Agents in the city, in a room to manoeuvre lined by their structural positions, make their lives and livelihoods with moral orientations and organization of their actions that impact their capabilities. The resulting inequalities in capabilities are not simply the result from the heterogeneity of people and hence the variations in their assets. The city in the making implies the making of a social infrastructure that also *creates* spatial variations (or, in Sen's terms, variations in non-personal resources and environmental diversities). In much of the social sciences over the last 20 years or so, the stuff people can use to make things work for them has often been discussed as forms of capital (overview: Field 2003; Blokland and Savage 2008). In this book, we chose instead to talk about capabilities as the realization of life chances rather than of the forms of capital, even though the latter concept has dominated much of the work on urban inequalities. We did so because we believed that through the notion of capabilities, we would be better equipped to see how opportunity hoarding of possibilities to make a life and livelihood in the city could be exclusionary. In particular, following Bourdieu's theory as laid out in *Distinction* (1984) social, cultural and economic capital have often been discussed as to be protected, and exclusion from access to capital as an active act of distinction: of boundary drawing aimed at making access to these forms of capital impossible for others defined as 'different' (or as 'othered') outside of those who share a homogeneous social position. There is much to say for this perspective, and as Butler (2003) has shown for the middle class residents whom they interviewed in London, there seems to be at least some evidence that such active protection through 'othering' indeed takes place. But it is not the whole story, and this approach to forms of capital did not fit with the empirical observations we made, observations that forced us to re-theorize. We have seen how middle class parents attempted to reduce the instability they feared their children were facing. They worried about the flexibilization of the labour market and their jobs, and about their own unstable partnerships in the case of divorces or separation. They hence sought elementary schools that provided their children with the same social ties as their kindergarten, so that they ensured their children's sense of existential safety, as they did not have to face transformations and new faces, and gave them a sense of home within institutions. Such practices are exclusionary: they meant that the parents withdraw from the catchment area school in ways non-middle class parents could not do. To ensure the capability to learn well for their child who felt safe, they used, as we have seen, symbolic and social capital. But it is difficult to read this practice of parents as one that aimed at distinction from other classes for the sole reason of keeping others out. We have also seen that, especially in *Lichterfelde*, the *Swiss Quarter* provided a residential environment where such practices were hardly necessary. Residential choice and residential structural inequalities in the city had already pre-given a context in which they could get the best for their children without further considerations or choices to make. Spatial profit, then, is not simply a notion that merely connects location and position, but, and here we refine Bourdieu's concept, a relational result of the inward orientations and practices expressed spatially by some groups at the expense of others, and unintentionally so.

We have also opted to speak of capabilities rather than capital because the notion of capital seems to imply that 'a lot' of capital provides ways of getting things done whereas 'less' capital does not. The problem with such an approach is, however, not only that an 'amount' of capital is difficult to measure. As we have seen, highly educated Sub-Saharan immigrants or Sub-Saharan immigrants with retail experiences elsewhere could be 'measured' to have a certain amount of cultural capital, as they would fill out a certain educational degree on a survey form, but this capital became severely devalued upon arrival in Germany. Even when their degrees were considered valid by the state, they did not land them in jobs that would bring them significant economic capital, as Hannah Schilling shows in her chapter. What is hence a 'lot' or 'little' capital is so context-bound that what it means has to be seen in practice. Our study shows then that, rather than the amount of capital forms, the qualities of relationships, personal ties, durable engagements and fluid encounters influence whether people can make such connections to others effective for getting things done. To 'have' capital does not equate the realization of capabilities, as for example also acknowledged in what the social capital literature often describes as actual and potential social capital (Völker 1995). However, how potential becomes actual has been little discussed: our discussion of practices of getting things done, whether among the middle class parents, the Sub-Saharan job seekers or the young women trying to establish an educational perspective for themselves, they all turned potential resources into actual ones.

The empirical case studies in this book provide unusual comparisons of places and people scattered over Berlin. We purposely did so. We have tried to take the plea for a 'comparative gesture' (Robinson 2011) informed as a 'mode of thought' (McFarlane 2010) seriously. Within this framework we thus brought together, to mention only some examples, the middle class mothers in *Lichterfelde* and the Turkish girls in *Neukölln*, allowing a mode of comparison between social groups that did not only highly differ in terms of social status but also in lifestyles. Our chapters have shown that the mechanisms of applying moral orientations, developing practices within their own group with an inward orientation, and realizing capabilities through the use of various social ties was not different for the various groups that we studied: opportunity hoarding occurred in each of our instances, even among the *drinkers* on *Leopoldplatz* or the girls in the youth club (for example when they labelled various types of students in their school).

Social groups within the city, as we have seen, do not necessarily need to interact directly to influence or hamper other people's capabilities. The middle classes gave the Sub-Saharan immigrants in the city never any thought. Yet the absence of their presence is exactly where the practices of urbanites are *implicitly* connected and the resulting social infrastructure needs to be seen through a 'relational lens' (Blokland 2012). As Bourdieu (1999, 124) notes:

> [agents] are situated in a site of social space that can be defined by its position relative to other sites (above, below, between, etc.) and by the distance separating it from them. As physical space is defined by mutual exteriority of its parts, so social space is defined by the mutual exclusion (or distinction) of the positions that constitute it, that is, as a juxtapositional structure of social positions.

Although the agent's position in the city is relatively defined by the distance to the social position of others (Bourdieu 1999), we cannot assume wilful attempts to exclude and form boundaries. Whereas radical urban scholars have been keen to blame the middle classes for wanting to exclude the 'other' (the poor, the immigrant, the gay person) without much evidence for this intentionality, some seem to presume that to acknowledge that one cannot produce the empirical data that the middle classes *intentionally aim* to punish the poor is all but the end to critical urban theory. On the contrary, it forces one to think how the actual patterns of exclusion come about *while* being seen as undesirable. The simple answer to that is that it is 'class that's dunnit' and that Capitalists are to blame. A more subtle, less comfortable answer is provided in this collection of case studies: exclusions can, and may often be the unintended consequences of intended behaviour. This does not release the middle classes of any of their societal responsibilities, nor does it conflict with radical urban theory it only implies the radical realism, that changing the ways in which urban inequalities are reproduced requests a different set of interventions than simply pointing to the wrongs of middle classes and Capitalists.

In fact, the inward orientation of social groups to make resources work for them has a substantial outward effect. The chapter of Carlotta Giustozzi, the chapter of Talja Blokland and Georg Große-Löscher as well as the chapter of Carlotta Giustozzi, Talja Blokland and Nora Freitag showed how middle class parents created their islands in the city and secluded themselves from others, hence creating disadvantages for others. But this practice and its resulting dynamic was not 'reserved for' middle class residents. Marginalized residents also organized in durable engagements at *Leopoldplatz*, where the *drinkers* met, or at Church and excluded others from their resources without intention, but through their inward orientation, i.e. through cultivation of durable engagements in Stephan Simon's chapter on Sub-Saharan immigrants in the church, or the stigma-management in Daniela Krüger's chapter on the *drinkers*. These places then became social infrastructures that created spatial profit for those who had (claimed) the right set of moral orientations and practices to access, be it the same cultural capital, the same religious belief or the same quest for moral decency, as in the case of the *drinkers* Daniela Krüger wrote about. We saw that *German drinkers* forming durable engagements with a social worker had the spatial profit to access a social project like the *Drinking Room* while excluding other groups at the *Leopoldplatz* from using it. The *Drinking Room* enabled them to preserve their symbolic community vis-à-vis the groups that, in their experience, put a threat to their group identity.

We discussed these relations as durable engagements rather than as social ties, as is commonly done in social science and urban studies. Again, we think this intervention is necessary to sharpen a use of concepts that has become too vague and blurred. The use of terms like 'interactions', 'contacts' and 'networks' have not always been precise, leaving us in the dark as to what exactly are the types of urban bonds we are talking about, and deem to be valuable for getting things done in the city (Blokland 2003). First, especially in the church, as Stephan Simon showed, the more than incidental engagement with the church as an institution, or with the collective of church members, guided the practices of support and sharing of resources, not the personal connections. We thus need to rethink the ways in which people's ties are usually conceptualized.

Second, as put forward by Rebecca Arbter, the sociology of social ties has so far mostly neglected the relevance of absent ties, or has not taken much account of the role of more fluid, instantaneous encounters in the city. Durable ties of networks of people who know each other, often measured through letting interview partners name these friends, family members and acquaintances, are seen as crucial for the development of capabilities: they constitute the social capital that people access to develop lives and livelihoods in the city, or so the mainstream literature on social capital maintains (i.e. Putnam 2000; Völker and Flap 1999; Van Eijk 2010; Franzen and Freitag 2008). Arbter's case study of Sub-Saharan immigrants elaborated on the ways in which fluid encounters work, and which benefits they can bring. In contrast to durable engagements, where the resourcefulness is based much on practices that are informed by moral orientations, fluid encounters rely much more on casual, random rubbing shoulders in the city and the settings in which people, unplanned and accidentally, get together. Whereas Wirth (1938) feared that the city would make all forms of community of real close relationships impossible and the urban way of life produce a moral emptiness and lack of solidarity, Simmel (1950 [1903]) saw the city as the site where the sheer volume of encounters urbanites had on a daily basis could only close them and make them *blasé* for the presence, and the fate, of others. It seems that once we take a lens from the 'Global South' as a comparative gesture, they were both wrong.

But fluid encounters do not unconditionally just occur everywhere. A feeling of safety may be important for opening up to fluid encounters, as Hannah Schilling discussed in her chapter on religiosity as a resource in the face of institutional discrimination. Safety can thus be seen as a precondition that enables the organization of social infrastructures, and the creation of capabilities (see also Blokland 2008). At the same time, safety is also a resource that middle class residents value and seek for. It helps them to establish a resourceful social infrastructure. In all that, we see how feelings of safety are spatially distributed, stabilized in discourses and daily practice as Mirjam Lewek demonstrated. This then can explain the difficulties for some to create or associate to social infrastructures that provide them resources.

In what concerns the establishment of durable engagements the chapters of Stephan Simon and Daniela Krüger showed the importance of interaction rituals. Constitutive for the establishment of durable engagements is also the boundary work. In particular when identities and social positions are threatened or resources are scarce, these symbolic boundaries become social boundaries (Tilly 2005) that fix groups and lines of exclusion, as the chapter of Daniela Krüger and Talja Blokland with Georg Große-Löscher show.

In the analysis of fluid encounters and durable engagements, we also pointed to the centrality of foci (Feld 1981) – as sites where these social infrastructures can emerge, like the public square in Daniela Krüger's analysis, or institutions like churches, job centres and youth clubs – foci for organized interactions that urban scholars need to take more seriously while analysing urban inequalities. For instance, Imogen Feld, Stephan Simon and Hannah Schilling showed how institutions work. They explained through their cases that actors need particular sets of moral orientations and practices to make institutional settings work for themselves.

Yet we should be careful to not turn these sites of foci for social interactions into black boxes: internal processes of differentiation, marginalization within institutions and in public spaces like the square are important for understanding the city in the making. Internal differentiation is crucial within institutions, yet the study of urban inequalities has often stopped at assessing who has access to an institution and who does not, without questioning what happens once inside of those. In institutions like state bureaucracies then, this internal differentiation is mainly mediated through street level bureaucrats who accentuate a situation of marginalization for immigrants for example, as pointed out in Hannah Schilling's chapter. Meanwhile, these public institutions also compensate for the lack of the right set of practice and moral orientations, as Imogen Feld discusses in her chapter on the role of the youth club. Here, young Turkish girls could access resources that otherwise would not be available to them.

The unusual combination of cases showed that even citizens positioned and located very different in the city, from White German middle class residents in *Lichterfelde*, poor White German residents at *Leopoldplatz*, or newly arrived Berliners from Ghana in *Neukölln*, engage in a *similar* 'making of the city' – they deploy similar strategies in the creation of social infrastructures.

The contrasting cases then showed also how similar mechanisms in the end nevertheless stabilized patterns of urban inequalities. Core sites of resources like job centres, schools and public spaces, or neighbourhood-based personal networks, do not work in favour of the marginalized. Middle class families can use their voice, political clout and social and cultural capital to ensure high quality institutions and living environments – privatized through home ownership and collectively owned commons – and as a consequence exclude others from these institutions and places. Those on the other side can do no such things.

As a result, social fringes of the kind that are important for the Sub-Saharan immigrants and alcohol- and drug-using disadvantaged Berliners to get by do not necessarily help them to get ahead. As far as our book showed that these social fringes are indeed resourceful, we don't claim that seeing the city in the making approves that social groups do actually help each other out anyways and public policy should withdraw from redistributive interventions, hence supporting a neoliberal trope of everyone helping themselves. Rather, as the chapter of Imogen Feld showed, public social policy programmes like after school activities might be core sites for the marginalized to access resources that otherwise would be difficult to attain.

Social analysis should be as nuanced as possible, in order to understand the processes and mechanisms that marginalize, and this neither by playing down the agency of the disadvantaged, nor by blaming the middle class for their presumed bad intentions. This is not to say that middle class people never do 'bad' things, as do people of other social classes – the right-wing racism is only one direct example of this. We take issue, however, with locating exclusionary practices in the 'heads' of people doing 'bad' things because they are morally 'bad'. In this sense, this book has sought an implicit dialogue with some of the radical urban scholarship published over the last few years.

The structuring structures that Bourdieu wrote about structure us all; they do not determine. But we act in structured situations: not just our positions are structured. Limitations on choice, also on progressive choice for a more equal world, affect each of the individuals we have brought to word in this book. The art of anticipation, Bourdieu writes (1992, 259), depends on the practical sense of what is to be done in a given situation: the feel for the game. Anticipation of the future of the game, he continues, is inscribed in the present state of the play. To surf on the wave with those who slate the middle classes for their practices in their structured positions or to stay on a more meta-level and say that it is the class that is revanchist against the poor and not the actual people making up the social class, that everyone is acting under the big pressure of hegemonic punishment of the poor, revanchism and the Neoliberal project, does *nothing* to suggest what else one could anticipate, what different future of the game may be possible, and how one could learn the art of anticipating a different game. Yet a truly radical urban study would do exactly that.

References

Blokland, Talja V. 2003. *Urban Bonds. Social Relationship in an Inner City Neighbourhood.* Cambridge: Polity Press.

———. 2008. *Oog voor elkaar: veiligheidsbeleving en sociale controle in de grote stad.* Amsterdam: Amsterdam University Press.

———. 2012. 'Blaming Neither the Undeserving Poor nor the Revanchist Middle Classes: A Relational Approach to Marginalization'. *Urban Geography* 33 (4): 488–507.

Blokland, Talja V. and Michael Savage. 2008. *Networked Urbanism: Social Capital in the City.* Aldershot, England; Burlington, VT: Ashgate.

Bourdieu, Pierre. 1984. *Distinction. A Social Critique of the Judgement of Taste.* Cambridge, MA: Harvard University Press.

———. 1992. *The Logic of Practice.* Palo Alto, CA: Stanford University Press.

———. 1999. 'Site Effects'. In *The Weight of the World: Social Suffering in Contemporary Society*, edited by Pierre Bourdieu, Alain Accardo and Priscilla P. Ferguson, 123–9. Stanford: Stanford University Press.

Butler, Tim. 2003. 'Living in the Bubble: Gentrification and Its 'Others' in North London'. *Urban Studies* 40 (12): 2469–86.

Feld, Scott L. 1981. 'The Focused Organization of Social Ties'. *American Journal of Sociology* 86: 1015–35.

Field, John. 2003. *Social Capital.* London: Routledge.

Franzen, Axel and Markus Freitag. 2008. *Sozialkapital: Grundlagen und Anwendungen.* Wiesbaden: VS Verlag für Sozialwissenschaften.

McFarlane, Colin. 2010. 'The Comparative City: Knowledge, Learning, Urbanism'. *International Journal of Urban and Regional Research* 34 (4): 725–42.

Putnam, Robert D. 2000. *Bowling Alone. The Collapse and Revival of American Community.* New York: Simon & Schuster.

Robinson, Jennifer. 2011. 'Cities in a World of Cities: The Comparative Gesture'. *International Journal of Urban and Regional Research* 35 (1): 1–23.

Simmel, Georg. 1950. 'The Metropolis and Mental Life'. In *A Free Press paperback. The sociology of Georg Simmel*, edited by Karl Heinz Wolf, 409–24. New York: Free Press. Originally Published as Georg Simmel. *Die Großstädte und das Geistesleben.* (Dresden: Zahn & Jaensch 1903).

Tilly, Charles. 2005. *Identities, Boundaries and Social Ties.* Boulder, CO: Paradigm Publishers.

Van Eijk, Gwen. 2010. *Unequal Networks. Spatial Segregation, Relationships and Inequality in the City.* Delft: Delft University Press.

Völker, Beate. 1995. *Should Auld Acquaintance be Forgot ...?: Institutions of Communism, the Transition to Capitalism and Personal Networks: the Case of East Germany.* Amsterdam: Thesis Publishers.

Völker, Beate and Flap, Henk D. 1999. 'Getting Ahead in the Former GDR. Human and Social Capital in the Status Attainment Process under Communism'. *Acta Sociologica* 37 (1): 17–34.

Wirth, Louis. 1938. 'Urbanism as a Way of Life'. *American Journal of Sociology.* 44 (1): 1–24.

Appendix

Map of Berlin

Source: © albertherrmann.de, based on authors' fieldwork sites

Index

Bold page number indicate figures.